Florence and the Medici

J. R. Hale

Florence
and the Medici
THE PATTERN OF CONTROL

with 36 illustrations

THAMES AND HUDSON

Printed in Great Britain by
Latimer Trend & Company Ltd, Plymouth

Contents

V   Grand-Ducal Tuscany

VI   The Decline of a Dynasty and the Growth of a Legend

Preface

This book attempts to explain the relationship between the most provocative of Italian cities and the most famous of Italian families. Both city and family have attracted copious attention. In particular, some of the most stimulating research of the past decades has been undertaken to answer questions about Medicean power: How was it acquired? In what way did it function? Why was it accepted? Yet there is no up-to-date history of Florence that covers the three centuries during which the relationship endured, no account of the Medici which keeps the string of biographies steadily connected with the life of the city. Much detail, of course, is lost when following over so long a period the points of connection between personal and institutional life which constitute the core of that relationship. But as we shift from a time when personality conditioned the nature of power to one when power simply adhered to personality by hereditary right, what emerges is, I hope, of compensating significance: a pattern of political control that (not without violent oscillations) led Florence from a republicanism uniquely energetic in its cult of liberty to the drowsy acceptance of near-absolutist rule.

I have worked almost entirely with material produced by others, as the bibliography will make clear. I owe a great deal to the generous patience with which Professor Nicolai Rubinstein has given me advice, and to the care with which Dr Michael Mallett and Mr Stanley Baron read successive drafts of the typescript.

J. R. H.
University College, London.
March 1977.

The Medici as Leaders and Rulers in Florence

1	Cosimo *Pater Patriae*	1434–1464
2	Piero di Cosimo	1464–1469
3	Lorenzo the Magnificent	1469–1492
4	Piero the Younger	1492–1494
	[Republican regime	1494–1512]
5	Giovanni (later Leo X)	1512–1513
6	Giuliano, Duke of Nemours	1513
7	Lorenzo, Duke of Urbino	1513–1519
8	Giulio (later Clement VII)	1519–1523
9	Ippolito and Alessandro	1523–1527
	[Republican regime	1527–1530]
10	Alessandro	1531–1537
11	Cosimo I	1537–1574
12	Francesco	1574–1587
13	Ferdinando I	1587–1609
14	Cosimo II	1609–1621
15	Ferdinando II	1621–1670
16	Cosimo III	1670–1723
17	Gian Gastone	1723–1737

CHAPTER I

The First Steps to Power

The founding of a dynasty

In the early fifteenth century the Florentines, never slow in self-congratulation, had much to be proud of. They had survived an attempt by Duke Gian Galeazzo Visconti of Milan to encircle and defeat them. By war or purchase they had acquired the ports of Pisa and Livorno, and the important inland cities of Arezzo and Cortona, thus coming to control all Tuscany apart from Lucca and Siena. Though there was no writer in the vernacular who bore comparison with Dante or Boccaccio, intellectual life had never been more vital, nor classical studies more stimulatingly attuned to problems of individual and public life, than in the brilliant circle of such scholars as Coluccio Salutati, Poggio Bracciolini, Niccolò Niccoli and Leonardo Bruni. In the arts, achievement was literally epoch-making: after Masaccio's frescoes in the church of the Carmine (1425–28), Donatello's S. George (1418), Ghiberti's baptistery doors (completed in 1424) and Brunelleschi's foundling hospital (begun *c.*1421), painting, sculpture and architecture definitively curved away from medieval models on to a course that is still discernible today. The most widely-felt source of pride, however, was the apparently flourishing state of a centuries-long tradition: Florence's republicanism.

The city's constitution was intricately designed to spread political power among a large group of responsible citizens. It was filigreed with legal devices to prevent the formation of political parties or the domination of affairs by a single family – let alone by a single man. And the prevailing political philosophy overwhelmingly supported this intention. 'Liberty is equal to all,' wrote Bruni in 1428. 'The hope of attaining public office and rising to higher status is equal for all.'

Yet six years later, in 1434, Cosimo de' Medici, a middle-aged banker with scholarly leanings, returned from a year's comfortable exile in the rival city of Venice to a reception from the Florentines that Machiavelli was to see in quasi-military terms. 'Rarely,' he wrote, 'has a citizen returning in triumph from victory been received by his country with such demonstrations of joy . . . All saluted him as the benefactor of the people and the father of the country.'

THE MEDICI

Simplified genealogical table*

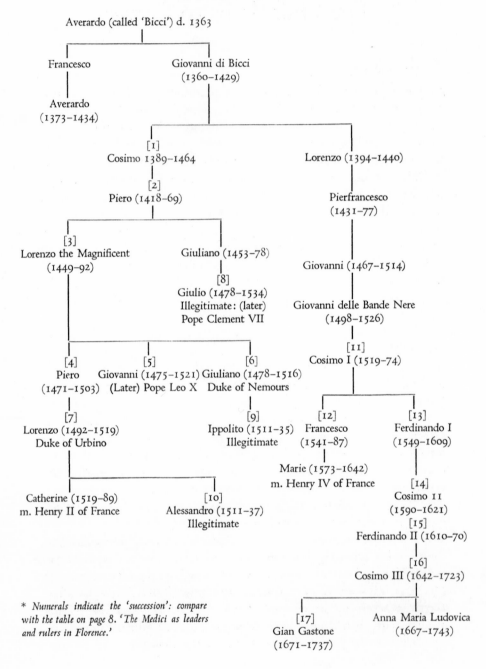

Averardo (called 'Bicci') d. 1363

Francesco

Averardo
(1373–1434)

Giovanni di Bicci
(1360–1429)

[1]
Cosimo 1389–1464

Lorenzo (1394–1440)

[2]
Piero (1418–69)

Pierfrancesco
(1431–77)

[3]
Lorenzo the Magnificent
(1449–92)

Giuliano (1453–78)

Giovanni (1467–1514)

[8]
Giulio (1478–1534)
Illegitimate: (later)
Pope Clement VII

Giovanni delle Bande Nere
(1498–1526)

[4]
Piero
(1471–1503)

[5]
Giovanni (1475–1521)
(Later) Pope Leo X

[6]
Giuliano (1478–1516)
Duke of Nemours

[11]
Cosimo I (1519–74)

[7]
Lorenzo (1492–1519)
Duke of Urbino

[9]
Ippolito (1511–35)
Illegitimate

[12]
Francesco
(1541–87)

[13]
Ferdinando I
(1549–1609)

Marie (1573–1642)
m. Henry IV of France

Catherine (1519–89)
m. Henry II of France

[10]
Alessandro (1511–37)
Illegitimate

[14]
Cosimo II
(1590–1621)

[15]
Ferdinando II (1610–70)

[16]
Cosimo III (1642–1723)

* *Numerals indicate the 'succession': compare
with the table on page 8. 'The Medici as leaders
and rulers in Florence.'*

[17]
Gian Gastone
(1671–1737)

Anna Maria Ludovica
(1667–1743)

This reflected the clarifying exaggeration of hindsight. Nevertheless, it was between 1428 and 1434 that something theoretically impossible and historically highly improbable happened: that a hitherto un-remarkable family created a party and threw up a leader. That this leadership would endure and become hereditary and eventually near-absolutist was long in doubt. Machiavelli himself saw the family twice forced to pack their bags and leave the city. But 1434 can be taken as the founding date of the Medici as one of the great dynasties of European history.

The early Medici to Giovanni di Bicci

The family came from the valley of the Mugello, some twenty miles north-east of Florence, and the first documentary reference to a Medici in the city itself dates from 1216. That within the next 150 years certain members of the family became reasonably prosperous is clear: between 1291 and 1343 the name 'Medici' appears on the chief council of the city no fewer than twenty-eight times. On the other hand they were rarely called upon, as were the oldest and wealthiest families, to give advice to the government in times of crisis; accepted as responsible workhorses, they were not yet counted among those whose support was considered necessary to the well-being of the republic. Some figures will show their financial status. Towards a forced loan in 1364 the Strozzi family was assessed at 2,063 florins, while the Medici were only expected to pay 304. Some of them would have been thought to be moderately wealthy men, others lived at the level of artisans and shop-keepers.

In the decades after 1343 Medici names continued to occur frequently among the membership of the leading offices of the state, but the coveted consultative role still continued to elude them; their prominence was not matched by their political standing in the eyes of their fellow-citizens. In part this may have been due to a riotousness that brought a plethora of lawsuits upon them and led to five death sentences in the seventeen years 1343–60. But violence and lawbreaking were common in fourteenth-century Florence. More important, in all probability, were quarrels among the nine branches of the family who had by now moved in from the countryside, their inability to project, as did families like the Strozzi and the Albizzi, a coherent image of what they stood for politically as a clan. Nor did the political record of the next genera-tion improve matters. In 1378 Salvestro de' Medici played a prominent

role in the Ciompi Revolt, supporting the demands of the disenfran-
chised woolworkers. Towards the end of the century Antonio de'
Medici was exiled for plotting against the government. In 1400, after
two more attempted plots against the state, this time with the backing
of the Duke of Milan, there were more exilings and only two branches
of the family were permitted to accept public office for the next twenty
years; with such kinsmen, it is not surprising that the members of both
determined to devote themselves to their own concerns and behave as
little like Medici as possible.

In 1400 these branches were represented by the sons of Vieri de'
Medici and the sons of Averardo ('Bicci') de' Medici. Their relative
wealth can be judged by their assessment for a tax a few years previously: 220 and twelve florins respectively. It was nevertheless the
family of Averardo that was to emerge as the economic and political
leaders of the Medici clan during the next generation, and, in particular,
it was Averardo's son Giovanni di Bicci whose banking activities
founded the Medici fortune and whose solid and cautious political
career refurbished the Medici reputation. He died the second richest
man in Florence, and left to his son, Cosimo, a training and an organization that were to make him not only the wealthiest man in Florence
but probably in Europe.

Giovanni's father had died in 1363 reasonably well-off, but his
money had been left equally among his five sons. Vieri, however, was
among the most successful of the seventy-odd bankers in Florence
towards the end of the fourteenth century and it was with him that
Giovanni received his early training. By 1385 he was managing the
Rome branch of Vieri's bank, buying a junior partnership with the
dowry brought to him that year by his wife, Piccarda Bueri. From 1393,
on Vieri's retirement, Giovanni was in business on his own, though
always with partners who added to the bank's capital. In 1397 he
moved his headquarters to Florence where it stood among its rivals at
the junction of the via di Porta Rossa and the via dell'Arte della Lana,
not far from Or San Michele. The initial capital was 10,000 florins,
more than half coming from Giovanni himself, the remainder from
two partners.

The Medici firm, like its contemporaries, acted as a deposit bank,
cashed bills of exchange on behalf of foreign banks, made advances and
invested its own funds. By 1408 there were branches in Venice and
Rome, with a sub-branch (under Rome) at Naples. Giovanni had also
entered into partnerships for the running of two cloth-making enter-

prises. The profits for the years 1397 to 1420 came to 151,820 florins, of which Giovanni's own share was 113,865.

The Rome branch was easily the most profitable. Indeed, the greatest coup in Giovanni's career was in 1413 when he became the chief papal banker and thus handled, for a commission, the greater part of the revenues of the Church. This near-monopoly only lasted for two years, until his friend and patron Pope John XXII was deposed by the Council of Constance in 1415. Giovanni's bank was for a while reduced to competing once more with its chief rivals in Rome, those of the Spini and Alberti, but its business slowly improved and the bankruptcy of the Spini in 1420 left it once more predominant. The consequence was of deep significance. As George Holmes, the most recent student of Medici business affairs, has put it: 'That the Medici bank became the greatest business organization of the world and Cosimo reputedly the richest man was primarily due to the superior position of the Medici in the financial affairs of the Curia.'

As his prosperity increased, Giovanni had been careful not to appear politically ambitious, though he did not refuse public office when it fell to him; given the current ideal of dutiful service to the community, abstention would have been more conspicuous than participation. In 1402 he was for the first time elected to the Signoria. In 1403 he went on an embassy to Bologna. Later he represented Florentine views at Venice and before Popes John XXII and Martin V. He was governor of the subject city of Pistoia in 1407 and a member of the warfare commission in 1419. In 1421 he became gonfalonier of justice. In 1424, at the age of sixty-four, he was sent on another embassy to Venice. It was an honourable, above all it was an uncontroversial record. 'He never sought honours', Machiavelli summed up, 'though he possessed them all . . . He died very rich in treasure, but far richer in fame and goodwill.' More controversial was a fact that eluded Machiavelli's somewhat cursory treatment of his sources: Giovanni's undercover role in building up a political party to safeguard his fortune and to bring the Medici clan for the first time into the mainstream of civic politics.

To take the measure of that role depends on an understanding of the nature of the Florentine consitution and of the political class that staffed its committees and carried out the functions of government. For the moment, however, let us look at the other moves made by Giovanni that affected the triumphant reception accorded his son in 1434.

Apart from his own character and political record, a man's repute in Florence was determined by the antiquity of his family's connection with public affairs, the standing of his wife's family and the size of his fortune. Giovanni's political career was at least a reminder that in spite of their traitors and cutthroats the Medici had supplied responsible office-holders to the republic over two centuries. He married his son Cosimo to Contessina, who belonged to the more ancient and consistently reputable family of the Bardi. Having suffered himself from the initial setback of a divided inheritance, he left his fortune intact to Cosimo: some 180,000 florins, together with the banks and much of the land he had been buying both around Florence and in the old Medici homeland in the Mugello.

In addition, Cosimo's prestige, if not his power, was enhanced by his reputation as a patron of scholarship. Here, too, Giovanni prepared the way. He had the boy carefully educated under the guidance of Roberto de' Rossi, one of the first Florentines to read Greek and a friend of humanists like Bruni and Niccoli, both of whom were to become friends of Cosimo's. Nor did he plunge him into the affairs of the bank until he had had ample time to develop his relationships with these men and other respected figures in humanistic studies, among them Poggio, Carlo Marsuppini and Ambrogio Traversari. There is no evidence that Giovanni himself shared the intellectual excitement of early fifteenth-century humanism. He appears to have been entirely dedicated to his business and his family. But a classical education had become *à la mode*. Indeed a number of leading scholars were themselves members of ancient and honourable Florentine families. Classical learning now added lustre to wealth and Giovanni was determined that Cosimo should share it.

He also did something to interest Cosimo in the patronage of art. Giovanni was one of the judges in the competition for the bronze doors of the baptistery of St John, which Ghiberti won by a hair's breadth from Brunelleschi. In 1418 or shortly afterwards he agreed to put up the money for the building of the sacristy (now called the *sacrestia vecchia*, or old sacristy) in the new church of S. Lorenzo. The architect chosen, undoubtedly with his approval, was Brunelleschi, and sculptural decorations were ordered from Donatello. Again, John XXII's executors – among them his faithful banker – had been charged to arrange for his burial in a Florentine church and to erect a monument there. They chose the baptistery as the place, and, as designers and sculptors of the tomb, Donatello and Michelozzo, who created one of the most influential funerary monuments of the fifteenth century. Of Giovanni's own interest in these projects as works of art there is no evidence. It is only possible to guess at the debt which Cosimo the patron owed, among so many others, to his father.

The social and political framework

The physical arena in which Giovanni and his relations made their first moves towards power was not a large one. Primarily as a result of two severe visitations of plague, in 1400 and 1417, the population of Florence shrank from some 60,000–65,000 in 1380 to about 40,000 in 1427; by the end of the fifteenth century it had recovered, possibly reaching 65,000 again in 1500. But by this date the populations of Naples and Venice were in the neighbourhood of 100,000. These were among the largest cities in Europe. Florence was more on a par with Seville or London, both of which had about 50,000 inhabitants. These figures not only emphasize how remarkable were the extent and variety of the cultural achievement of the city in Giovanni's lifetime, they do something to explain the exposure of governmental affairs to the Florentine populace as a whole. The city took twenty minutes to cross on foot from side to side, and the hub of both business and government was the small inner grid bounded by via Tornabuoni, via Cerretani, via del Proconsolo and the Arno. The leading figures in Florence were constantly to be seen as they walked from their palaces to the cathedral, to their place of business or to the centre of government, the Palace of the Signoria. The chronicles and memoirs of the time show the liveliest interest in political issues and personalities, and though political representation was not normally very wide, as we shall see, the sense of involvement in public affairs, through gossip, through sheer physical proximity, penetrated into all sections of society.

For purposes of local administration Florence was divided into four districts, each divided into four sub-districts. One of the purposes served by this sub-division was to facilitate the speedy raising of the civic militia in case of danger. The men mustered about a flag (*gonfalone*) and it was these flags, each painted with a different emblem, which gave their name, gonfalons, to the sub-districts.

These local divisions were reflected in the organs of central government. The most important of these was the Signoria. It comprised eight priors, two appointed from each of the districts, and a ninth member, the gonfalonier of justice. Though he acted as chairman his power was no greater than that of his colleagues, but from long tradition this was the position that carried with it the greatest prestige of all governmental posts.

The Signoria met daily in its palace, commonly together with two other bodies whose opinion they were required to canvass and whose assent to any proposed legislation was mandatory, that of the twelve good men (*dodici buonuomini*) and of the sixteen standard-bearers (*sedici gonfalonieri*). These three bodies were known together as the *tre maggiori*, the three leading offices, and represented the core of the decision-making function of government.

The supervision of specific aspects of administration was vested in a number of committees. Some of these served only in times of emergency, like the ten-man Warfare Commission (*Dieci di Balìa*) which contracted for mercenaries and acted as a channel both for military orders and for diplomatic contacts in time of war; others were permanent. Of these, the most outstanding was the eight-member Security Commission (*Otto di Guardia*), which was responsible for detecting and preventing crimes against the state. With its guards and spies it functioned on the lines of a secret political police and had been created after the shock of the workers' rising in 1378. Other commissions were responsible for the supervision of various aspects of trading activity, taxation and public works. All were responsible to the Signoria but some had very considerable executive and judicial powers of their own.

Legislative powers were vested in two councils whose members were elected by the Signoria: the three-hundred-strong Council of the People, and the Council of the Commune, which had two hundred members. All legislation had to be approved in these bodies by a two-thirds majority but they had no initiatory powers: they were competent only to debate and vote on proposals passed down to them by the three leading offices.

The way in which the various organs of government were staffed was based on the principle of distrust. In order to prevent power from being concentrated in too few men, or for too long, officers of the state (except for the bureaucrats centred on the Chancery) served for a strictly limited period, usually from two to six months; and most of them were chosen not by majority election nor with regard to professional qualification, but by lot. Their names, even those of the priors and the gonfalonier of justice himself, were drawn, literally, out of a bag. Not least among the reasons for a constant public interest in politics was the element of chance. The fortunes of the city which housed some of the wealthiest businesses and the most vivid culture in Europe depended, month by month, on a form of roulette.

The priors and gonfalonier of justice served for two months, the good men for three, the standard-bearers and the members of the Councils of the People and of the Commune for four. Each year these organs were staffed by 1,650 different men. When to this are added the rotations among the membership of the commissions and among the officials who controlled public order and the military and financial affairs of the Florentine possessions in Tuscany, there was a total of well over 3,000 posts falling vacant and being refilled annually. The co-operative nature of Florentine government emerges clearly from these figures, but so does a question: how did a system of chance provide a measure of effectiveness and continuity? What, in fact, were the croupier's rules which ensured that the enterprise of government was not run with ruinous inefficiency, that lengthy wars could be conducted, enormous sums of money raised and a consistent foreign policy pursued?

Certainly the rapid turnover of personnel was to some extent compensated for by the existence of a civil service which kept and filed records of precedents and procedures, and which provided notaries to act as secretaries of commissions and to help them in the conduct of their business. There were, moreover, procedures which enabled the advice of experienced men to be sought on a semi-official basis. To assist the Signoria in questions of great moment, *ad hoc* bodies of citizens were summoned to aid their discussions in assemblies known as *Consulte* or *Pratiche*. Their function was to debate and advise and the Signoria was not bound to follow their recommendations.

Though the names of candidates for government office were drawn from a bag, the name tickets in the bags had been placed there by committees, one for the three leading offices and another for appointments to positions in the city and throughout the domains in Tuscany. These committees followed certain rules when, every few years, they emptied the bags and refilled them. To qualify for a name ticket for the three leading offices, for instance, a man could not be bankrupt or in arrears with his taxes; he had to be over thirty years old; and he had to be enrolled in one of the seven *arti maggiori* or major guilds (judges and notaries; two cloth guilds, the *Calimala* and the *Lana*; bankers; furriers; silk dealers; doctors and apothecaries), or one of the fourteen minor guilds which comprised various sorts of craftsmen, shopkeepers, and the providers of services – innkeepers, for example. Nor could a man be appointed to the Signoria if he had already served on it less than three

17

years before or if any member of his family had served within one year.

Further checks lay in the discretion left to the men who filled the bags (called *accoppiatori* for the three leading offices). Appointed by the Signoria, they tended to favour new admissions only from families which had already gained a responsible place in the city, and as their selections had to be approved by an electoral commission consisting of the three leading offices and a number of co-opted advisers, the system as a whole was weighted against the admission of new blood or of potentially unreliable candidates. In times of crisis, moreover, through a practice known as 'election by hand', the number of name tickets in the bags for the most important organs of government could be sharply reduced in such a way that political homogeneity could be almost, but never totally, assured in the interest of continuity.

The Florentine governmental system produced what was proportionately the largest politically conscious class in Europe, for to those qualified for the bags the opportunity would come, and come repeatedly, to plan policy on one body, to pass it into law on another and to oversee the administrative consequences of it on a third. It also led to something like an ideal of public service, a political ethos which took for granted the collaboration of responsible citizens as equals in the conduct of public affairs, condemned political alignments on party lines and deplored the concentration of power in a few hands. But it was far from being democratic. Something between five and six thousand individuals were of a status sufficient to be considered for office, not all of whom would be entitled to hold office, under the terms of disqualification, at any given time. This is the bald numerical significance of 'republic'. And of these men, many belonged to the minor guilds whose members could occupy only one quarter of the places on councils and magistracies; in the Signoria, for example, six priors were elected from the major and only two from the minor guilds. The gonfalonier of justice could never be a minor guildsman. Political power, then, corresponded to social gradations: men outside the guild system were excluded; men in a small way of business had some influence; the majority of important posts, especially those concerned with the making of policy, were in the hands of the smallest and richest section of the community, some two and a half thousand men. And even here, because of gradations in wealth, family tradition and personal effectiveness and ambition, there were diminishing circles of increasing power, from a group of about seven hundred men whose names constantly recur in the three leading offices and on the most influential commissions, like those of war and public security, to an in-group of some seventy-five, whose association with major offices and key embassies, and whose constant attendance at *Consulte*, was so taken for granted that in the eyes of contemporaries the tone of government as a whole was determined by the attitude to domestic and foreign affairs they were known to share. This was the political core of Florence, the oligarchal power base the Medici were to infiltrate and finally dominate in the 1420s and '30s.

In reaction from the traumatic lower-class revolt of 1378, its mood was strongly conservative. It stood for the protection of the privileged classes as a whole by a group trusted to safeguard their interests. Given continuity by the need for coherent leadership during the wars of the late fourteenth and early fifteenth centuries, it constituted an 'old guard' anxious to preserve its own position and deeply suspicious of any threat from families outside what contemporaries called the 'stato' or regime. Its leaders, the heads of families like the Uzzano, Capponi, and, most notably, the Albizzi, repeatedly stressed the need for unity – that is, the continuation of their own influence – and the dangers that would arise from outsiders forming factions or parties to promote their own interests. The sense of surprise when an outsider did find himself elected to one of the leading offices is well conveyed – as is the consequent, speedily repressed ambition for still more power – in an entry for 1412 in the diary of Gregorio Dati, a moderately successful silk merchant:

On 28 April my name was drawn as standard-bearer for the militia company [i.e., he was elected to the *sedici gonfalonieri*]. Up till then I had not been sure whether my name was in the bags for that office, although I was eager that it should be both for my own honour and for that of my heirs. . . . On the very day my name was drawn, I had taken advantage of the reprieve granted by the new laws and finished paying off my debt to the commune. That was a veritable inspiration from God, may His name be praised and blessed! Now that I can obtain other offices, it seems to me that, having had a great benefit, I should be content to know that I have sat once in the colleges and should aspire no further. So, lest I should ungratefully give way to the insatiable appetites of those in whom success breeds renewed ambition, I have resolved and sworn to myself that I shall not henceforth invoke the aid of any or attempt to get myself elected to public offices or to have my name included in new bags. Rather, I shall let things take their course without interfering. I shall abide by God's will,

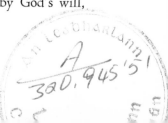

accepting those offices of the guilds or commune for which my name shall be drawn, and not refusing the labour but doing what good I may. . . . And if I should depart from this resolve, I condemn myself each time to distribute two gold florins in alms within a month.

It was largely through following the course Dati refused to follow, and by gratifying the ambition of men like him who were too timid to depart from the prevailing political ethos on their own, that the Medici were able to build up a party. Such an attempt was considered a grave political crime. Yet its success was to bring honour to them and to their heirs.

The Medici party

The decision to acquire political power arose with the need to protect the growing fortunes of Giovanni's bank and the associated one of his nephew Averardo. The time was partly unfavourable, because of wars which justified the devices used to keep key political offices in the hands of a few in the interest of continuity, and partly favourable, because the costs of war were so high that to pay them required the willing co-operation of all Florence's richest citizens.

The campaigns against Gian Galeazzo Visconti came to an end with his death in 1402. But it was not the end of war. In 1404 Florence began a campaign of its own choosing, which ended with the capture in 1406 of Pisa. In 1408 a new danger arose, this time from Naples, whose king, Ladislao, struck up from the south with intentions similar to those which had led Gian Galeazzo to strike down from the north. The conflict was resolved in a similar way: it was brought to an end by Ladislao's death in 1414. Ten years later, Florentine armies were again in the field, this time against Gian Galeazzo's successor, Filippo Maria Visconti. Peace came in 1428 and with it came security. Nevertheless, late in 1429 the flywheel of militant emotion and war-oriented finance carried Florence into yet another conflict, an attempt to conquer its old rival Lucca.

In that year Giovanni di Bicci died, leaving Cosimo leader of the Medici interests in Florence, with Averardo, who had also gained a quiet eminence through embassies and attendance at *Consulte*, as his lieutenant. And by that time the advancement of those interests was being actively carried forward by a Medici party.

The core of that party was formed by the various branches of the family itself, which fell in line behind the superior financial weight and political experience of Giovanni's family. It was broadened by a series of careful marriages which linked the Medici with poorer but more prestigious families: Bardi, Salviati, Cavalcanti, Tornabuoni. It was broadened still further by acquiring a circle of less influential but numerous body of 'friends', men who came to identify their interests with those of the Medici in return for their support.

None of these elements was suspect in itself. Family pride was one of the intensest emotions of the age. Social and political advancement was the chief consideration behind the choice of marriage partners. Enough of the feudal instinct to seek the protection of men more powerful than oneself remained to encourage a dependency best described as clientage. It was the active fostering of all these elements in combination with a specific political goal that ran counter to the intention of the laws.

The party was built up and kept together by an assiduous correspondence with members who were temporarily absent on business or in exile as well as through day to day contact within the city. The means adopted to advance the party's power were unspectacular but cumulatively effective. Its members solicited votes, which was illegal. They advocated enlarging the numbers of names in the electoral bags in order to dilute the ranks of their opponents. They helped one another to administrative posts as far as personal influence and the electoral laws permitted. The richer members of the family offered loans to members of the party who were in arrears with their taxes and thus ineligible for office; they also offered advice on business and legal matters. The style of party management was canny and avuncular. The enterprise was in itself corrupt, but it involved neither outright bribery nor coercion. The aim was to plait together an increasing number of influential men who would vote on Medici lines when chosen for the leading offices and commissions, of lesser men who would create a pro-Medicean atmosphere within the guilds, and a solid bloc of all classes within the district where most members of the family lived, in the parish of San Lorenzo.

The credibility of the party arose not only from Giovanni's wealth but from his and Averardo's prominence as office holders, and the regularity with which they were summoned to *Consulte*. Its opponents mustered a more illustrious roll-call of names, but they were divided, a divisiveness increased by criticism of the way they conducted the war with Lucca in 1429–33 and the deaths of some of their senior and most respected leaders in the same years. When the war ended there was a clear confrontation within the regime or political core of the republic between the smaller group which looked to Cosimo de' Medici for leadership and the larger but less unified old guard who looked to Rinaldo degli Albizzi.

Exile and triumph, 1433–34

Short of armed rebellion, there was no way in which either side could eliminate the power of the other. The two-monthly rotation of the Signoria meant that on each re-election the number of Albizzi and Medici supporters could be guessed at, but not known. But Rinaldo – taking a leaf out of the Medici's own book – took one precaution at least to ensure that the system would favour him. One of the name tickets in the bag for the gonfaloniership of justice was that of a man he knew he could rely on, Bernardo Guadagni. But Guadagni was behind-hand with his taxes and, were his name drawn, would be disqualified. Rinaldo paid off the arrears for him. The election of the Signoria for September and October 1433 produced a majority of Albizzi supporters with Guadagni as gonfalonier.

Late in his life Cosimo wrote a laconic account of what happened immediately after that election.

> The gonfalonier advised me that I ought to return for some important decisions. As a result on 4 September I returned to Florence and on the same day called on the gonfalonier and on one of the priors whom I thought to be a friend. I told them about the reports I had heard but they denied them. . . . On the 5th a meeting was convened of eight *richiesti* [i.e. citizens summoned to a *Pratica*], two from each quarter, with whose counsel the Signoria wished to arrive at certain decisions. Rinaldo and I were among the *richiesti* . . . On the 7th, in the morning, I was sent for on the pretext of attending a new session. In the palace I found the greater part of them already deep in discussion. After a short while the Signoria asked me to go up to them. I was led by the captain of the guard to a room called 'Barberia' and incarcerated there.

He remained there until 3 October. Meanwhile, Rinaldo strained ever nerve to get him condemned to death as a traitor who had planned to overthrow the legally constituted regime. The utmost he could obtain, after a month of argument and bribery, was an increase in the severity of the original sentence. Cosimo was banished to Padua for ten years, his cousin Averardo to Naples also for ten years, his brother Lorenzo to Venice for five. Moreover, almost the whole clan was excluded from all public office for ten years. Divided opinions among the Florentines, and diplomatic pressure on Cosimo's behalf by other cities where his services as a banker had gained him friends, notably Ferrara and Venice, whither he was allowed to move from Padua, saved his life, but Rinaldo appeared to have secured at least his political death. Moreover, the enormous sums demanded as sureties for good behaviour – Cosimo had to produce 20,000 gold florins – show that Rinaldo and his supporters were also determined to destroy the financial base of Medici influence.

Almost at once, however, Rinaldo found himself fighting to preserve his own authority. The months that followed were a demonstration of every device that could be used to subvert the constitutional arrangements of Florence in order to keep its offices and commissions favourable to a powerful but increasingly unwanted faction: threats, bribery, the use of armed force. But nothing could stop the rotations from throwing up men who represented the steady drift away from Albizzian loyalties. Cosimo, meanwhile, was in touch with both the Medici exiles and with the 'friends' in Florence who were confidently planning his return. From the end of the Lucchese war he had taken precautions against the rancour that could break out on the domestic front. Bank funds were quietly shifted to storm-proof shelters: to the Hermits of S. Miniato, to S. Marco, to the branches in Venice and Rome, to accounts in others' names. Commingled with relics, fragments of Christ's winding cloth or His crown of thorns, protected by legal separateness, the family fortune was secured, and the help of friends in providing guarantees for the surety sums meant that its capital was not gravely affected. Calm, rich, respected by the heads of other states, a friend of the pope, invested with the aura of undeserved political martyrdom: the contrast with the bullying death-throes of the Albizzi faction was alone sufficient to gain further recruits for Cosimo's party from those who wanted a return to order in the city.

At last, in August, 1434, the election for the Signoria for the next two months produced three pro-Medicean priors and a pro-Medicean gonfalonier of justice. It at once called for a *Parlamento* (an open meeting of all Florentine males, apart from clerics) into whose hands the Signoria surrendered its powers while begging the assembly to 'elect' an emergency committee, or *Balìa*, with authority to steer the city out of its present crisis. Theoretically a democratic safeguard, a device for transferring power to the people as a whole when rival groups within the more powerful families were deadlocked, the *Parlamento* was in practice usually employed to accelerate a shift of power within the regime of the moment. On this occasion its members were overawed by the presence of armed men – many from the farms cannily purchased by Giovanni in the Mugello – and passively 'elected' a list of names read out to them. The Albizzians had also brought in soldiers from their estates, but though there was disorder, it stopped well short of civil war. Pope Eugenius IV was residing in the city and was a supporter of the family who acted as his banker. Rinaldo had already alienated some of his more militant associates. The *Balìa*, moreover, contained a sufficient number of names belonging to the old regime to appear a guarantee that the Mediceans' revenge would be moderate, and other Albizzians thought it more prudent to wait and see than to have recourse to arms.

Early in October, hardly more than a year from his banishment, Cosimo returned to Florence. 'On October 6th', he later recalled, 'we arrived at our own house, Careggi, for dinner, and found many people. The signori sent to us to tell us not to enter the city until they told us, and this we did. At sunset they bade us come and we set forth with a great following. But as the road we were expected to take was crowded with men and women, Lorenzo and I with one servant and a mace-bearer of the commune rode round the walls. Going behind the Servi, and then behind S. Reparata [the cathedral] and the Palace of the Podestà [the Bargello], we entered the Palace of the Signoria without being seen, as everyone was in the Via Larga, waiting for us near our house. The city was quiet, though the people crowded the piazza, and in the palace were many armed men for security.'

The opportunity for the Medici to become a dynastic power thus came into being undramatically and – for all the show of armed force during the *Parlamento* – constitutionally. And as what use Cosimo could make of it depended not only on what he stood for but on what he was like, before taking the political story forward to his death thirty years later, it is helpful to look at the man himself.

Cosimo, 1434–64. Character and interests

Cosimo comes into view with any clarity only after his father's death in 1429, when he became head of the bank and campaign manager for the emerging Medici party. He was then already forty. Childhood disposition, early influences, the formation of character traits: we know almost nothing of these. As for his physical appearance, he is already an old man when we first see him clearly represented in works of art, wrinkled, the cheeks sagging, the pursed lips and baggy eyes giving an impression of rueful watchfulness. Even this expression cannot be trusted as an indication of personality; he suffered long and serious pain from gout, he was often bedridden or carried about within his palace on the via Larga in a special chair. The anecdotes about his private life give a picture which is quietly attractive. He was devoted to his children, including the son Carlo he had by a Circassian slave girl – the one moral lapse recorded of him, and a common one in a society where many well-to-do families kept slaves as domestic servants. Carlo was brought up with his father's legitimate sons Piero and Giovanni and went on to a highly successful career in the Church. In later years Cosimo showed the same steady concern for his grandchildren; according to a contemporary story, he once interrupted a conference with ambassadors from Lucca to whittle a whistle for one of them and said to the raised ambassadorial eyebrows, 'You are surprised that I should have made the whistle; it is as well that he didn't ask me to play it, because I would have done that too.' His wife, Contessina, married to the richest man in Florence, was the sort of woman who haggled over the price of meat. Lorenzo, his brother, who died in 1440, was a cultivated and unforceful character. There was no challenge within the family to the role in which Cosimo's friends liked to cast him, that of a kindly patriarch.

The role is most fully developed in the memoir of Cosimo written by the learned bookseller and manuscript contractor Vespasiano da Bisticci:

Of agriculture he had the most intimate knowledge, and he would discourse thereon as if he had never followed any other calling. . . . In all his possessions there were few farming operations that were not directed by him . . . moreover, when the peasants came into Florence, he would ask them about the fruit trees and where they were planted. He loved to do grafting and lopping with his own hand. One day I had some talk with him when, being then a young man, he had gone from Florence – where there was sickness – to Careggi. It was then February, when they prune the vines, and I found him engaged in two most excellent tasks. One was to prune the vines every morning for two hours. . . . Cosimo's other employment, when he had done with pruning, was to read the *Moralia* of St. Gregory, an excellent work in thirty-five books, which task occupied him for six months. Both at his villa and in Florence he spent his time well; taking pleasure in no game, save chess, of which he would occasionally play a game or two after supper. He knew Magnolino [Vespasiano adds with one of the circumstantial remarks which refresh belief in his narrative], who was the best chess player of his age.

Cosimo's practical wisdom was expressed in a number of tough little sayings which achieved the status of proverbs in Tuscany. 'You can't govern a state with paternosters'; 'better a city ruined than lost'; 'a gentleman can be made with two yards of red cloth'. This is philosophy for the market-place and its pungency has led to some underplaying of Cosimo's concern for scholarship, even to the suggestion that he was more interested in the bindings of the books he bought than in their contents.

His wealth, of course, enabled him to be of use to scholarly humanists. He bought manuscripts for Niccoli, Florence's foremost bibliophile, and he paid off Poggio Bracciolini's debts. Nor did he stop making new humanist acquaintances as the cares of political leadership came to press heavily upon him. In 1439 he sought out Gemisthos Pletho, inspirer of the circle who were to call themselves the Platonic Academy and who met with Cosimo in his palace; he helped Argyropoulos to come to Florence in 1456 to lead their discussions. He presented Marsilio Ficino, whose education he had already paid for, with a house in Florence and a small farm near the Medici villa at Careggi, so that discussions on humanistic topics, particularly on Plato's views about the immortality of the soul, could continue wherever the ageing statesman-banker found himself. In gratitude for the hospitality he had received in Venice during his exile, Cosimo gave a collection of books to the great island monastery of S. Giorgio Maggiore. After Niccoli's death Cosimo procured his manuscripts, gave six hundred to the monastery of S. Marco and paid the architect Michelozzo to build there what was in effect the first capacious public library in Italy. He continued to add to it and, using the nucleus of Niccoli's books which he had retained, he built up a new collection of his own, now known as the Laurenziana from the cloister of S. Lorenzo which houses it. He amassed yet a third collection for the Badia of Fiesole. Vespasiano described how, on Cosimo's orders, he engaged forty-five scribes and produced 200 volumes in less than two years. And that Cosimo was not merely ordering by the yard is shown by the fact that purchases for both his own library and that of the Badia followed a plan drawn up for him, at his request, by his friend Tommaso Parentucelli who, as Pope Nicholas V, was to found the Vatican Library. Moreover, Cosimo underwrote some of the key manuscript searches of the age, helping to finance the European travels of Poggio and the expeditions made to Constantinople, Syria and Egypt as well as to Greece by the antiquarian merchant Cyriac of Ancona.

Certainly he derived some excellent publicity from men associated with the revived interest in ancient literature and ideas – and also some that was embarrassing and of dubious benefit to him at the time. According to the humanist Niccolò Tignosi, Cosimo's wisdom was as natural to him 'as flying to a bird, leaping to panthers, racing to horses and savageness to lions'. The absurdity of applying such comparisons to a gout-ridden old banker is obvious. So were the parallels drawn between him and the Emperor Augustus and even the somewhat more moderate view of Argyropoulos that Cosimo represented the sort of philosopher-ruler whom 'divine Plato wished to govern cities and public affairs'. If the eulogies of Cosimo are analysed, however, it becomes clear that the most abject, and those that stress his 'imperial' status, come from men who were either foreigners, like Tignosi, who was a native of Foligno, or of low social status. The humanists who were Cosimo's social equals, like Carlo Marsuppini, or who, like Bruni, had themselves sat on the Warfare Commission and the Signoria, wrote of him as a man from whom they needed no favours and whose world they knew well. The qualities they stress are Cosimo's magnanimity and the way in which he combined a devotion to learning with an active and conscientious concern for public affairs: he exemplified, in fact, that blend of the active and contemplative life which was a leading theme of Florentine humanist discussion in the first half of the fifteenth century.

Cosimo was not himself a scholar. He had no Greek, did not edit a text, showed no interest in classical poetry, drama or history. But his interest in classical philosophy and in the researches and commentaries of his humanist contemporaries was not just a continuing lip-service to an excellent education. He probably met the Greek scholar Manuel Chrysoloras and Poggio at Constance in 1414; certainly he contracted lasting friendships with both men. Cosimo was one of the speakers in a dialogue written by Poggio in 1440, the others being Niccoli and Marsuppini. Cosimo's book-collecting enthusiasm can be traced back to at least 1418, by which time he had a respectable library of his own. In 1427 he went with Poggio to examine the remains of the ancient Roman site at Ostia, near Rome. And as the tone of Florentine humanism shifted from a concern with discovering and editing texts and with moral philosophy (the rationale behind the good citizen's behaviour), towards a more speculative and Platonic view of man's place in the universe as a whole, Cosimo remained at the centre of intellectual life, as sponsor and as learner. The spirit of his relationship to this later humanist philosophy can be seen in a letter written by Ficino to Cosimo's grandson the young Lorenzo de' Medici. Shortly before his death, Cosimo had written to ask Ficino to bring his Latin translation of Plato's *De Summo Bono* to Careggi, a translation made from a text Cosimo had bought for him. As Ficino wrote afterwards:

> I, my Lorenzo, for more than twelve years gave myself up to philosophy with him. He was as acute in reasoning as he was prudent and strong in governing. Certainly I owe much to Plato, but must confess that I owe no less to Cosimo. Inasmuch as Plato only once showed me the idea of courage, Cosimo showed it me every day. . . . Even till the last day when he departed from this world of shadows to go to light he devoted himself to the acquisition of knowledge. For when we had read together Plato's book dealing with the *Origin of the Universe* and the *Summum Bonum* he, as you who were present well know, soon after quitted this life as though he were really going to enjoy that happiness which he had tasted during our conversations.

His knowledge of Plato and Aristotle, his feeling for their relevance to his own life, his interest in having the ancient world alongside the Christian on his shelves: these things entitle him to be called not merely the patron and friend of humanists but a humanist himself, albeit an unprofessional and uncreative one.

This interest in the thought of the pagan past involved no conflict with religion. When Cosimo commissioned Ambrogio Traversari to translate Diogenes Laertius' *Lives of the Philosophers*, Traversari, a monk, expressed some doubts about the propriety of his undertaking so exclusively pagan a work. Nevertheless, there is no reason to doubt Vespasiano's picture of Cosimo reading St Gregory while he relaxed in the country. In the mid-fifteenth century Christian faith and observance were taken for granted, both in the sense that atheism was almost literally unthinkable and that the religious atmosphere was in general somewhat easygoing. Into what moral dilemmas Cosimo's private life led him, apart from his bastard Carlo, we do not know. His patronage of the arts was largely concerned with monasteries and churches, but his activities as a banker took him amidst the usury laws of the Church, and his love of ancient learning led him among systems of thought and conduct that owed nothing to Christianity and could – though the danger was hardly realized yet – lead to conflict with it. Anything, therefore, that throws some light on his religious temperament is of interest.

He certainly was capable of expressing a mystic's contempt for the thick web of affairs in which he was involved. Answering a letter of condolence on the death of his second son, Giovanni, in 1463, he said 'This, which we call life, is death, and that is the true life which is everlasting. . . . For what is my power now worth? What worth has it ever had? Nay, my purpose in caring for my life is that I may be found not to have despised the precious gift of God, nor to have forgotten the mercies which I have received from the divine love.'

But this was within a year of his own death and he was writing to a pope, Pius II. It seems likely that Cosimo saw his religion in the light of a philosophy rather than as a spiritual experience, a source of wisdom arming a man against disappointments and griefs, speaking more to the will than to the heart or conscience, and that he studied St Gregory in the same spirit as that in which he discussed Plato – in order, as he said, 'to know the best road to happiness'.

Cosimo was also closely involved with another aspect of cultural life where the Florentine contribution was as remarkable as in the sphere of humanistic learning: the fine arts. Here, however, his interests were more selective. As far as is known, he personally commissioned no paintings. A member of the bankers' guild, Cosimo had been concerned, as one of a committee of four, with the choice of Ghiberti for the statue of St Matthew in the guild's niche in the wall of Or San Michele. He commissioned him to make a reliquary for Traversari's monastery and to mount a gem for his own collection of antiquities. His favourite sculptor, however, was Donatello. The names of the two men are indeed so frequently linked that it is baffling to find no clear evidence for even one work directly commissioned by Cosimo after the stucco reliefs and the two pairs of bronze doors in the old sacristy in S. Lorenzo, for whose decoration Cosimo had become responsible on his father's death. Both Donatello's *David* and his *Judith* are first heard of in the courtyard of the Medici palace, but it is not known when they were placed there, nor by whom they were originally ordered. Cosimo's personal interest in the sculptor is suggested by Vespasiano's story of his giving him 'a red mantle and a cowl, with a cloak to go under the mantle' because he 'was wont to go clad in a manner not to Cosimo's taste'. Donatello put up with this finery for only two days, thus challenging Cosimo's dictum about the effect of two yards of red cloth. Another story describes how Cosimo helped him get back one of his young assistants with whom he had had a lovers' quarrel. As executor of Cardinal Rainaldo Brancacci, Cosimo must have had a hand in arranging for Donatello and Michelozzo to execute his monument in Naples. He was asked by the cathedral authorities of Prato to persuade Donatello to accept the commission for their singing gallery. He was said by Vespasiano to have commissioned Donatello's last, unfinished, and most boldly expressionist work, the bronze pulpits in S. Lorenzo. So many links and no chain. And perhaps this is not just an accident of the sources. The impression that does emerge is one of benignant interest in a master craftsman and a powerful influence which could put work in his way, rather than a real feeling for sculpture as an art.

It was to architecture that he gave his interest and his money most freely. He was one of the judges for the various designs submitted in 1436 for the lantern which was to top Brunelleschi's cupola of the cathedral. That cupola itself, the trickiest piece of engineering called for since the Pantheon was roofed in ancient Rome, had enabled a large number of Florentines to talk knowledgeably about stresses and strains and thrusts in the long years (1420–36) during which it was inching upwards. Cosimo came to know building as he knew agriculture, and the tradition that Michelozzo voluntarily chose to accompany him in exile is in no way an unlikely one. His choice of Michelozzo rather than Brunelleschi as the designer of his own dwelling has been explained by a less likely tradition: that Brunelleschi's design was too grandiloquent for a man who shunned an ostentation that could harm him politically. The less daring, the less subtle architect was a man whose plans Cosimo could follow without having to take an imaginative leap into the dark, who would be careful with his money and who, unlike Brunelleschi, did not have quarrels with his construction team. Cosimo had 'inherited' Brunelleschi, as it were, from the old sacristy in S. Lorenzo, where his parents were buried. That the marvellous clarity of Brunelleschi's work, the sense of architecture giving a lucid shape to the air men breathe inside a building, appealed to him is shown by his persuading the chapter to choose him to carry out the rebuilding of the church as a whole. But to Cosimo Brunelleschi may have seemed to be above all an exhibition architect. When he wanted a house to live in, whether it was in the country, at Careggi or Cafaggiolo, or in the via Larga, he chose the man he knew would listen to him when he spoke of such mundane matters as storage space for sacks and bales.

Work began on the Medici palace in 1444. It was some ten years before Cosimo and his family were able to move in, and even then the top storey was not finished. Narrower than it is today, it had something of the old street-fighting days, when a man's home had to be a castle if he were to survive, and something of the merchant's sanctum: strong-box as well as stronghold. It also had as powerful an influence on the city's domestic, as Brunelleschi had on its ecclesiastical, architecture, the Pitti and Strozzi palaces being but the most impressive of the buildings patterned on it. It was also, with the exception of the church of the Badia of Fiesole, the only building for which Cosimo was wholly responsible. He rebuilt much of S. Marco. He financed a dormitory at S. Croce. He was connected with the re-structuring of the church of the Annunciation. At S. Lorenzo, though Vasari was later to show him as the imperious director of the new building, he pledged himself only to lend money free of interest for the choir and part of the nave, out of deference to the other families in the neighbourhood who might also want parts of the church for chapels and for the display of arms of their own. No architect's name can be firmly attached to the Badia church. As at S. Marco, there was a room in the monastery beside it set apart for Cosimo's use. The church is small, the interior Brunelleschian in style but not in effect, as though the ideas of Brunelleschi, the 'exhibition' architect, have been domesticated, brought down to the realm of usefulness.

Architecture, with its teasing combination of the ideal and the useful, was probably the only form of artistic expression with which Cosimo could feel personally involved. Certainly he spent more on buildings than did any of his contemporaries not only in Florence but in Italy as a whole. What did he get from this patronage, apart from places to live in? Fame, certainly: 'Cosimo himself', wrote a Florentine in 1463, attempting to persuade a distinguished foreigner to visit the city, 'a most famous man, builds now private homes, now sacred buildings, now monasteries, inside and outside the city, at such expense that they seem to equal the magnificence of ancient kings and emperors.' Advertisement for his family: the saints particularly dear to the Medici – Stephen, Lawrence, Cosmas and Damian – top the 'Martyrs' Door' of the old sacristy; the *palle* of the Medici label the loggia of the Badia as possessively as they identify the Medici palace. Conscience money? Banking depended on interest. Canon law had, under pressure from bankers, under the pressure of papal need for loans, formulated rules by which interest could be taken, and though a smear of pre-capitalist indignation still clung to the process of allowing money to breed profit, this generated only a residual guilt. But there were taxes, and Cosimo, like most rich men, underestimated his assets; and there were, the taking of interest apart, instances when sharp practice edged aside a steady calculation of risk, as when creditors died or disappeared without agents to reclaim their deposits. Giovanni di Bicci had consulted the Pope on this last problem, and had been advised that his account with God (or conscience) could be settled by a donation to Roman churches in need of repair. Cosimo kept an account book which itemized his non-productive expenditures, listing buildings along with taxes and donations to charities. Was this only tidy-mindedness or, as has been suggested, was part of this account book 'concerned with the settling of debts to the Supreme Creditor'? As domestic buildings were presumably included with such items as the S. Croce dormitory, and as Cosimo's temperament was as much stoic as Christian, it is difficult to see him bribing his way through the gates of Paradise with architectural good works. He acted as banker to a pope who treated alum deposits on papal territory as a monopoly. His social position was unassailable. A rich man with a sturdy pride in his family's social position, a real pleasure in building, happily shouldering the responsibilities of wealth and not so imaginative as to disregard convention: it is in these terms that Cosimo the architectural patron should probably be seen.

These intellectual and artistic interests were, of course, but hobbies compared with the running of the largest banking house in Europe. Since Cosimo had taken it over on his father's death, the bank had steadily expanded. The head office was in Cosimo's home; the office in the via Porta Rossa was only the Florentine branch of an international organization. It was in his house on the via Larga and later in the palace he built there that Cosimo interviewed clients, received the reports of his branch managers and planned the strategy of investment with his general manager. In 1440 there were five other branches. The Rome branch was at that time actually in Florence itself, for the Pope, Eugenius IV, was there from 1439 to 1443, and the Rome branch – usually referred to as the branch 'that follows the court of Rome' – was temporarily established in the Piazza S. Maria Novella. When the Pope was in residence at the Vatican the branch operated from the via del Banco di Santo Spirito. There was a branch in Geneva (in 1464 it was transferred to Lyons, through which an increasing proportion of Geneva's international trade was passing), another in Bruges and another in Ancona. And in the years that followed, Cosimo continued to expand. He bought a palace in Pisa in 1441 and opened a branch there in the following year. In 1446 a branch was opened in London, where business had formerly been organized from Bruges, and in the same year one was founded in Avignon, then the chief trading city in France south of Lyons.

The latest branch to be founded was in Milan, in 1452. Unlike the other branches, which Cosimo set up on his own initiative and purely to tap business where economic life was at its most brisk, in Milan he was responding to pressure from Francesco Sforza, the *condottiere* who had recently fought his way to the throne left vacant by the death of the last Visconti duke, and who continued to need the Medici loans which had been in no small part responsible for seating him there. Among the least profitable, the Milan branch was easily the most splendid. Sforza had given Cosimo a site near the Como gate and, under Michelozzo's direction, a palace was built there, second in magnificence only to Cosimo's own. Lavishly appointed for guests, decorated by a number of local painters, including Vincenzo Foppa, its office walls were covered with the emblem Cosimo had chosen to sum up the qualities he needed for success: clear-sighted watchfulness and endurance, represented by a falcon clutching a diamond and the motto *Semper*.

Under Cosimo's direction, the bank's catchment area included the whole of Europe west of the Rhine with the exception of Spain and Portugal. On the trading side, the variety of goods handled became ever more exotic: apart from staples like wool, cloth, alum, olive oil and spices, Medici agents handled silver and jewels, tapestries, manuscripts and choirboys – recruited in the Low Countries for St John Lateran in Rome. Almonds, bedsteads, paintings, ginger, gold bullion: it is difficult to think of a commodity that Medici enterprise did not handle, either with the general policy of spreading risks through diversity, or to satisfy the demands of special clients.

There was industrial expansion as well. In 1438 Cosimo made a fairly heavy investment (4,200 florins) in a silk manufactory, and in the following year acquired a further clothmaking business. The profits from these concerns, though satisfactory, were never large, and among the motives for their purchase was probably the traditional one of providing employment, for there was some social pressure against the notion of building up a fortune solely by banking and exchange. Certainly these activities complicated the running of Cosimo's financial empire. Wool and silk manufacture was not then run on factory lines, most processes being carried out in private houses or in small specialized yards which dealt with such stages in the path from raw wool to finished cloth as fulling and dyeing; day-to-day control was left to professional managers. Cosimo chose them with care; one prospered so well with the firm and made so responsible an impression in the city that he became gonfalonier of justice. Indeed, with an organization of that size – the bank assets were in the neighbourhood of 100,000 florins at mid-century – and at a time when poor communications meant that the head office was forced to leave considerable initiative with the branches, a careful choice of managers was essential. Much of the bank's success was due to Cosimo's shrewdness in this respect and to his appraisal of the local situation when setting limits to the credit his managers could extend without consulting him.

Most important was his choice of a general manager. This post was occupied from 1435 by Giovanni Benci, who had started his career as office boy and then became chief accountant in Rome. He had been sent to prepare the way for the establishment of the Geneva branch and from 1435 had been in charge at the via Porta Rossa. Before his death in 1455 he saw the bank rise to what was probably the peak of its prosperity and, because Cosimo made all his managers partners, he died a rich man. Each branch was, in fact, a separate legal entity, keeping its own books and charging the others interest on inter-branch loans. The sole personal link was Cosimo who, as the controlling partner in all of them, was the directing influence in the organization as a whole. Professor de Roover has pointed out that 'in studying the organization of the Medici bank, one cannot fail to notice how closely it resembles that of a holding company'. There was, however, no board of directors. Policy and control lay in Cosimo's hands. If he consulted his general manager it was because he chose to.

His involvement in politics benefited from the bank, which gave him an unrivalled information service and contacts with influential men throughout western Europe. But this involvement in turn added to his work as a banker. Had he not been linked politically to Francesco Sforza he would not have opened the branch in Milan; the Ancona branch, too, in all likelihood was opened to aid Francesco, who was then Lord of the March of Ancona, under military pressure from Filippo

Maria Visconti and the Pope, and in need of loans. Giovanni di Bicci had been firmly set against loans for military purposes to rulers: there had been too many banks broken by reneging monarchs. More politically committed, Cosimo could not afford to be so cautious and thus had decisions of a particularly worrying kind to make. Nor could he afford to be purely business-like in his dealings with influential Florentines. Undoubtedly the bank enabled him to grant favours and win supporters, but his office day was the more onerous as a result.

Pater Patriae

Ideologically, the city's mood was as republican as ever on Cosimo's return. The humanist patricians and state officials – men like Roberto Rossi and Bruni – who welcomed Cosimo's return did not do so as potential courtiers. The strands in Florentine political self-consciousness that had been woven together during the wars of Cosimo's youth, both praise of republicanism and scorn of despotic rule, and the belief that a man's moral potential was best realized through public service: these held firmly. That Cosimo's sentence had been quashed was part of the rejection of a regime that had become unpopular. It was a symbol of change, not an invitation to leadership. Political life had become unworkable, but there was not the degree of disintegration that looked (as Florence had sometimes looked in the past) for a solution in one ruler. Again, though crisis by crisis the constitution had hardened into its 'emergency' form, that is, with special powers given to *Balìe*, the suspension of certain of the normal rotations and restrictions on the number of names placed in the lottery bags, at the end of each crisis the constitution had been readjusted to its 'open' peacetime form. However big the crowds in the via Larga, there was no indication from ideology, from the nature of the ruling class, or from the forms of government, that the city saw itself as entering a new, a Medicean period in its history. Yet, thirty years later, when Cosimo died, his son Piero, far from the cleverest or most experienced of men, very far from being the most charismatic, was accepted almost without question as the city's natural leader. By then the notion of dynasty was in the air as it had not been when Rinaldo degli Albizzi had succeeded to *his* father's position in the then dominant oligarchical group.

The *Balìa* elected in September 1434 had been granted full powers until the end of the year. Nearly seventy more Albizzi sympathizers were exiled. Some of them left the places to which they had been banished, grouped themselves about Rinaldo and followed him in an attempt to return by force with the aid of a Milanese army. The attempt failed and, though the exiles were not captured, they were sentenced, *in absentia*, to death, their names inscribed on the walls of the Palace of the Podestà and their portraits painted there, probably by Andrea del Castagno (whose nickname 'degli Impiccati', of the hanged men, came from this employment). And there were a few subsequent banishments – again of men associated with the previous regime. The circle of possible leaders was shrinking.

Exile, however, was too provocative a weapon to use on a large scale once the atmosphere of crisis was past. To help narrow the new regime's circle still further until it contained no one who was likely to oppose it there were a number of other devices that could be used. One was the appointment of temporary *Balìe* which could suck away most of the legislative power from the Councils of the People and of the Commune, bodies difficult to control because of their large size. A second was the creation of new councils of intermediate size, which, again, could draw off some of their power. Most effective of all, however, because least dramatic, was manipulation of the procedures whereby names were drawn for the key offices. All these devices could be used with the greater freedom because they had good precedent in the past.

While Cosimo was still on his way to Florence, the *Balìa* decided to burn the electoral lists that had been used by the Albizzi regime for filling the bags and to draw up new ones; the determination to re-start political life with a clean slate could not have been expressed more literally. On the 1433 lists there had been only one Medici name, Nicola di Vieri, who had represented the 'safe' branch of the clan. The new lists included nineteen Medici names. Apart from readjustments of this sort, however, the lists left comparatively undisturbed the roster of families accustomed to being eligible for office. To know that one might be merely considered for office was in itself an important status symbol, and for many this was sufficient. The art of narrowing the circle of men who could exert effective authority within the republic was to combine the maximum show of eligibility to office with the minimum choice of those actually appointed. The quiet revolution was to consist not so much in the drawing up of the lists, as in the way they were used.

While the new lists were being made and name-slips apportioned among the bags both for the leading offices and for other appointments within the city and throughout its territories in Tuscany, it was

36

natural for the *accoppiatori* appointed by the *Balìa* to produce short lists for the Signoria bags as a stop-gap measure. Normally, the bags contained a total of some two thousand name tickets. It was decreed that the short-list bags might for the time being contain as few as seventy-four. The political complexion of the Signoria, therefore, if not the actual names of its members, could be fairly accurately determined. And though the original justification for this restricted suffrage was the incompleteness of the revised electoral lists, by pleading a succession of states of emergency the regime was able to continue the use of this device until 1455, with only two intervals, in 1441–43 and 1445–52. The military preparations of the exiles constituted such an emergency until their army was defeated in 1440 at Anghiari. From 1443, the nervous state of Italian politics, caused by the failing power of Milan and the jockeying by Venice, Naples and Francesco Sforza for dominion in northern Italy and the Romagna, was used as a further excuse. The determination of Naples to challenge Sforza's rule in Milan constituted yet another emergency, for which the excuse failed only with a general Italian peace league in February 1455.

Within months of this event the demand for dismantling the emergency, or 'closed', structure and restoring wide representation had become so strong that constitutional forms were restored to the state they had been in before the crisis of 1433–34. What happened in the next three years is of particular interest, for it gradually became apparent that the 'open' constitution was no longer capable of working. The government's main task was aiding economic recovery after long years of mounting indebtedness caused by military preparations. This involved tax increases and these were naturally unpopular. Successive Signorie were unable to prevent a growing restlessness within the city which, in September 1457, burst into outright conspiracy. The plot was discovered, its leader, Piero Ricci, was executed, and his supporters fled. But the atmosphere became still more highly charged when a particularly heavy tax bill was passed in January 1458. Though its effect would have been felt by the moneyed class as a whole, and though it was supported by a number of rich men, including Cosimo, the shock it caused polarized into a debate about the nature of government as a whole: the merits and demerits of wide representation versus the advantages and disadvantages of the form of narrower representation with which the city had become familiar since Cosimo's return. The issue was not merely whether the inner circle representing the men of 1434 was to be enlarged, or to what extent, but whether the constitu-

tion was to lose its oligarchical tone altogether by admitting large
numbers of men of secondary station to the major offices.

For a few months the Signorie remained favourable to a wider representation, or at least to a formula which would dilute the regime without swamping it with men whose attitude towards such topics of
crucial concern to the rich as taxation was uncertain. *Pratica* after
Pratica was called to try to find some middle ground. What emerged
from these meetings was a growing pressure for a conservative reform
bill that would insert, between the three leading offices and the
Councils of the Commune and of the People, a new body which would
provide stability: a sort of permanent *Balìa*, with its membership
changing every six months but representing the families now habituated
to taking the lead, the *ottimati*, or 'best' men. 'There are two alterna-
tives,' one speaker argued. 'Should we allow the *ottimati* to be ruled by
the others, or should the others be ruled by them, as is right and just?'
The bill was repeatedly put to the councils. It was always turned down.
In August 1458 a more conservative Signoria was appointed which was
not content simply to try the reform bill on the councils. The bell of
the palace was rung for a *Parlamento*; the 'people' drained into the
heavily guarded piazza; a scarcely audible proposal was read to them
and a *Balìa* was 'elected' to put into permanent form the programme to
which the regime had, with increasing steadfastness, been reaching
since 1434. Electoral controls for the Signoria, via the *accoppiatori*, were
reintroduced after new election lists had been prepared by the *Balìa*.
And a new Council of One Hundred (the *Cento*) was formed. Reflecting
the hectic mood of the past months, this body was a compromise. It
was to formulate legislation concerning war, taxation, elections and
other constitutional matters before – this was the concession – they
were passed to the Councils of the People and the Commune for con-
firmation. But the Hundred could also be given power (as *Balìe* had
been) to appoint to key organs, such as the security and public debt
commissions. To ensure its loyalty to the organizers of the *Parlamento*,
it was to be elected for the first two six-month periods from lists
specially prepared by the *accoppiatori*, and thereafter from names which
had already been drawn for the leading offices and the gonfaloniership
of justice: a thoroughly conservative group though, again, not an
entirely calculable or homogeneous one.

This compromise form of government lasted to the end of Cosimo's
days, and Piero de' Medici was expressing a feeling general to the
supporters of the 1434 regime when he said in 1461, at the beginning

of his own first term of office as gonfalonier of justice: 'The state finds itself in such peace and happiness as not only the present citizens, but also their ancestors, had never witnessed or recalled. Business and public revenue are constantly growing, and bestowing greater glory and dignity upon the city.'

In the same year Alessandro Strozzi wrote with mild bitterness to his exiled brother that 'whoever keeps in with the Medici does well for themselves'. But how far can the regime of which we have been speaking be equated with a Medicean party? Cosimo was the richest man in Florence. But wealth was only one criterion of leadership. He moved among families – Pandolfini, Ridolfi, Capponi – whose lineage and experience in government forced him to treat them as equals. Moreover, the men linked with his over-all views did not always share them in detail. He was qualified for office in the normal way through his membership of the money-changers' and silk guilds. But the list of public offices he actually held could be matched with ease by several of his contemporaries. He was gonfalonier of justice three times, and sat on the Warfare Commission seven times. Once he sat on the Security Commission. He served for two long periods on the Public Debt Commission, some five years in all (personal exceptions to the rotation rules were not unusual). He also was a member of three of the *Balìe* that had been part of the regime's 'programme', twice because he was on the Warfare Commission at the time and once because he had been an *accoppiatore*. He did not sit on the *Balìa* of the crisis year 1458 but he was consulted about the *Parlamento* that called it into being. Spaced over thirty years, this does not, taken by itself, look like the record of a ruler. He was frequently asked to advise the Signoria in *Pratiche* but there is nothing in their records to distinguish him from others in the effect of what he said.

As a family the Medici (Cosimo, his brother Lorenzo and his sons Piero and Giovanni) were in a position to grant favours, offer protection and sponsor lesser men in the guilds and thus assist them to qualify for office. They were, indeed, accused of introducing 'new men' in this way as they had been in the days of Giovanni di Bicci. But there is no evidence that they could buy supporters into the area of power guarded by the *accoppiatori*, the inner circle (actually referred to as the *cerchio*) of the leading offices and the key commissions. Both Lorenzo and Piero served as *accoppiatori*, but only once. Several other families had been represented by more than one member; several individuals, such as Luca Pitti, served twice. Cosimo himself served for only a short period, taking Lorenzo's place on his death. Known friends also served, but, as Professor Rubinstein puts it, 'without more evidence to go on, they appear as "representatives" of the inner circle of the regime rather than as tools used by Cosimo'.

Thanks to the bank, however, he was on terms of some intimacy with popes and princes. His alone was the cachet of having acted as host to two emperors, Frederick III of Germany and John Paleologue of Byzantium. In 1439, largely due to his own powers of persuasion, he had made Florence the meeting place of a general council of the Church (and as a result it was in the cathedral of Florence that the short-lived decree of union between the Latin and Greek churches was proclaimed). Increasingly, therefore, foreign policy was left to him to conduct in the informal atmosphere of the Medici palace, though only when his steady urging of a Milanese instead of a Venetian alliance had become accepted, if grudgingly, as in Florence's best interests. The Milanese ambassador, Nicodemo da Pontremoli, actually lived in the Medici palace. It was this aspect of Cosimo's life that led foreigners to see him as a *signore*, the effective leader of Florence.

An antagonistic mid-century comment reveals the success of the policy of restricted representation on the chief organs of government: 'the commune was governed at dinners and desks rather than in the Palace; many were called to office, but few were chosen to govern.' But this refers to the regime as a whole, not specifically to the Medici; 'Cosimo and Piero', wrote Angelo Acciaiuoli to his son in 1464, 'do what they can, but they cannot do all that the city needs.'

The distinction of Cosimo's role in the eyes of outsiders and the difficulty of detecting the precise working of his authority within the city lend colour to Vespasiano's famous description of Cosimo as the concealed puppet-master of Florentine politics. 'He acted privately with the greatest discretion in order to safeguard himself, and whenever he sought to obtain an object he contrived to let it appear that the matter had been set in motion by someone other than himself.' Pius II said more or less the same thing. 'Although Cosimo is practically *signore* of the town', he wrote towards the middle of the century, 'he behaves in such a way as to appear a private citizen.' Cosimo himself had an opportunity to comment on this definition some years later when Pius wrote to ask him to persuade Florence to provide two galleys for crusading purposes. 'You write to me', Cosimo replied (this is in the year before his death), 'not as a private man who is satisfied with the mediocre dignity of a citizen, but as though I were a reigning prince . . .

Well you know how limited is the power of a private citizen in a free state under popular government.' Old and ill as he then was, this was not necessarily hypocritical; 'Cosimo has put an end to the worry of being one of the Eight [the Security Commission],' his wife had written to Giovanni in 1460. But by then the consolidation of 'his' regime had been reasonably assured.

In spite of its aura of creativity and experiment in the arts, Florence was politically a conservative city, cautious about change, constantly looking over its shoulder for precedents. As a conservative man, dignified, 'close', having a large stake in the city's internal order and its prosperity, Cosimo was a natural leader for those who stood for moderation and saw it in terms of a method of government that would remain substantially true to the forms of the past while damping down new ambitions and sudden changes of front. Head of the party of order he may have been, but because his own career and standing represented its ideal, not because he gave the orders.

Above all, Cosimo's figure cannot be sharply contrasted against the background of his age because his interests and ambitions flowed deep in the channels cut by its strongest currents. He did not create the conditions that produced the marvellous efflorescence of early *quattrocento* humanism and art. He responded, he encouraged, but, save in the scale of his building programme, he did not initiate, nor was his patronage different in kind from that of other individuals and groups. Save perhaps for the close relationship with Rome for which he was primarily responsible and which permitted a fruitful interchange of posts and ideas between Florence and the papal court, and, more conjecturally, for his encouragement of Ficino, the city's leading Platonist, the development of Florentine humanism can be described with little reference to Cosimo, as can the direction taken by the arts.

In political life, in spite of the lip-service still paid to the ideal of wide representation, the current had long been set in the direction of a taut oligarchic control. Social mobility was probably slowing; certainly rapidly acquired fortunes that demanded access to the political core were becoming rare. Recurrent use of emergency powers had sapped the vitality of the 'open' form of the constitution. Heavy investment in the city's public debt produced a desire for caution and continuity in the office-holders responsible for paying interest to the many who had lent money to the state during its long series of wars.

We cannot be present at the dinners and round the desks where party management and policy decisions were discussed. In a small city, much of domestic history evaporates in talk. As for Cosimo's role, we must beware of seeking analogies with the conduct of larger princely Renaissance states, though the fame of Florence makes this tempting. If analogies there must be, they could more profitably be sought in the municipal government of the newly prosperous towns of early nineteenth-century England or even in the 'bossism' of American cities between the wars.

Cosimo died on 1 August 1464, and was buried in S. Lorenzo, simply, as he had requested. The inscription on his tomb, voted by public decree, was as guarded as it was generous:

PATER PATRIAE

CHAPTER II

The Medicean Regime

Piero di Cosimo, 1464–69

That Florence posthumously adopted Cosimo as its father threw little light on the position it was to accord his son. Piero inherited Cosimo's fortune, his palace and his villas. To the outside world it seemed obvious that he would inherit his influence as well. The Pope wrote at once to condole with Piero on the death of such a father: 'His life was full of honour, his glory extended beyond his own city to Italy, nay, to the whole world.' The king of France, Louis XI, sent letters patent appointing him a privy councillor to the crown and granting permission to blazon the *fleur de lis* of France on one of the *palle* of the Medici. To the Florentines, however, the inheritance to a position which had depended in part on Cosimo's character and attainments and which, while it had assumed the nature of a habit, had never been institution-alized, was not a foregone conclusion. All the same, Piero's place in the regime did at first appear to be analogous to Cosimo's. And then, two years later, it seemed likely that he would follow in his father's foot-steps only in one direction: into exile.

Piero's role was a brief one – he died five years after Cosimo; he lived in the shadow of an illustrious father and was succeeded by the most brilliant secular figure of the age. This should not obscure the realiza-tion that it was during Piero's occupancy of the palace in the via Larga, and thanks to his surmounting a grave constitutional crisis in 1465–66, that the Medici were given their second chance to become a dynasty of princes.

Nicknamed at some uncertain but much later period *Il Gottoso*, the Gouty – he had inherited his father's uricaemia – Piero was forty-eight when Cosimo died. Though crippled, much of the time bedridden and forced to be carried in a litter when he went out, he was by no means an unimpressive figure, certainly not to be considered as a mere ligament connecting two great careers. His education, as one would expect of the son of Cosimo, had been thorough, and he had been responsive to it. He was a good Latinist, a collector of manuscripts and of those little objects, coins and cameos, which were both precious in themselves and, to the sensitive ear, transmitters of the pulse which had given life to the manners and ideas of antiquity. While Cosimo built, Piero decorated; it is almost as though Cosimo had deputed the responsibility of dealing with painters to him. Domenico Veneziano and Filippo Lippi wrote to him asking for employment. From a letter Matteo de' Pasti wrote to him we get the impression that his taste in painting was for the precious: 'I have learnt something for the work you commissioned me to do, a technique of using powdered gold like any other colour.' It was possibly Piero who ordered Uccello's three great battle scenes for a room in the Medici palace. It was certainly he who commissioned Benozzo Gozzoli to decorate the chapel there.

'Yesterday I had a letter from your Magnificence', Gozzoli wrote in 1459, 'from which I understand that you think that the seraphim I made are out of place. I have only made one in a corner among certain clouds; one sees nothing but the tips of his wings . . . I have made another on the other side of the altar but also hidden in a similar way . . . Nonetheless, I'll do as you command; two little cloudlets will take them away.' This obedient tone encourages a cautious trust in the fidelity of the portraits of Cosimo and Piero in the frescoes.

Piero was also responsible for the tabernacle in S. Miniato and for the *tempietto* by Michelozzo in SS. Annunziata which bears the inscription 'Costò fior. 4 mila el marmo solo' (the marble alone cost 4,000 florins). Piero's reputation as a patron has suffered from this evidence of his predilection for the pretty and the costly. But his taste had its pioneering side. Michelozzo decorated the *tempietto* with an anticipation of the taste for architectural fantasies so dear to painters like Filippino Lippi later in the century. Piero helped spread the taste for polychromed terracotta by being among the earliest patrons of Andrea della Robbia, as he was of Verrocchio, whose bronze David was made for him.

Affectionate, if stern, with his children, proud of the Medici name and determined to advance its prestige, he carried all the weight contemporaries expected from the head of a wealthy family. He was lucid and persistent in his diplomacy and held firmly to the special relationship Cosimo had established with Milan. This alliance with Florence's traditional enemy still rankled in the city, but apart from its being arguably a rational link both commercially and diplomatically, it served as a personal lifeline for the Medici; Piero knew, as Cosimo had demonstrated, that he could turn to the Sforza for support if his own position in the city were endangered. And in the person of the Duke's representative, Nicodemo da Pontremoli, who continued to reside in the Medici palace, the link brought the advice of a man who had been deep in his father's confidence. Certainly Piero acted from the start on the assumption that he was carrying on where his father had left off, both as politician and banker. In both roles, however, ill health and its consequence, irritability, took their toll. With no reserves of nervous energy to draw on, he lacked Cosimo's patience and the human insight this had enabled him to cultivate.

In an initial burst of stocktaking, he ordered a review of the bank's assets on Cosimo's death. The result showed a serious over-extension of credit. He ordered retrenchment in London, Bruges and Milan, took steps to close the Venice branch altogether, and began calling in debts in Florence. This caused surprise and resentment, unjustifiably but understandably, for Cosimo had treated debtors gently and had thereby increased the number of his political supporters. Piero was doubtless influenced by a general financial panic which gripped the city in 1464–65. War between Venice and the Turks had broken out in 1463 and the Levantine trade came temporarily to a standstill, bringing loss or downright bankruptcy to firms whose interests in the eastern Mediterranean had helped offset the worsening balance of trade with northern Europe. There is no evidence that Piero was responsible for any of these bankruptcies. Indeed, he helped one or two companies stay on their feet. But the atmosphere was such that his precautions were seen as threats. His manner, moreover, was not reassuring. His son Lorenzo complained privately to Nicodemo that his father's unfortunate temperament lost him friends every day. Yet Piero weathered the financial depression and was to emerge from the constitutional crisis more influential than ever. Lorenzo's comment and the complaints of Piero's creditors should be judged against the background of his invalidism rather than being attributed to any fundamental weakness of judgment or common sense.

During his father's lifetime Piero had played a part in city politics, though it was not an outstanding one: he served as an *accoppiatore*, attended *Pratiche* and once, in 1461, was gonfalonier of justice. On the eve of his death, as Piero wrote to Lorenzo, Cosimo

> began to recount all his past life. Then he touched upon the government of the city and then on its commerce, and at last he spoke of the management of the private possessions of our family. . . . Two things he deplored. First, that he had not done as much as he wished or could have accomplished; secondly, that he left me in such poor health and with much irksome business.

What Cosimo had not done, and could not have done, was to ensure that Piero would be treated with the same deference that he had himself received. Cosimo had been the leading spirit in a regime that contained many others, including some who had been more or less openly resentful of the deference paid to his opinions. Straightforward jealousy, dislike of 'Medici' policies, especially the Florence-Milan axis, genuine or more or less genuine concern that the constitution had lost much of what democratic flavour it had once had: Piero inherited opposition on all these fronts. There was again pressure from below to restore open elections to the Signoria and to broaden the spectrum of those whose names could be drawn for it. And it soon became apparent that a significant number of men who had hitherto accepted the regime were willing to yield to this pressure as an excuse to regroup in a form that would displace Piero. In September 1465, a year after Cosimo's death, a proposal to restore election by lot for the Signoria was snapped up with huge majorities in the Councils of the People and of the Commune, and a surprisingly large one in the more closely controlled Council of One Hundred.

In the next months, debate moved well beyond the issue of equality within the regime itself to the number of men who were to be added to it, to a complete reappraisal, indeed, of how Florence was to be governed. Frightened by this development, the men who had become accustomed to leadership competed desperately to build up parties on the Medicean model for themselves. Piero's own position worsened when the power of controlling elections was taken from the Hundred. Old watchwords like 'liberty' and 'equality' were brandished at the ruling group as a whole. 'The foundation of peace in democratic cities is equality in matters of offices and taxes,' a speaker in a *Pratica* observed. 'Our ancestors had provided for it, among other things, through rotation of offices.' And as, Signoria by Signoria, the electoral controls continued to dissolve and, *Pratica* by *Pratica*, the principle of liberty of speech and criticism was stressed, the wealthier protagonists of a freer constitution themselves became more alarmed about their position within it. Political discussion, traditionally secret to governmental bodies and *Pratiche*, was being openly reported. The making and breaking of political parties, a grave sin in traditional Florentine eyes, went on publicly and restlessly.

The situation had become so volatile by May 1466 that the Signoria ordered all those citizens who were known to be eligible for the three leading offices to swear an oath of allegiance to the constitution as it then stood, that is, partially dismantled of the safeguards that had protected the closed regime of Cosimo's last months in 1464. They were to promise to keep state matters secret, to abstain from canvassing for support. Politics was to be brought back from the streets into the Palace. Three weeks later, as fearful of a reaction back towards Piero as of a more democratic form of government, all those to the left of the 1464 regime swore another oath to keep their backs firmly turned on it. Nothing was said about Piero, much was implied about the constitutional position he stood for. 'The city is to be ruled in the customary way by a just and popular government, the Signoria is to be elected by lot in future, as it is nowadays, and in no other way, and the citizens should not suffer any violence, so that they may be free to debate and judge public affairs.' Agnolo Acciaiuoli, Luca Pitti and Dietisalvi Neroni signed the oath, and so did some four hundred others, including Pierfrancesco, Piero's cousin, who felt that, as heir to Cosimo's brother Lorenzo, he had been defrauded in the apportionment of Cosimo's property.

This apparently solid front was run up in a panic to cover the rifts between the anti-Medicean groups until enough support for abolishing the Council of One Hundred could be mustered. Though they had passed the law freeing the Signoria from electoral controls, the members of this council were on the whole loyal to Piero. If the Hundred went, as men like Agnolo Acciaiuoli and Dietisalvi Neroni urged, the movement against the constitution of 1464 might well consolidate itself by exluding Piero altogether instead of merely shouldering him away from the centre of affairs. But if the left had a historical tradition behind it and a political philosophy of sorts, so did the right: the example of peace and prosperity in the last years of Cosimo's lifetime, the efficiency of a government that was not subject to the constant changes of direction and competence brought about by unrestricted rotation. The Council of One Hundred, then, had its supporters, and the more 'open' the constitution was seen to be getting, the more they rallied behind Piero. Moreover, the more forcibly Luca Pitti and his wealthy supporters urged the popular cause, the greater the number of men who deserted it as offering no secure niche for themselves. In late August 1466 matters came to a head with the election of a Signoria which on balance favoured Piero.

By this time, behind both Piero and Pitti lay the possibility of armed support, for Piero from the Duke of Milan, anxious that the diplomatic axis should not be broken, for Pitti from the Duke's enemy, the

Marquess of Ferrara, who was equally anxious that it should be. Clouded by the threat of civil war, the atmosphere was suddenly cleared by a change of front on Luca Pitti's part. Conscious that opinion among the less ideological of his supporters was tilting back towards the ideas of 1464, he declared his loyalty to Piero and suggested in a *Pratica* early in September that matters should be settled no longer by oaths but through a *Parlamento*.

With varying shades of enthusiasm this was agreed. That Piero could operate with skill and resolution in a time of crisis was demonstrated to the citizens when they assembled; the piazza was ringed with some three thousand troops. Lorenzo was there, on horseback, and witnessed in full armour the first stage in the reconstruction of the system he was to inherit, tighten and dominate.

In such circumstances there was no doubt about what would happen. A *Balìa* was appointed. It exiled Agnolo Acciaiuoli and Dietisalvi Neroni together with Niccolò Soderini who, as gonfalonier in the October of the previous year, had led the assault on controlled elections. Other signatories of the May oath were banished or debarred from office, but on the whole Piero remained content merely with the show of force. The constitution of 1464 was restored with the added safe-guard that election by lot for the Signoria should be suspended for twenty years. That Piero's should be the controlling voice once more in governmental decisions was accepted, not only because he was Cosimo's son but because he had shown patience and strength and now – a rarer gift in the annals of Florentine leadership – magnanimity. The ruling class had looked down into the pit of free discussion and change, and closed ranks once more about him.

Nevertheless there was still no move to institutionalize his position. The exiles tried to collect armies to oust him as Rinaldo degli Albizzi had hoped to oust Cosimo. Within the city not all the May signatories had undergone an unreserved change of heart and Piero made no attempt to woo them; it is from his last year that Lorenzo's concern about Piero's knack of alienating supporters comes. By his death, on 1 December 1469, many were thinking again of change, especially as his heir, Lorenzo, was of incalculable temperament and was not yet twenty-one.

1   Palazzo Vecchio

2 Piazza della SS.
Annunziata, Ospedale
degli Innocenti, and
the statue of
Ferdinand I

3 Palazzo Riccardi

4   Old Sacristy, S. Lorenzo
5   New Sacristy, S. Lorenzo

6   Villa Poggia a Caiano

7   Fortezza da Basso

8   Florence in 1584, engraving by Bonsignori

ORENTIÆ TOPOGRAPHIA ACCVRATISS. DELINEAT

RI MO
PERILL ET EXC. D.D. IACOBO DANIO
MI
SER FERDINANDI
MAGNI ETR DVCIS
SECRET.
Donatus Rascottus obs ergo D.D.

LVOGHI NOTABILI

9   Palazzo Pitti

10   Portico of the Uffizi

11   Ponte Vecchio and
the elevated corridor
connecting the Uffizi
with the Pitti

12 Palazzo Vecchio: the
   studiolo of Francesco I

13 Princes' chapel, S. Lorenzo

14 Detail of the ceiling of the
   Galleria in the Palazzo
   Riccardi, painted by Luca
   Giordano

Lorenzo the Magnificent*, 1469–92. Character and interests

Lorenzo had been fortunate in his education. From the age of five, Piero had put him in the care of Gentile Becchi, a priest, a sound Latinist, a poet of enthusiastic if meagre talent and, above all, a lovable and amusing man. Becchi was no pedantic humanist. Apparently he made no attempt to teach his pupil Greek, but by the age of twelve Lorenzo was reading Latin with pleasure, and combining the study of Ovid with that of Dante; he began to write poems of his own when he was about sixteen. It was probably from listening to the lectures given at the *studio* (university) by Cristoforo Landino that Lorenzo was introduced to the rules of rhetoric and was taught the serious nature of the poet's calling. For Becchi's tuition was no more than a base from which Lorenzo could reach out and learn from the men of real genius who came to lecture at the *studio* and were entertained in the Medici palace or at Careggi. Landino later described the group which from 1462 had referred to itself with more or less seriousness as the Platonic Academy as discussing such topics as true nobility, the virtues of the active as opposed to the contemplative life and the nature of God, discussions in which the young Lorenzo listened to Ficino, Leon Battista Alberti and the famous Greek scholar, Argyropoulos. Lorenzo's education owed as much to his family's way of life as to the formal hours he spent reading Latin literature with Becchi, and he was lively enough to take advantage of it. Indeed, far from determining the tone of Florentine intellectual life, Lorenzo was its product. To pursue his own chief interest as a youth, for instance, the vernacular poetry of Tuscany from Dante's precursors to his own day, he could turn for advice to Landino and Ficino, both fervent admirers of Dante, and to the scholarly young poet Angelo Poliziano.

From the time Lorenzo was fifteen Piero had begun to coach him for the responsibilities to which it was hoped he would fall heir, by sending him on courtesy missions to some of the ruling families with whom he would have to deal. In this way he was entertained at Bologna, Ferrara, Venice, Rome, Naples and Milan. 'Remember to be civil and alert,' Piero primed him before his meeting with the Duke of Milan. 'Act as a man and not as a boy. Show sense, industry and manly endeavour, so that you may be employed in more important things, for this journey

* *Magnifico* was a common title of respect, used in correspondence with or in descriptions of men of standing. It was only when Lorenzo came to be seen (wrongly) as responsible for the cultural splendours of the late fifteenth century and as presiding over an age of gold on the eve of the Italian wars of 1494–1559, that the title came to be applied to him with a special significance – and that with any regularity only in the nineteenth century.

is the touchstone of your abilities.' Invalid as he was, though, Piero preferred to keep Lorenzo at home; without him, he explained, he was like a man without hands.

Lorenzo also had much to learn from his mother, Lucrezia Torna-buoni, with whom his relationship was warm and easy. Unlike his grandmother, the *Hausfrau* Contessina, Lucrezia was an original and highly intelligent woman, a copious writer of verse, mostly on religious themes, and a shrewd businesswoman; at a time when invalids (rightly) trusted nature more than doctors, she bought the decayed sulphur baths at Morba, ten miles south of Volterra, re-piped the springs, re-built the bath-houses, and turned them into a flourishing concern. Little is known about Lorenzo's feeling for his sisters but he was closely attached to his younger brother, Giuliano. He grew up at a time when wealthy clans had chosen to live apart, when the older custom whereby several families belonging to the same stock lived a more or less communal life within a single palace, or a huddle of adjacent buildings, was breaking down. The result was greater privacy, closer contact both between parents and children and between brothers and sisters. And the Medici palace was one of the first to reflect, in its architecture, this turning in of a family upon its own members and pursuits. Instead of emphasizing semi-public forecourts open to the street, it and its successors in Florence were built round a spacious inner courtyard which gave added light to the rooms surrounding it and acted as an open drawing room. The change was not so much in the direction of providing individuals with rooms that offered greater privacy or comfort as in emphasizing the right of the family as a whole to withdraw from civic to domestic life.

Impressive as it was, the Medici palace was one of something like one hundred new palaces built during the fifteenth century. Though planned in the main for single families, they were broader than the buildings they replaced, squeezing out the tenants of shops and work-shops and creating areas in the city, such as via dei Servi, via Torna-buoni, borgo Pinti and piazza Strozzi, that were overwhelmingly domestic and patrician. That these new constructions were increasingly referred to as palaces rather than houses reflects in terminology as well as in style of living the shift towards a more aristocratic self-conscious-ness on the part of the governing class.

To an affectionate family life in the via Larga was added the friend-ship of a number of boon companions. They were chosen because they echoed Lorenzo's more extrovert tastes, but all had talent, and one, the poet Luigi Pulci, genius. Most came from patrician families; all the same, it is remarkable to watch how the gay companions of his youth matured into the loyal and sober government servants of his manhood. Pulci himself served on the Warfare Commission, Luigi Alamanni sat on the Signoria four times and in 1490 became gonfalonier of justice, Sigismondo della Stufa also became gonfalonier, Bernardo Rucellai one of Lorenzo's most trusted ambassadors. Though subject from an early age to the arthritic symptoms which ran in the family, Lorenzo, like the others, was a keen sportsman, a connoisseur of hawks and horses, a huntsman and a fisherman.

In all this there was not only a natural love of exercise and sport, encouraged by humanist educational theories which pioneered the long-lasting ideal of *mens sana in corpore sano*, but the influence of the chivalric models which were lightening the texture of the social life of the Florentine *haute bourgeoisie*. It was a generation which moved from the stony patrician precincts where their fathers' palaces stood to a country-side charged with the atmosphere of knight errantry. The fusion of neo-Platonic ideas about beauty providing a means of ascent from the carnal to the spiritual with a revived taste for the verse romances of medieval France, meant that love, now a matter of philosophico-chivalrous speculation as well as of sex and hard-headed dowry negotiations, was very much part of that atmosphere and of the discussions and intrigues that it engendered. Lorenzo's name has been coupled (on fair con-temporary evidence) with Lucrezia Donati, aged eleven when the six-teen-year-old Lorenzo was first thought to be in love with her; Simonetta Vespucci, toast of the Florentine 'courtly' poets before her early death; and Bartolomea de' Nasi. All are shadowy figures. There is no painting which certainly shows what any of them looked like. There is no way of telling whether Lorenzo's love for them was merely a form of literary artifice or whether he actually seduced them. The truth, indeed, is only of importance if Lorenzo's sexual appetite aroused political opposition – or if its over-indulgence proved fatal; both accusations were levelled within twenty years of his death by the greatest of all Italian historians, Francesco Guicciardini. For neither accusation is there the slightest evidence. Citizens did not bar their doors against Lorenzo. He died, like his father, of uricaemia and its complications. In any case, to create scandal is largely the prerogative of those who know themselves to be secure, and Lorenzo did not. He wrote marvellously about love, from the buoyant obscenity of the carnival songs to the *canzone a ballo*, 'Donne belle, io ho cercato . . .', which gives in the briefest form the mood of *Romeo and Juliet*: the birth of love at a dance, the gratitude and the amazement, but all that can be said usefully and with certainty about his sex life is that he had eight children by a wife chosen for him – with his assent – by his parents and is not known to have fathered any bastards.

He was married to Clarice Orsini six months before his father's death. It was the first time the Medici had married outside their own class and it was an indication on Piero's part that the Medici were transforming themselves into something different from the solid burgher stock represented by Cosimo. The Orsini were one of the out-standing clans in the Papal States; their castle at Bracciano remains the most impressive monument of the tough seigneurial life of central Italy. They had large properties in Naples, and, above all, they were soldiers. For armed support Piero had had to rely on a political alliance; he was determined that Lorenzo should have the security of a family army. With Piero ill, the negotiations were left to Lucrezia. She met the girl – then fifteen or sixteen – in Rome.

> She is reasonably tall [she wrote to Piero], and fair-skinned. She is gentle in manner without the ease we are used to, but she is biddable and will soon conform to our ways. Her hair is not blonde – they are not blonde here – but it is reddish and plentiful. Her face is on the round side, but I find it pleasant. Her neck is slender, almost per-haps on the thin side, but graceful. We didn't see her bosom – the women cover it here – but it gave the impression of being well formed.

Dutiful, full of common sense, unimaginative, Clarice became a loving wife without ever being a stimulating companion or a figure of note in the city. The Ferrarese ambassador to Florence wrote to Duke Ercole on 1 August 1488 that 'she died three days ago, but I did not send the news at once as it did not seem to me of much importance.'

Marriage at first made little difference to Lorenzo's life or interests. 'I trust God may convert you during Lent and cause you to behave as a Christian', Pulci wrote shortly afterwards in a letter from Naples, thus combining personal advice with a hint as to what he thought Lorenzo's attitude should be to falling in with Neapolitan plans for a crusade against the Turks in conjunction with Venice and the papacy. Co-inciding with political cares, marriage indeed saw Lorenzo increasingly eager to get away from Florence, frequently on the move between the Medici villas and Pisa, hunting, writing, and talking about poetry. His relationship with Ficino became particularly close at this time. There was an exchange of letters in which the philosopher urged, and Lorenzo seemed to accept, the idea that, Socrates-like, the older man could use their friendship to protect Lorenzo from the preoccupations of the city and of power, and to help him fix his eyes on truth and beauty. Power was to make Lorenzo less considerate of others and increasingly self-important. But if Ficino's ideas had no effect on his behaviour, they continued to move his imagination as a poet, sometimes, as in the *Altercazione*, to an almost pedestrian literalness.

This is not the place to examine Lorenzo's verse, though its quality, uneven as it is, makes him one of the major literary figures between Petrarch and Ariosto and the only man to figure in popular anthologies who was also head of a bank and of a state. It is enough to mention its variety. Lorenzo experimented with every Italian verse form and mood. Wild parody of his masters, Dante and Petrarch; vivid portrayals of the sights, sounds, even the crops, beasts and farmhouse meals of rural life, with an occasional direct and joyous observation of nature itself; an intense realization of love as an experience, muted by rather conventional descriptions of the objects of his love; religious yearnings and religious anguish: the range of feeling is even more impressive than the level of accomplishment. Perhaps his finest effects are those when he felt behind his verse neither philosophy nor Petrarch nor nature, nor the chase, but music, as in the deeply spiritual:

> *O Dio, o sommo Bene, or come fai,*
> *che te sol cerco e non ti truovo mai?*

and the marvellously worldly:

> *Quant'è bella giovinezza,*
> *che si fugge tuttavia!*
> *Chi vuol esser lieto, sia:*
> *di doman non c'è certezza.*

The range was such as to amount to a working out of his early defence of the vernacular in a letter, composed when he was seventeen, in which he had claimed that Tuscan could master as many subjects and moods as could Latin. It may even be that the unevenness of quality in his verse results as much from the deliberate attempt to carry out such a demonstration as from his desire to describe scenes and characters traditionally the province of prose.

The range indeed is such as to compound the difficulty of assessing the character of this most celebrated member of his family. Nor do his portraits help. The attraction of his personality, part sneering confidence, part intent, saddened self-watchfulness, breaking across the years from that well-known sallow face with its squashed nose (he had no sense of smell), hooded gaze and firmly pouted lower lip presents a puzzle that no contemporary source resolves. Instead, Machiavelli's famous shorthand description has been seized on. 'To see him at one time in his grave moments and at another in his gay,' he wrote at the conclusion of his *Florentine History*, 'was to see in him two personalities, joined as it were with invisible bonds.' Lorenzo's life did lend some colour to this interpretation. In 1476 Poliziano, who had become tutor to his young son Piero, wrote the following letter to Clarice:

> Yesterday, after leaving Florence we came as far as San Miniato al Tedesco, singing all the way and occasionally talking of holy things so as not to forget Lent. At Lastra we drank *Zappolina*, which tasted much better than I had been told. Lorenzo is brilliant and makes the whole company gay – yesterday I counted twenty-six horses of those who are with him. When we reached San Miniato yesterday evening we began to read a little of St. Augustine; then the reading resolved itself into music and watching and giving directions to a well-known dancer who is here. Lorenzo is just going to mass. I will finish another time.

Gaiety – then Augustine; dancing – then mass: the shift of mood during a lightheartedly described twenty-four hours can be made to bear out Machiavelli's analysis. But Machiavelli was merely expressing surprise at the contrast between Lorenzo's public and private moods, saying little more than he had said about Cosimo in the tale of the grandchild – possibly Lorenzo himself – who interrupted a conference with a request that the banker-statesman make him a whistle.

The two-persons-in-one formula is at once too dramatic and too simple. Lorenzo had a temperament in which thought and emotion were closely linked. He followed ideas with a nimbleness of which there is no trace in Cosimo and Piero. He was in fact, in the modern sense, an intellectual. Yet at the same time he was creative. He did not just enjoy the philosophy of his friend and mentor Marsilio Ficino, he felt it; it suggested themes for his poetry. In the hands of thinkers like Ficino and Pico della Mirandola (whom Lorenzo also came to know well), philosophy v as no longer a matter largely of understanding the thought of Plato, Aristotle and Cicero more clearly and deriving wisdom from it, as it had been for Cosimo and his generation. It had become at once more systematic – a new way of looking at the traditional subject-matter of philosophy, the nature of reality, the purpose of existence, and what could be known – and more transcendental, exalting the soul's struggle to soar past the mesh of sensual appetite and social convention. It had become more emotionally demanding, to a creative ˙·idual more relevant – and at the same time potentially more

˙iquity had, of course, always been relevant: it would ˙ ʰad it not been. But in the first half of the ˙e had above all been to the nature of ˙·ty. The neo-Platonists were not so ˥imal as in man as a self-ˌir speculations on the nature ˌ of friendship, on the divine ˌse provided matter for painters, musicıaˌ ˌasis on the nature of creativity itself, while ıˌ ˌssumption that God alone created while man could meˌ ˌroducing the strain in their thought which has been dubbed ˙tıˌ ˌssance philosophy of man', made the act of creation itself self-conscious. It is from this same generation that the notion of genius began to take shape, together with the idea that genius is allied to feelings of alienation and despair. Again, while not un-Christian, and certainly not the product of neo-pagans, neo-Platonic philosophy could look less religious because it did not buttress every argument with citations from the Bible or the Fathers of the Church. And in its search for the nature of the divine it tended to by-pass the Christ of the gospels in an attempt to decode the pre-Christian messages from God to be found in what were thought to be the extremely ancient 'Hermetic' writings of the Greeks, in the Jewish Cabala, even in Egyptian hieroglyphics. Pico was to be declared a heretic for casting his net too widely in this way. Finally, its implications were not yet popularized; even to sense them was to feel kinship with an elite of initiates. Thus as a poet and a man of strong religious feelings Lorenzo's sensibility exposed him to aspects of the culture of his mentors and friends which contained at least the possibility of inner conflict.

An additional obstacle to understanding is the fact that Lorenzo's interests – philosophy, the collection of antiquities, patronage of the arts, music, the use of the vernacular as a medium of literary expression instead of Latin – were precisely those that have preoccupied scholarly debate within the last two generations. Inevitably, there has been a tendency to use Lorenzo as an example of, or a trait within, one or other of the approaches to these subjects and thus prise a particular facet apart from the man as a whole. Equally confusing is the fact that his talents and interests can be seen in two ways: as sincere preoccupations, or as means to increase his standing as a politician. He organized elaborate festivities, tournaments which called on the skills of men like Antonio Pollaiuolo, Verrocchio and Botticelli for the chasing of armour and the painting of standards. Tens of thousands thronged to see them; literati celebrated them; word of them was spread all over Italy. These have been seen as inspired contributions to a genuine Renaissance art form, the festival – and as circuses to divert the Florentines from brooding on their loss of liberty.

He arranged for Florentine painters, sculptors and architects to take up commissions outside Florence. He recommended the architects Giuliano da Sangallo to the King of Naples and Andrea Sansovino to the King of Portugal. He at least did nothing to hinder Verrocchio from going to Venice to make the equestrian monument of Colleoni or Botticelli and Domenico Ghirlandaio from helping to decorate the walls of the Sistine chapel in Rome. Was this a genuine interest in artists and their careers – or cultural propaganda for Florence and thus for its leading citizen? Lorenzo wrote verses to be sung at carnival time in the streets, verses which catch the ribald flavour of the traditional ones to perfection: because he was interested in the tone and verse forms of popular poetry, or because he was seeking popularity by identifying himself with the taste of the commonalty? His poem *La Nencia di Barberino* contains a list of market towns through which the lover has searched in vain for a rival to his mistress's beauty. The list both sets the slightly mocking tone appropriate to the narrative and establishes the poem quickly and firmly as a rural tale. Yet one of the most erudite of Lorenzo's biographers expects us to see it as a way of making the Florentines proud of their possessions scattered throughout Tuscany and thus support Lorenzo's desire (itself unproven) to increase his authority there.

In his grandfather's day the newest, the most fashionably attractive ideas had been directly relevant to social and political life; they stressed involvement in public affairs, they supplemented the ethical imperatives of the Bible with a moral philosophy suited to a dignified and materially purposeful way of life. They were given currency by men like Leonardo Bruni who were themselves part of the governmental machine. In

Lorenzo's day the most interesting ideas decried the counting house and the duties of office holding, and they were expressed by men quite outside politics. Yet from the age of fifteen, when his infirm father needed his support, Lorenzo had known that there was no escape from his becoming a banker and a politician. At just about the time when Lorenzo succeeded to his father's position, Giovanni Rucellai, the father of his friend Bernardo, a man whose wealth put him almost in the Medici class, who, like them, had built a new 'classical palace' (designed by Alberti) and who also knew and admired Ficino, advised his sons that unless they were deeply interested in business, they should get out of it. Moreover, 'I would not advise you to seek offices and political influence. There is nothing which I esteem less, or which seems less honourable, than to be involved in public affairs.' No such licence to follow his own bent could be granted to Lorenzo.

Again, there are many indications that Lorenzo felt a kinship with the style of life natural to young princes or the heirs to princedoms and which, while imitated by his young acquaintance, had, with them, an inevitable flavour of charade. To visitors he had the perilous knack of seeming to be a prince, possessed a presence that has led his household and his entourage of friends and protégés to be seen, misleadingly, as a court. It is tempting to see Lorenzo as a man born at the right time but in the wrong place.

But if precocious responsibility in a burgher republic forced his character somewhat against its grain, it cannot be suggested that in any profound way he resented being the descendant of Cosimo and Piero. He was not interested in the bank, and he neglected it. But he became just as proudly and possessively the patriarch as they had been with respect to his family and, if anything, even more concerned to keep in touch with every aspect of the city's life and with the personal affairs of those who helped him run it, even arranging their children's marriages with a zeal that led some up to, and some over, the verge of resentment.

In his poetry, Lorenzo had doubtless been supported by his father, who in 1441 sponsored, together with Alberti, a pioneering competition for vernacular verse in which the rival poets read their works aloud in the cathedral before a panel of judges. In art, too, Lorenzo took after his father. He was not, as Cosimo had been, an enthusiastic builder. He was interested in architecture; he was consulted when advice was sought for completing S. Spirito, which had been left without a façade on Brunelleschi's death, he submitted a design of his own for the uncompleted façade of the cathedral, he chose among the designs submitted to him for a new church in Prato. But the only surviving building of note for which he was personally responsible was the remodelling of his farmhouse at Poggio a Caiano into a villa, for which he commissioned Giuliano da Sangallo. Like Piero, he was in touch with a number of painters and his opinion on their behalf carried great weight. He recommended Filippino Lippi to Cardinal Caraffa, one of the most lavish patrons of the arts in Rome. 'Even had Master Filippo not been as sufficient as he is', the Cardinal wrote to a colleague, 'having been commended by the Magnificent Lorenzo, we would have placed him above an Apelles, or all Italy.'

When Lorenzo died, an inventory showed that hanging in the Medici palace were works by Fra Angelico, Squarcione, Piero and Antonio Pollaiuolo, Castagno, Pesellino, Filippo Lippi, Jan van Eyck, Petrus Cristus, Domenico Veneziano and Uccello. But he seldom ordered works on his own account; the only large-scale work he ordered was a set of frescoes for another villa at Spedaletto (on the site of thermal springs near Arezzo, which he frequently visited for his health), to be carried out by Perugino, Ghirlandaio, Botticelli and Filippino Lippi. They were unfinished at his death and have all perished. It was for Lorenzo's younger cousin Lorenzo di Pierfrancesco that Botticelli painted *Primavera* and *The Birth of Venus*. It was thanks to his uncle Carlo that Filippino painted the superb fresco series in the cathedral at Prato. In Florence, the chief fresco cycles of his day, in the Sassetti chapel in S. Trinita and in the chancel of S. Maria Novella, were commissioned not by him but by men who were his business associates. To the patronage of architecture and painting Lorenzo preferred an activity which was more private, more scholarly and, indeed, far more expensive: the collection of ancient gems, cameos, and *objets d'art*. The Tazza Farnese, for instance, was valued at ten times the fee given to Ghirlandaio for the enormous frescoes in S. Maria Novella.

Just as Piero had defended the vernacular while Lorenzo wrote in it, Piero had been known as the possessor of precious objects while Lorenzo was looked up to as a connoisseur, an arbiter of taste. Already at his birth the Medici palace was the most imposing private building in Florence and the *palle* of his family were brandished widely through the city and on the slopes of Fiesole. He left to others the commemoration of their names in stone and paint. Knowledgeable and discriminating, preferring not to chaffer with monastic chapters or fellow parishioners as Cosimo had done, he was content to exert an intellectual Maecenatism in the city and to spend his money at home.

Destined by circumstances to be a public servant, Lorenzo had moods in which he responded to the strain in Ficino's, and later Pico's, thought which stressed the otherworldly, contemplative side of ancient philosophy. When he could, he escaped to the country and hymned there – as in the *Altercazione* – his scorn of the town. When he could not, he used an escape route to the past offered by his gems, intaglios, ancient busts and statues. Many of these he bought from other collectors or from the organizers of the impromptu 'digs' men of his tastes stimulated up and down Italy. Many he received as presents, sometimes wrapped up in a petition. His antique vases, deeply cut with his name, LAU.R.MED., his purchase of over four hundred Greek manuscripts, none of which he could read: there is some indication that the objects in his collections had a talismanic force for him.

He recommended sculptors, as he did artists, to others, and decided between the models of rivals for a commission. With Giuliano he commissioned Verrocchio to design the monuments to Piero and his brother Giovanni in S. Lorenzo, and Verrocchio made terracotta busts of both the brothers. But the sculptor he most favoured was Bertoldo, whom he retained to look after the collection of antiquities begun by Cosimo and to produce bronzes, classical in style and subject-matter, which ministered to his taste for the thumbable and the evocative. In a man in so conspicuous a station, even this essentially private activity could not be without its effect and the collection of small bronzes became a habit strengthened by his example. The story of a 'Medici garden', where Lorenzo had young sculptors, including Michelangelo, trained in the principles of classical art, was an invention of the art historian and painter Giorgio Vasari, designed to impress his own patron, Duke Cosimo I, with the glory that came from protecting and educating artists. Lorenzo fostered no school. His patronage was neither copious nor consistent enough to encourage any particular style. His influence is not to be measured so much in terms of altarpieces as of an attitude, an attitude fusing his neo-Platonism with his visual taste: that 'art' is not the total of a myriad individual commissions, but, for the artist, the patron and the collector, a reflection in each work of something universal, man's creativity.

Though nothing is known of the commissioning of Botticelli's *Pallas and the Centaur*, it is possibly a flattering reference to the wisdom with which Lorenzo had calmed the political passions of Florence by the early 1480s, when it was painted. Signorelli's *Pan*, which almost certainly was painted for him, dates from ten years later, from a period when Lorenzo was expressing a longing to retire from politics altogether. He had always spent as much time as possible in the country. Among the Medici estates in their homeland, the Mugello – Trebbio, Scarperia, Sassuolo, Schifanoia, Gagliano – he preferred, as Cosimo had done, Cafaggiolo. At Careggi he planted a garden of shrubs, herbs and flowers which soon became famous. He frequently rode out to the Medici villa at Fiesole. But of all the Medici villas he preferred his own creation, Poggio a Caiano, the classical country retreat remodelled under his eye near the stream he personified as a nymph in *Ambra*, one of the loveliest of his mythologizing nature poems. Long before *Pan* was painted, Lorenzo's circle had identified the nature god with Cosmos, symbol of the world, and punningly (and somewhat gushingly) had twinned Cosmos with Cosimo, thus making of Pan almost a family deity. In Signorelli's painting the young god gazes at Syrinx, the nymph who had escaped him by being turned at the moment of capture into a reed by her fellow nymphs. To console himself the god had whittled the reed into a flute. But neither music, played by the young man on his left, nor philosophy, urged by the old man on his right, can console him now. Love is all-powerful, unattainable in its earthly fulness, not only by the young and the old who are both, like the shepherds in the foreground, in its thrall, but by the gods themselves. Just as there is sadness in the long shadows of approaching evening which move across the countryside, so the contemplation of love, naked but withdrawn, brings as much melancholy as desire. So many Laurentian themes are here – the classical myth, the rural setting, the Medicean god, philosophy, music (Cosimo when dying had asked Ficino to bring his lyre, and both Piero and Lorenzo were in touch with performers and composers), the theme of love as pursuit and loss – that it is difficult not to read the painting in a strongly personal sense, as the most revealing portrait we possess of Lorenzo's inner life.

Lorenzo, politician and statesman

Two days after Piero's death, Lorenzo wrote in a brief memorandum of some outstanding moments in his family's history,

> Although I, Lorenzo, was very young, being twenty years of age, the principal men of the city and of the regime came to us in our house to condole with us on our loss and to encourage me to take charge of the city and the regime as my grandfather and my father had done. This

I did, though on account of my youth and the great peril and responsibility arising therefrom, with great reluctance, solely for the safety of our friends and of our possessions. For it is ill living in Florence for the rich unless they rule.

This 'reluctance' was disingenuous. Already, the day before, he had written to the Duke of Milan, asking him to deal with him as he had dealt with his father and to support him in the same way. The day before that, with Piero hardly dead, the pro-Medicean members of the ruling class, seven hundred of them, met together and, in a discussion led by Piero's chief supporter, Tommaso Soderini, agreed to preserve the *status quo* by granting the same position to Lorenzo and Giuliano as their father had enjoyed; this formula meant that age-exemptions would be waived so that they could at once share in the city's government, and that Lorenzo would be consulted on all important decisions as Piero had been. The issue was not so much one of a transfer of power, as the maintaining of a regime the altering of which would have plunged the political – and thus the social and economic – life of the leading citizens into disorder and feud. Just how much power the rich young poet would exert as an individual was an unknown factor. He was needed for his family name and the preservation of the complex of personal alliances which had stabilized about it.

The decision to let Lorenzo step into his father's shoes created, however, a momentum of its own. A number of minor but significant constitutional changes were hurriedly made while the instinct to close ranks was still potent. A measure was passed whereby the *accoppiatori* who were to elect the Signoria were themselves to be elected annually by their predecessors and the Signoria in office each July or August, thus making the inner circle almost literally into a circle. Still more important was the action taken to increase the powers of the Council of One Hundred; a body of forty men elected by a strongly pro-Medicean Signoria and the *accoppiatori* was added to it, and the right of the Councils of the Commune and of the People to pass or refuse tax laws was cancelled. 'The reform of the *Cento*', Professor Rubinstein points out, 'thus constitutes a landmark in the history of the Medici regime, and the culmination of earlier and not always successful, attempts in this direction.'

None of this was Lorenzo's doing; at this early stage leadership was being forced upon him; but as the regime's unofficial chairman he came to know more and could initiate more freely than anyone else.

61

From being consulted about decisions it was an easy, indeed an inevitable step, to actual control over them. Once more the entrance of the Medici palace was worn by the tread of endless courtesy calls, endless petitioners. Invitations to exert power multiplied. How far he actually sought it through political patronage is not clear. He had had suitors before. At sixteen he had been approached by a man of good family who had fallen on hard times with the humble plea 'with four words you can give me a place in the world again. Lorenzo, I'll be your slave forever.' Such petitions were to multiply. In 1471 Piero Vespucci, believing himself to be victimized by tax laws passed in bodies from which he was excluded, reminded Lorenzo of his family's faithful support during the crisis of 1465–66. 'If I did not think that I shall be restored to office', he wrote, 'and relieved by your favour, I should not believe in Christ nor in any power on earth. It is enough to make a man burst with rage; it is only for love of you that I can be patient.' Yet in suggesting names for the offices which the regime as a whole was determined to control – the Signoria, the Council of One Hundred, the Warfare and Public Debt Commissions, for instance – Lorenzo's personal influence was limited. In the large number of other offices in the city and its territory, he possibly had a freer hand, but support here was less important to him. If he could not increase his power to any extent by outright patronage, however, and if Florence remained a republic, nothing could stop his image looming ever more impressively within the city.

The most important factor in his rise to real power was in any case the role he inherited in foreign policy. A successful foreign policy and good personal relations with other rulers had been a mainstay of his grandfather's and father's influence; it was primarily misjudgment in foreign affairs that would lead to the exile of Lorenzo's son in 1494 and to the family's temporary eclipse. Lorenzo was fortunate in that he had already met and made a favourable impression on the heads of the chief Italian states. It was an impression that created difficulties; throughout his life diplomatic relations were plagued by their over-estimate of his freedom of action. They saw him in their own image, whereas he had to pursue a negotiation according to the make-up of each successive Signoria, slowing down a course of action when their members were unlikely to support it, forcing the pace when they might approve. Necessarily, Florentine diplomacy followed a different rhythm from that of other powers, and the distrust this engendered involved an added burden of correspondence both to ruffled princes and to the

personal agents Lorenzo used to persuade them to endure the disadvantages that arose from his position. The licence he was commonly
granted to nominate the republic's ambassadors did not provide a
solution. Members of the regime might agree in supporting Lorenzo as
a means of preserving their status within the city, but they differed
among themselves over foreign affairs. The aim of a negotiation might
start with Lorenzo and end near the target he had set for it, but it was
only in his last years that its course ceased to zig-zag between initiatives
emanating now from the via Larga, now from the Palace of the
Signoria.

His diplomacy on behalf of Florence was further hampered by his
faltering position as a banker. An ally would – as Duke Galeazzo Maria
of Milan did – hold him to ransom during negotiations by calling for a
loan, or for other private favours, that Lorenzo became less able to grant
for reasons he found ever more difficult to explain without eroding the
diplomatic value of his reputation for enormous personal wealth. The
conduct of diplomacy was always complex in Florence. The reliance on
mercenary armies meant that negotiations with princes had to proceed
in parallel with negotiations with condottieri. The principle of rotation
involved delays when it did not lead to positive contradictions. For
Lorenzo the complexity was compounded. The intelligence and the zeal
with which he plunged at once into these deep waters throws additional
doubt on his 'reluctance' to follow Piero, and is a warning not to place
too much emphasis on his desire to escape from the burden of office.

The awkwardness of his dual role became apparent as early as 1471.
In that year Sixtus IV became pope. Lorenzo himself was chosen to
attend his coronation as Florence's ambassador, and he described the
visit with satisfaction: 'I was received with great respect, and brought
back with me two antique busts, the one of Augustus, the other of
Agrippa, that the Pope gave me; the cup of carved chalcedony and a
number of cameos and medals I bought there.' A few months later,
Sixtus approached the ex-ambassador as a banker. The Pope was determined to take over more of the Romagnol towns which were nominally
part of the states of the Church but were in fact controlled by rulers
who gave the papacy neither money nor military support. An additional
motive was the fierce family pride which abetted his expansionist policy.
As the Pope who, above all, gave the word 'nepotism' its notoriety,
Sixtus was anxious to find territories for his lay nephews (he made no
fewer than six of the clerical ones into cardinals). Towns like Imola,
Sinigaglia and Urbino, which were among his objectives, were sensitive

pressure points in the rough and ready balance of power that had obtained in Italy since Cosimo's death. Venice, too, was interested in the Romagna and Milan was anxious to stop it expanding there. Florence distrusted any attempt at consolidation, preferring a Romagna that was weak and divided. It was an important source of grain for the city, and the routes across it to the port of Ancona were vital to Florentine commerce in the Adriatic.

Trouble began over Imola. Its ruler, Taddeo Manfredi, was prepared to sell his title so that he could live in greater style in his other possession, the large city of Faenza. Negotiations for its purchase by Duke Galeazzo Maria of Milan, intended to give Florence effective control of the town, were concluded when Sixtus IV persuaded the Duke to transfer Imola to himself, so that he could install his favourite nephew Girolamo Riario there as papal vicar. Part of the price was the marriage of Girolamo to the duke's illegitimate daughter, Caterina. For the cash, Sixtus turned, perhaps not disingenuously, to Lorenzo, who instructed the Rome branch of the bank not to lend him the purchase price and urged the Pazzi bank to adopt the same attitude. As a result, Lorenzo was identified as an enemy by the Pope, not only because he represented Florence's traditional policy of keeping the Romagna divided but because he had used his own bank to strike at the Pope. It was an issue that stamped the Medici image more firmly than ever on policy-making.

Lorenzo was at the same time concerned with what seemed a more urgent task, to help keep the peace between Milan and Venice, for Florence could hardly avoid being sucked into any conflict which might break out between them. In 1474 a league was concluded among the three powers, but while bringing peace in the north, the league produced an enhanced tension in Italy as a whole, the Pope and the King of Naples allying with one another in defiance of it. Two years later the tension increased still further when Galeazzo Maria was assassinated and the government of Milan was taken over, unsteadily, by his wife, acting as regent for a young and sickly son.

Ever since Francesco Sforza had become Duke with Cosimo's financial backing a strong Milanese state had been an essential support to Medici power. That support was now in doubt, and Lorenzo was to that extent more vulnerable. He became vulnerable in the second place because of the affair of Volterra. This city, while within Florence's sphere of influence and paying an annual tribute, was to all intents and purposes independent. In 1470 a private company was formed to mine for alum in its territory, three of its partners being Florentines. It was, in fact, a project of great concern for Florence and especially for Lorenzo. Alum was third only to salt and silver as one of the most sought-after products of the age. It was used in the glass and leather industries and, more important still, it was essential in textile manufacture both to cleanse the wool and to fix the dye in cloth. And it was in short supply. The only source of any importance in Europe was on papal territory, at Tolfa near Civitavecchia, and from 1466 the Medici bank had controlled its output and sale as papal concessionaires. It was clearly in Lorenzo's interest to determine the supply of alum and thus to keep the price high, and he obtained an interest in the Volterran company, an interest great enough to offend the local businessmen who saw themselves as the victims of a big-city cartel. The facts of the financial situation remain obscure. Indeed, when considering this hotly debated phase of Lorenzo's career, it is useful to remember what his tutor, Gentile Becchi, wrote to him: 'This affair of the alum – it makes me think of the Trinity; I don't understand it.' But the affair led to war, a war which illustrates the problems that arose from Lorenzo's dual political role.

When the Volterrans protested against the cartel, the Signoria sent an ambassador to discuss the matter with them. The ambassador, Ridolfi, was so far from being a Laurentian nominee that he encouraged the Volterrans to persist in their objections and may have been responsible for their action in imprisoning Lorenzo's own representatives in the city. This act of defiance was aimed at suggesting a discrepancy between Lorenzo's personal interests and those of the republic, and he reacted by requesting troops from the *condottiere* Duke of Urbino and at least token forces from Milan, Naples and the papacy in order to show the range of political support he could muster. But the republic's own position was also threatened; the revolt could infect other cities, like Pisa and Prato, that did not ride easily under Florentine control, and the Signoria somewhat grudgingly followed Lorenzo's lead and raised an infantry and cavalry force, which, together with the others, was placed under the Duke of Urbino's command. Volterra was besieged and surrendered. The troops then got out of hand and sacked the town with a brutality that entered Tuscan folklore. The Duke of Urbino was held responsible by some. Others blamed the Milanese detachment. But some of the odium necessarily attached to Lorenzo, who had personally turned down the Volterrans' initial offer to capitulate on terms he thought too favourable to them, and who unwisely seemed to accept a share of the responsibility by offering two thousand florins to repair the damage inflicted on the town. Both the Imola crisis, such as it was, and the war of Volterra, had drawn attention to Lorenzo as an individual at a time when, because of his youth and the uncertain nature of his 'succession' to Piero, it would have been safer for him to have acquired less prominence.

He was vulnerable, moreover, simply through the publicity his position within the regime gave him and through the trust he reposed in men chosen from outside Florence for their fidelity and secrecy; especially unpopular was the Dovizi family from Bibbiena in the Casentino, one of whom, Piero, was his private secretary and another, Antonio, was frequently employed as a diplomatic agent. These were all factors which led to the progressive alienation of families which were unwilling to enter the orbit of his leadership and resented his bypassing the secretariat and diplomatic service of the government.

Such a family were the Pazzi. Pazzi was a household name well before the ancestors of Giovanni di Bicci came to Florence. As feudal magnates, representing the contemptuous militancy from which the medieval commune of merchants had struggled to free themselves, their residence in the city had been subject to the rules excluding men of their status from participating fully in civic affairs. Cosimo had sponsored their exemption from this disability, enabling them to qualify for government office and engage in banking. It was during his lifetime that, in their new-found prosperity, they commissioned Brunelleschi to build the Pazzi chapel beside S. Croce. But late entry into the mainstream of political and economic competitiveness brought resentment. During the affair of Imola they had chosen to show in Rome their impatience with the role Lorenzo was assuming in Florence by lending Sixtus IV the money refused him by the Medici bank. Their growing virulence found a wide response among Girolamo Riario's circle of anti-Medicean friends and kinsmen. By 1477 Lorenzo himself was aware that there was a widely-based conspiracy against his life. In 1478, with the help of hired assassins (one a Volterran) and confident of support from the Pope, they attempted to kill both him and his brother.

The moment chosen was high mass in the cathedral. The attack on Giuliano succeeded; he was stabbed to death. Lorenzo's assailants were less dexterous. He beat them off, ran past the altar, and was hurried by onlookers into the north sacristy. The doors were slammed shut, and one of his rescuers sucked a wound in his neck in case the weapon that had caused it had been poisoned. From that moment the hue and cry was up. By nightfall three of the Pazzi and the archbishop of Pisa himself, a Sixtine appointee and a leading spirit in the plot, were dangling upside down from the windows of the Palace of the Signoria. Botticelli was paid to paint them as they swung – and Lorenzo wrote verses to go underneath their heads. During the next few days something like seventy more conspirators were rounded up and killed. By the end of the following year, the last of the actual assassins, Bernardo Bandini, had been brought back from as far afield as Constantinople and executed. But by then Florence was at war. Sixtus, as behoved a pope, had not felt able to give the assassination plot his public blessing, but he could call on God and the King of Naples to arbitrate between him and Lorenzo on the battlefield.

The goal of both the crime and the war was the same: to help the city see reason by cutting off its head. 'For I well know,' Lorenzo wrote in answer to a letter of sympathy from the King of France, Louis XI, 'and God is my witness that I have committed no crime against the Pope save that I am alive and . . . have not allowed myself to be murdered.' As the troops of the Pope and his ally pressed further north – they crushingly defeated the Florentine army near Poggibonsi and occupied Colle, only thirty miles from Florence – Sixtus repeated that the war was directed not against the city but against Lorenzo and that by expelling him his fellow-citizens would obtain forgiveness.

This attempt to isolate Lorenzo failed, as had the paler attempt preceding the war of Volterra. Resistance to any increase in the territories either of the Church or of Naples was an instinct shared by nearly all Florentines, and in his diplomatic correspondence Lorenzo now took especial care to point out that communications relating to war and peace should go to the Signoria or the Warfare Commission, and that matters of this importance could not be settled by him personally. Clearly the Pazzi were not alone in disliking Lorenzo, but within Florence they were alone in trying to do anything about it. When Jacopo dei Pazzi, the head of the family, rode through the streets after the failure of the assassination plot shouting the old popular rallying call of 'Liberty and the People' he had been greeted with curses and 'Palle, Palle!' Sixtus represented Florence as a tyranny. This was not how the city regarded itself.

As the war dragged on, however, it brought humiliation through losses of territory and a mounting impatience with the heavy taxation that was imposed to pay for mercenaries. Time and time again in the past Florence had reacted to lack of success in war by a change of government. Similar military failure and similar heavy taxes in the

Lucchese war had brought about the fall of the Albizzi. If this could not with justice be called Lorenzo's war when it began, it might well come to be seen as such if it continued. This consideration, as well as the welfare of the city, must have been in his mind when he determined to try to end a Florentine war with a Laurentian peace.

Having privately ascertained that King Ferrante would treat with him directly, Lorenzo left for Naples in December 1479, confiding in an *ad hoc* assembly of members of the regime but letting the Signoria officially know of his intentions only when it was too late for them to stop him, had they so wished: 'as I am the person against whom the attack of our enemies is chiefly directed, I may by delivering myself into their hands be the means of restoring peace to my fellow-citizens.' By acting more or less independently, and by identifying himself so clearly with the war, Lorenzo was taking a major risk in case he failed. There was also some measure of physical risk involved in putting himself in the King's hands; Ferrante had already murdered one man, the great *condottiere* Jacopo Piccinino, who had visited him with a Neapolitan safe-conduct in his hands. But again, this physical risk would redound to his credit if he succeeded. Probably the greatest risk was one of time: how long would the regime stay together in his absence?

Ferrante proved open to negotiation. He had over-extended himself in a war that was more in Sixtus's interest than his own, and by now Lodovico Sforza had replaced the weak regency of the young Duke of Milan's mother by taking over the government himself and was in a position to help Milan's now traditional ally. There were signs that France was at last prepared to intervene rather than merely show sympathy. By March 1480 Lorenzo was back with his peace treaty.

How far the regime had been actually threatened by men emboldened by Lorenzo's absence is difficult to know. Within weeks of his return, however, a *Balìa* was appointed to consider further constitutional changes. The urgency of the city's financial position was used as an excuse, and the *Balìa* promised a review of tax burdens. Financial reforms were indeed carried out, but the *Balìa*'s chief purpose was to make the control of the inner circle still tighter by creating a new council of seventy members, carefully chosen and not subject to rotation. The Seventy was designed to add its weighty corroboration to bills sent down to the Councils for what was hoped would be automatic enactment, especially those affecting finance, war, foreign policy and the constitution. It was also made responsible for electing the Signoria. At the same time the executive powers of the Signoria were reduced by the appointment of two permanent commissions to be responsible for the daily conduct of foreign and internal affairs respectively: the *Otto di Pratica* and the Twelve Procurators. The membership of these bodies was to change every six months, but only members of the Seventy could be elected to them. While the constitution looked the same from a distance – the Council of One Hundred remained, the Warfare Commission was still appointed in times of crisis – seen more closely it was clear that yet another step had been taken towards a narrowly based control of the republic. The Seventy, it is true, was created for a five-year period only, but, as had happened in the past with extensions to the term of office of the *accoppiatori* or the use of *Balìe*, emergencies could be invoked to prolong the existence of the exceptional, and the Seventy remained the heart of the regime until it fell in 1494.

Emergencies, indeed, were not far to seek. In 1482 Venice, in alliance with Sixtus's most militant nephew, Girolamo Riario, declared war on Ferrara. By now Florence and Naples were at one in their opposition to any extension of papal authority and, together with Milan, sent troops to the aid of Ferrara and to break up the army the Pope was assembling around Rome to send to his nephew's aid. The success of this second aim, during which a Florentine contingent occupied Città di Castello, and the Pope's mounting alarm at the prospect of Venice's taking possession of the Duke of Ferrara's territories entirely on its own account, led him to join Lorenzo, the Duke of Milan and the King of Naples in what he promptly dubbed 'The Most Holy League'. Determined to continue fighting, but now isolated, Venice widened the diplomatic scene and escalated the sense of alarm with which the rulers of Italy as a whole watched the progress of the war, by appealing to the French Dukes of Lorraine and Orleans to reactivate their families' long dormant claims to Naples and Milan. It was the spectre of foreign invasion that produced a peace settlement, but not until the summer of 1484. And almost at once Florence was involved again in war, this time as the ally of Naples when Ferdinand was attacked by Sixtus's successor, Innocent VIII, backed by a number of his own rebellious barons. Once more there was the fear of French intervention, and equally perturbing was the Duke of Milan's reluctance to back his allies, Florence and Naples. It was largely Lorenzo's urging that brought Ferdinand and Innocent to terms in 1486.

These campaigns were fought far from Florence itself, but the need to raise money for troops was continuous. To deal with this problem, and in effect to restrict the control of the city's tax structure and the public debt to a very small group within the regime, the Council of One Hundred was repeatedly given special powers that emasculated still further the role of the Councils of the People and the Commune.

Even when the financial emergency was over, Lorenzo's gift and energy for diplomacy were still required. Once raised, the spectre of French intervention could not be exorcized, only kept at bay by denying it the wars or threats of war that would bring it to life. Milan had to be kept within the fold of the triple alliance, Innocent VIII to be transformed into a friend – and the achieving of this was perhaps Lorenzo's greatest accomplishment. And lastly there were small fires to be ringed against getting out of control. In 1488 alone the murder of Girolamo Riario in Forlì was followed by moves from Milan and Rome to take possession in his stead, moves stilled predominantly by Lorenzo's mediation; the murder of the ruler of Faenza, Galeotto Manfredi, led to the threatened takeover of the city by Bologna with Milanese support, until an agreement reached in Lorenzo's presence at Cafaggiolo restored, as in the case of Forlì, its independence; a plot to assassinate the ruling Bentivoglio family of Bologna could, without Lorenzo's refusal to aid the conspirators, have had a greater chance of involving the whole of North Italy and the papacy in taking sides. And these are but examples, if the most dramatic ones, of the advantages Lorenzo's influence in Italy brought to a city of traders and manufacturers who needed open roads and welcoming cities for the transport and sale of their goods.

In spite of drastic interruptions in the Levantine trade caused by the Turks, the Florentine economy had remained fairly buoyant. The cloth industry, once the basis of its wealth, was still suffering from a shortage of wool available for import, but silk manufacture was increasing in its stead. Investment in land, with its slow but sure return, rather than in business, is a sign of failing confidence in a mercantile community, but there is no indication that it increased to any important extent in Lorenzo's lifetime. The urge to build large new private palaces brought its casualties, and a number remained unfinished through lack of funds, but given energy and luck, fortunes could still be increased.

While the domestic economy remained reasonably sound, however, the position of international banks, like that of the Medici, became increasingly difficult. Branches in northern Europe found it difficult to buy commodities that would appeal to Italian consumers, or the raw materials that Italian industries were geared to process. And licences to export wool were increasingly conditional on loans to the government granting them, so that cash became locked up and unavailable for transfer. Most Florentine banks were hit in this way by forces beyond their control; it was the reason why Giovanni Rucellai retired from business. It led to failure after failure. In 1460 there had been thirty-three banks in Florence; shortly after Lorenzo's death there were less than half a dozen, and the Medici bank itself slid towards a general collapse which involved banks of its type all over Italy. It was, in fact, particularly vulnerable. The family's political prestige, and the quasi-aristocratic style in which its branch managers had accustomed themselves to live, made it uniquely liable to requests by rulers for loans. The London branch, for instance, was forced to lend so much to Edward IV in return for the granting of export licences that Lorenzo had to close it down as incapable of rendering the parent company a profit. A few years later, in 1481, he withdrew from Bruges as well.

How far the bank's prosperity would have been preserved had Lorenzo mustered the steady control that Cosimo had exerted over its operations, it is impossible to say. Apart from being urged by Piero to look into the running methods of the Rome branch on his visit there in 1466, there is no evidence of Lorenzo's being groomed to be more than the bank's nominal chief. When he did throw himself into business affairs it was to lighten a ship which was already sinking. Like Piero, though with less excuse, he left the day-to-day running to subordinates without checking either their methods or their balances. By the time the Bruges branch was closed, it was clear that without a major rethinking of the bank's constitution and a massive redeployment of its interests, little could usefully be done either by Lorenzo, who lacked the time, or by his general manager, Sassetti, who lacked the necessary talent. In that year, 1481, Lorenzo, in filling out his tax return, wrote: 'In making out this report, I shall not follow the same procedure as my father in 1469 because there is a great difference between that time and the present, with the consequence that I have suffered many losses in several of my undertakings, as is well known not only to your Lordships but to the entire world.'

The Medici fortunes were, of course, not dependent on the bank; Lorenzo was a very wealthy man simply in terms of buildings, land and possessions. But he was poorer in terms of potential earning power than either Piero or Cosimo had been, and the influence wielded by free money became less and less available. With a family account-book before him, he noted that between 1434 and 1471 'we have expended an incredible sum of money, not less than 663,755 florins, in public works, charity, and contributions to the taxes. Though many may think we might have better kept a part of the amount in our own purses,' he went on, 'I do not regret the expenditure, for I think the money well laid out in the promotion of great public objects.' And, indeed, this tradition of public benefaction would have been an awkward one to break.

His enemies had prophesied that Lorenzo's influence in Florence would wane if the bank fell on lean days. There was some foundation for this view. His glamour in the eyes of the populace as well as his usefulness to the regime as chief negotiator and spokesman for the republic's foreign policy, involved his acting as master of ceremonies as well as host to visiting rulers and their ambassadors, arranging public festivities and inflating the normally somewhat Spartan housekeeping of the Medici palace. 'The reputation of Lorenzo,' noted a Ferrarese ambassador, 'depends upon the consideration with which he is regarded by the powers of Italy and foreign monarchs. If he did not possess this, he would not be so highly valued in Florence.' And that consideration depended, in part at least, on his ability to entertain princes *en prince*.

When the lean days came, however, Lorenzo continued to entertain important visitors after they had paid their respects to the Signoria, and to contribute to the popular festivities associated with public holidays in the manner that led him, in retrospect, to be accused of attempting to divert the Florentines' attention from their progressive loss of liberty. To recompense himself he was accused of diverting money from the public treasury to his own. Whether true or not – the evidence is far from clear – the charge at least suggests another of his sources of strength: that he shared and reinforced the view of the leading members of the regime that the state's fiscal policy should support their own standing. This tendency was not new, but increasingly the costs of war were met not by issuing new low interest bonds secured on the national debt, the *Monte*, but by inviting subscriptions to special loans bearing a higher interest: loans floated by members of the regime in office at the time and subscribed to by them and their friends. In this way wars were paid for while the privileged few were offered an excellent investment guaranteed by the state. But the interest rate made these loans costly, and it became necessary to raid the *Monte*, cutting the rate payable on its bonds and lowering their redemption price, as well as to raise some of the taxes which bore on the incomes and consumption of Florentines and the population of the subject territories as a whole. The planning of the state's finances, therefore, became a form of conspiracy. And conspirators need a chief, however uneasy their relationship with him may be.

Lorenzo's position in Florence and in Italy

It is easier to estimate Lorenzo's stature than to describe his status, to sense, rather than to pin down in a phrase, the nature of his power within Florence.

He was referred to as a tyrant by political enemies in the city as well as by Sixtus IV. After his death, the diarist Piero Parenti wrote that he was a man who 'with a single gesture was able to bend all the other citizens to his will.' Lorenzo himself was always careful to emphasize, as had Cosimo, that he was not a *signore*, it was merely that among his fellow-citizens he had been granted a special degree of privilege. After 1481, when another plot to assassinate him was uncovered, a law was passed identifying anyone who conspired against Lorenzo with conspiracy against the state. Apart from this, no law or 'right' defined his position. At his death he was referred to in an official decree simply as 'the leading citizen of Florence.'

With others, he passed in and out of the key commissions and councils: he served at various times on the Hundred, the Seventy and the Seventeen. He had been a member of the *Balìe* of 1471 and 1480; he had served as *accoppiatore*. In all this he was still one among many who had comparable records of public service. The inner circle was at least three hundred strong. Governmental records are not full or complete enough – there are none at all for the Seventy, no records of meetings in the Medici palace – for proposals and decisions to be proportioned between him personally, men prepared to be his spokesmen, and others of more independent views. What is known suggests that decisions did not always go the way he wanted, and that when they did, the majorities were sometimes small. Even when the conciliar 'system' was complete it is best described as pro-Medicean rather than Medicean *tout court*; it certainly cannot be dubbed Laurentian. And it was volatile on two counts; Lorenzo's relationship to the regime was subject to change. So was the regime's relationship to the community as a whole; the great majority of offices were still filled by lot – not the crucial ones, but the traditional principle was there in practice as well as, potentially explosively, in theory.

That he was by far the most influential and, especially after Giuliano's murder, the most conspicuous member of the regime, there is no doubt. Nor is there much doubt that in the field of foreign affairs he was not primarily a figure to rally about but to depend upon. Just how far his initiatives carried the day, his personal agents render those appointed by the Signoria superfluous, will not be known until the vast mass of his correspondence has been analyzed. From 1469, some twenty-one thousand letters to him, getting on for two thousand from him, are known to have survived. As it is, the question of how far he was free or wished to pursue an 'Italian' policy, a deliberate and conceptualized maintenance of a balance of power among the states, remains a matter of debate. So does the extent of his personal responsibility for the comparative peacefulness that possessed Italy from 1486 to his death. What is beyond debate is that he was accepted as one of the great figures of Italian statecraft and that he was able to draw the government into a peninsular diplomacy that went beyond the aims of the most immediate of Florentine interests. But none of this makes him into a man who wanted or felt himself able to transform Florence into a princely state. Indeed, given the security of sons to succeed him within the system as it stood, the very single-mindedness with which he could turn from politics to become absorbed in other interests, his family, gems and bronzes, poetry and philosophy, country life, might seem to weaken the likelihood of his thinking of the future in such terms on the evidence of his character alone.

But while it is difficult to see Lorenzo as projecting forward from the realities of each moment coherent plans for the future of Italy, or even of Florence or of Tuscany (though he fostered the university and the economic life of Pisa and bought properties which served as foci of personal loyalty at a number of points in the countryside), his devotion to his family was naked.

Lorenzo was even more zealously a Medici than Cosimo or Piero had been. His family memoranda are almost exclusively preoccupied with honours gained by the family, and one of his earliest ambitions after Piero's death was to have one of his sons made a cardinal – as genuine princely families could manage almost as a matter of course in pre-Tridentine Italy. As early as 1472 he had sounded Sixtus IV. Then came the Pazzi conspiracy and war. But in 1489 Innocent VIII agreed to appoint Lorenzo's second son, Giovanni, to the cardinalcy. He was then thirteen, even in those days an unusual age at which to be promised the red hat. 'This', wrote Lorenzo to the Medici representative in Rome, 'is the greatest achievement of our house.' And when the teen-age cardinal finally went to Rome in 1492 to meet his colleagues at the

Vatican, Lorenzo advised him to devote himself, of course, first and foremost to the interests of the Church. However, he added, 'while doing this it will not be difficult for you to aid the city and our house.'

Early in 1492 Lorenzo's long campaign against the disease he had inherited abruptly faltered. His father and grandfather had died at Careggi, and he had himself carried there. Sustained by the companionship of two men he had protected, Poliziano and Pico della Mirandola (as the dying Cosimo had kept with him his protégé Ficino), he called for Savonarola. The decision has been found strange. From the previous year, Savonarola's sermons had portrayed Lorenzo, in all but name, as a tyrant, the perverter of law, the exploiter of the fisc, the oppressor of the poor. Neither by roundabout threats nor outright bribes nor by the calling in of another famous preacher, Fra Mariano, to draw his congregations away from him, had Lorenzo been able to divert the friar from using him as a symbol of the unjust ruler. But Savonarola had been recommended to him, on account of his learning as well as his religious zeal, by Pico. Moreover Lorenzo had gratified Pico by not interfering when Savonarola was elected prior of S. Marco, the foundation that was, above all others, identified with the benefactions and the devotions of Cosimo and Piero. Savonarola was the antithesis of a household chaplain, but there was something atavistic about Lorenzo's calling for, and receiving, absolution from him. He died on 8 April, at the age of forty-three, and was buried, again as his ancestors had been, in the old sacristy of S. Lorenzo. In 1559 his coffin was transferred to Michelangelo's new sacristy and lies in a vault under the statue of the Madonna.

CHAPTER III

Towards the Principate

Into exile. Piero di Lorenzo, 1492–94

When Lorenzo the Magnificent died in 1492 it looked as though the place of the Medici in Florence had become secure. Giovanni had made the money; Cosimo gained the influence; Piero the Elder had weathered the constitutional challenge to the concentration of so much authority; Lorenzo had demonstrated the advantages to Florence of such a concentration. The form of government associated with Lorenzo meant that his passing was a relief to many, but his twenty-year-old son Piero was admitted without challenge to the place Lorenzo had occupied on the Council of Seventy and among the *accoppiatori*, the age-limit being specially waived for him. In addition to this, he had already been briefed by members of the regime on the assumption that, were Lorenzo to die, he would take his place among them.

He had been given the usual carefully supervised Medici education and shared his father's interest in poetry and manuscript collecting. Lorenzo had continued the family practice of sending the eldest son on unimportant diplomatic missions. Thus Piero had been to the court of Milan and had met Lodovico Sforza, and had been to Rome where he met Innocent VIII. During Lorenzo's absences, sometimes prolonged, from Florence, Piero kept him in touch with political news and with the affairs of the bank. But he had been prepared for a position beyond the range of his talents unless all went smoothly. He lacked the ferocious concentration which allowed Lorenzo to be effective on so many fronts. He lacked his father's gift for anticipating opposition and soothing it. Lulled by the fluency with which Lorenzo's position had been passed on to him and with little awareness that this position had to be earned as well as accepted, he thought it safe to act on impulse.

Piero was an example of a not uncommon type: the young man who feels that early success excuses him from continuous effort. Lorenzo had realized that the stability of the regime depended on its leader's ability to harmonize the tensions and rivalries within it. He had favoured certain especially reliable men, but he had made it his business to be on reasonable terms with others as well, men whom Piero neglected and alienated. This was a defect. Still, it was one which Piero the Elder had had (though with greater excuse because of his invalidism); and he had survived. Graver was Piero's unprofessional approach to the hand-ling of the Medici's special province, foreign policy.

He started, it is true, with a disability. He inherited a banking com-pany which was on the verge of bankruptcy, and showed little interest in it. Piero was the least wealthy of the fifteenth-century Medici. Lorenzo's success as a statesman had depended, to some extent at least, on spending money. Piero did not have the advantages of display or bribery. Above all, he lacked the imagination to see that a change of allegiance in foreign policy wrenches apart scores of filaments glued to the main body of a pact. Lorenzo had worked with some desperation in his last years to keep the Milan-Florence-Naples axis stiff enough to support the peace of Italy as a whole. It had always been threatened by antagonism between Milan and Naples, and Piero, by weighing down on Naples' side too obviously, probably at the urging of his mother and his wife, both belonging to the pro-Neapolitan Orsini clan, let it snap. A *frisson* of alarm was registered throughout Italy – but not by Piero. In itself, his action was not disastrous. He was merely intensifying, though thoughtlessly, an aspect of Lorenzo's policy. But it alarmed Lodovico Sforza, and Milan made another of its almost ritual requests to a French king to take up the dormant Angevin claim to the throne of Naples. This time, however, there was a new urgency in Milan's urging and a new and reckless monarch to listen to it. Charles VIII of France, like Piero a young man impatient with the caution of his predecessor, crossed the Alps in the autumn of 1494 with the largest army that had ever been brought into Italy. It was an action that was to make Italian historians a generation later, and for centuries afterwards, see that year as a watershed between a time of comparative peace and one of violence and humiliation.

It is only fair to say that neither did Piero's associates in government see his pressure to favour Naples as a link in the chain that was at last, after so many twitches – previous invitations not only from Milan but from Venice – actually to haul the armour and the artillery of France over the mountains. Hindsight saw it thus, but only after the lapse of some years. What alienated them was Piero's reaction to the French invasion.

Charles, to Lodovico's relief, kept his aim fixed on Naples. He crossed Lombardy with an army of some 30,000, heading for the Tuscan border with a deliberation that gave Piero time to reflect that Florence was now identified as an enemy of France. One lesson from

Florence's past was impossible to ignore: peril endangered the regime of the moment, defeat was likely to destroy it. Scapegoatism was a Florentine vice. There is considerable pathos in the action which Piero – still, at twenty-two, a youth, a cosseted one – took. He remembered what Lorenzo had done at a similar moment when Florence (and still more acutely, his own position) was in great danger during the war that had followed the Pazzi conspiracy. His father had risked going into the enemy's jaws, and they had not snapped but smiled. But Lorenzo's had been a calculated risk. Piero, purely on impulse, went to meet Charles at the border, sending, as Lorenzo had done, a *post facto* letter of explanation to the Signoria. And there the father-son resemblance ends. Charles did not want to conquer Florence or expel the Medici. He wanted, however, to ensure his lines of communication up and down Italy, by land and sea. He wanted a friendly Florence and guarantees that it would remain friendly. So he asked for the key fortresses of Sarzana, Ripafratta, Sarzanello and Pietrasanta and the ports of Pisa and Leghorn to be put in French hands. Were this done, Florence and Piero would be left undisturbed. Piero, to the considerable surprise of the French, agreed.

Their surprise suggests that Charles would have settled for easier terms, but the reaction to the news in Florence makes it clear that it was not only the concessions but the fact that they had been made by Piero acting on his own that caused resentment. Two embassies were quickly sent to Charles to persuade him that an agreement with Piero was far from being the same thing as a treaty with Florence, but Charles imperturbably occupied Pisa and declared his intention of moving along the Arno to the city. Piero hesitated to return. When he did, early in November, he was summoned to appear before a Signoria which, though elected via the usual electoral controls, was prepared to be sharply critical of him. With yet another misjudgment of the political atmosphere, he chose to answer the summons accompanied by a retinue of armed men. The doors of the Palace were barred against him and the bell tolled to call the people to the piazza. The first strokes were enough to tell a politically conscious people what sort of change was in the air. A mob hurried to sack the Medici palace while Piero, together with his brothers Giovanni and Giuliano, fled through the S. Gallo gate towards Bologna.

From republic to duchy (1): the patriciate

The forty-three years from the exile of Piero in 1494 to the establishment in 1537 of Cosimo I as the first of a new line of hereditary Medici
dukes span a period which was arguably one of the most dislocating and
at the same time most formative between the collapse of the Roman
empire and the French Revolution. The Americas were revealed. Africa
was circumnavigated and a trade network stretched between the Atlantic
and the East Indies. Within Europe, political life was polarized, with
an urgency hitherto unknown, between the rival dynasties of Habsburg
and Valois; religious life, with a heart-searching formerly the painful
privilege of a few, between Catholicism and Protestantism. Italy, rich,
temptingly divided and hanging like a punching bag into the Mediterranean, was a predestined casualty of the strains caused by these
developments. Her trade was threatened, her soil became the chief
battleground for French, German, Swiss and Spanish armies, her popes
became responsible for stopping the spread of Lutheranism. And the
resulting confusion in the peninsula was all the greater because the
Italian states, unwilling to combine for more than a few months at a
time against the invaders from outside, fought desperately for local
advantages against one another.

Florence was not only stricken by the conflicts waged around and
against it, but experienced upheavals of its own. Piero's exile was
followed by a revival of republican government which lasted until 1512,
when the Medici were restored to their former authority by a papal and
Spanish army. In 1527 a last republican revival sent the family packing
once more and, by a vote of 1,100 to 18, Jesus Christ was elected king
of the city in their stead. Three years later they were back, this time –
though their first representative was assassinated – to stay. And meanwhile, the family produced the first two Florentine popes, Leo X,
darling of the intellectuals and identified with the Golden Age of
Renaissance Rome, and Clement VII, who saw one of his capitals,
Rome, atrociously sacked in 1527, and was heard to say of the other,
'Would that Florence had never existed!'

The history of the Medici in this period must, then, be imagined
against a disturbed European background and almost uninterrupted
warfare in Italy. From 1513, when Leo X was elected, it has both a
Roman and a Florentine thread. Moreover, no fewer than seven members of the Medici had a hand in the government of Florence itself.
Under this appearance of complexity, however, the period has an

underlying unity which emerges if, before turning to a narrative of events, we ask two questions: why did Florence cease to be a republic? and how was it that the Medici in particular, twice banished and at no time represented in the city by men approaching the calibre of Cosimo *pater patriae* or Lorenzo the Magnificent, were able to establish a dynasty of princes there? The answer to the first is to be found in the nature of the Florentine upper class; to the second in the consequences of Lorenzo's far-seeing action in having his second son made a cardinal.

By 1492 the inner circle of families closely involved with the running of the regime had come to look upon themselves as forming a ruling caste, men who by right, rather than by inclination or chance, took part in the making of decisions and seeing them executed. Among such families were the Acciaiuoli, the Capponi, the Davanzati, the Gianfigliazzi, the Guicciardini, the Pandolfini, the Soderini and the Tornabuoni. The old notion of service to the state still existed. But it had become more closely bound up than before with self-interest, especially through the control such men had over taxation and the raising of loans. It was they who decided how much money was needed; they or their friends who put up the cash for war loans; they who imposed taxes as security for the sum; they who made sure that repayment of their loans would be given precedence and at what interest. At a time when investment in business was hazardous and when the interest on normal government bonds was dropping, control over the workings of war loans was a distinct advantage for the minority that formed the inner circle, and it hastened a process whereby the gap between the self-protecting rich and the heavily taxed majority was growing.

The economic policy of the Medicean regime had thus been socially divisive. Resentment against it was one of the factors leading to the expulsion of Piero and the re-casting of the constitution in a more democratic form. But that more democratic constitution had to face military crises and decisions in foreign policy as grave as any in Florence's history. The relaxation of electoral controls from 1494 to 1512 brought inexperienced men into government, and the ex-inner circle, now become a species of conservative old guard, watched their inefficiency with contempt and alarm. Gradually a sense of nostalgia developed for the good old days when Lorenzo de' Medici had informally presided over a group of men whose wealth, possessions and family pride gave them a real stake in the city, men of experience under whose care Florence had earned the respect not only of the other Italian states but of rulers from France and Spain to the sultan in Constantinople. In all probability the difficulties Florence experienced were not due so much to the middle-class element in government as to the fact that events in Italy were now beyond the control of a small state. Nevertheless, the contrast between the golden days of Lorenzo and the iron years that followed them enhanced the *hauteur* of the old guard. And this increased sense of separateness from the middle reaches of society was further emphasized by a subtle change in the nature of their self-consciousness as a caste.

All over western Europe, in the early sixteenth century, traces can be found of a process of re-aristocratization, a return to the values, in places even to the forms, of feudalism. In Florence it had already appeared in the previous century as a form of play, a flirting with in-appropriate (to a republic) but attractive modes of behaviour. Country villas (baronial castles without the stigma of militarism), chivalrous poems, tournaments, an interest in genealogy: these betrayed the attractiveness to wealthy merchants and bankers of an exclusiveness based on blood rather than effort, transmissible in a way independent of the brains or the sense of application of an heir. The Florentine upper class knew about the manners of an aristocracy of blood from their business contacts with England, France and Burgundy; in the sixteenth century aristocratic mores could be seen at first hand as armies from France and Spain crisscrossed the peninsula. Pride of family, a hallmark of the burgher, was never far removed from pride in blood, hallmark of the aristocrat. But aristocracy implies a fount of honours: a monarch, a hereditary ruler.

It is possible, in fact, to present a fairly simple formula: a group of men, habituated to government and to the use of office for their own advantage, marked off from others by the cosmopolitan background of their wealth and a culture tinged with chivalrous interests, become in-creasingly scornful and fearful of the classes below them and are at last prepared to welcome a prince, to lose some power in return for security. Something like this did happen, but not so simply. There were personal and family rivalries within the group. Among some the nostalgia for Lorenzo's days – reflected in Niccolò Valori's glamorizing biography, written between 1517 and 1519 – did not, in itself, imply a desire to surrender to a prince. Lorenzo, as one writer put it, used 'to come to the public places every day and to give a friendly hearing to all who came to see him, to be an easy companion of the citizens, who saw him as a brother rather than a superior.' There was a tendency to imagine a Lorenzo-figure round which the upper class could rally but not surrender to. But this thinking of leadership in terms of a *primus inter pares* was the product of speculation about the internal organization of Florence. In the conduct of foreign affairs, the Medici had always been granted a special freedom of action, and there is little evidence of resentment at their being thought of as princes by other powers. As the political confusion in Italy grew, with Naples conquered first by France and then by Spain, Milan conquered by France, then controlled by the Swiss and later occupied for the Emperor Charles V, Venice stripped for a while of almost all its possessions, and as the vulnerability of Florence became more obvious, there were some to whom shared control within the city seemed less important than a form of government shaped above all to present a keen and formidable edge to the outside world. And that was a world in which the word and power of a prince were taken more seriously than the spokesmen for a parcel of flustered burghers.

It was not only Machiavelli who drew morals from watching force at work. Because of the acerbity of its thought and the tension of its style, *The Prince* remains the most telling example of early sixteenth-century political thought, but it is one of a large cluster of writings that shared certain assumptions. Among these, an outstanding feature was a giving-up of the fifteenth-century tendency to consider constitutional change in terms of what had worked best in the Florentine past. For this traditionalist approach was substituted a rational investigation of other polities, both contemporary and ancient, in order to discover what would meet the challenge of current events, and, loosened in this way, political theory could discuss class interests with a new freedom and frankness. Much of this discussion went on in the patrician circle to which Machiavelli's wit and interests admitted him, and constant debate about the role of the policy-making Senate in ancient Rome and the Senate-like *Pregadi* in contemporary Venice added yet another strand to the self-consciousness of the Florentine upper class.

Again, this self-consciousness could lead in two directions: to an enhanced sense of purpose that would admit a leadership only as politically emasculated as that of the Venetian doge, or to the acceptance of a prince, the absoluteness of whose power would give lustre to the circle of courtiers and officials connected with and protected by him. On the whole the older men held the former view; they remembered Lorenzo and had been brought up in the atmosphere of public service as a duty owed to the state as well as a function of their status. Among the younger members of the upper class, however, there was a growing tendency to look to a prince who, once and for all, would protect them from political pressure from below and present a monarch-like figure to the world outside. When the republican interlude of 1527–30 was over, the Medici pope, Clement VII, was able to take advantage of this attitude in his cautious but persistent determination to have his family installed as hereditary rulers.

It is, however, misleading to make such distinctions too precise. If the richer and older families were as a group becoming more conscious of their social separateness, more 'aristocratic' (which, in the Florentine context implied no contempt for business affairs) in their way of life, they were also becoming less involved with one another and less reliant on their shared control of the financial policy of the state. The extraordinary, indeed, for the time unique, technical competence with which individuals ran their business affairs, using double-entry bookkeeping with nonchalant expertise, reckoning with Arabic rather than the cumbersome roman numerals used elsewhere, and striking periodical balances to obtain an overview of their fortune: this competence nourished an individualism which reinforced the growing tendency of single families to build their own palaces and plan their own futures without reference to the stock or clan with whom they shared a name. To be a Capponi or a Guicciardini did not imply a political stance: that depended on the individual's calculation of his own prospects and preferences – a preference which could lead to forsaking civic politics altogether and concentrating on land, rural life and purely domestic and intellectual pleasures. Aided by the decreasing attractiveness of investment in the state debt, this shift from communal to personal self-definition made it easier for a steadily applied pressure from outside to gain support. Both those who feared a dilution of their status from below and those who merely wanted to be left alone could see the advantage of entrusting government to a hereditary princely family.

From republic to duchy (2): the Medici popes

Changes in the character of the Florentine upper class help to explain why Florence ceased to be a republic. They do not explain why it became a principate under the Medici. The line of Cosimo *pater patriae* was, as we shall see, petering out in an epigonate of clerics and bastards. There were other families, the Guicciardini and the Strozzi among them, whose standing now was not inferior to Cosimo's when he had replaced the leadership of the Albizzi. It was overwhelmingly the presence of the two Medici popes in Rome that kept the family in being as a political force and which produced a situation by the 1530s in which, if a Medici prince could not be found he would have to be invented – as, to all intents and purposes, Cosimo I was. At eighteen practically an unknown quantity, he was brought in from a branch of the family traditionally at odds with Lorenzo's. This establishment of the Medici as a dynastic family was the work of two bachelors.

It is possible to see the careers of Leo X and Clement VII as providing little more than magniloquent marginalia to the history of Florence. It is in Rome that they must be judged as popes, from Rome that they peered with little comprehension at the spiritual quickening in Germany and Switzerland, from Rome that they tried to harness papal interests to the ambitions of France and Spain. Yet amid these preoccupations, Leo and Clement never ceased to think of themselves as Medici, and the shift from the palace in the via Larga to the Vatican was one in space rather than in feeling.

When Lorenzo the Magnificent's son Giovanni became pope in March 1513, six months after the family returned to Florence from their second period of exile, the citizens, regardless of their political sympathies, rejoiced wholeheartedly; only one thing had hitherto been lacking from their civic pride, a Florentine pope. Bonfires blazed, the Medici arms were quickly hacked out of stone or painted on canvas for the façades of houses and churches. The city had never looked so festively Medicean. Pageant succeeded pageant, vast floats designed and painted by – among others – Andrea del Sarto and Pontormo rumbled through the streets. Most impressive, and most flattering to the Medici, was one representing the Age of Gold, painted by Pontormo and carved by Baccio Bandinelli; as Vasari was to write: 'In the midst of the float was a large sphere or ball, as it were the globe of the world, and on this was the prostrate figure of a man lying dead with his face to the earth, and wearing armour covered with rust. This armour was cleft, and from the figure there proceeded the figure of a child entirely naked, and gilded all over, to represent the age of gold reviving from the corpse of that of iron.' But it did not escape comment that the Golden Age himself died a few days later from the effects of the gilding on his skin.

Leo X and Clement VII were not only remarkable as the first Florentine popes; they were also the first popes and rulers of the Papal States who were at the same time heads, if not the formally appointed ones, of a state of their own. They determined Florentine policy through deputies, members of the family residing in the city but guided from Rome. The presence of these deputies kept a Medicean party in being. But they also attracted opposition. Seen in retrospect, their function was not so much to pass on orders from Rome and see them carried out as to provide an interim regime within which the shifts of mood in the upper class could produce a positive appetite for permanent Medici rule. Meanwhile, the papal Medici were helping the shift in mood by the glamour of their position and through the patronage they could extend.

Leo was careful to flatter the Florentines. Not long after they had honoured him by suggesting that his papacy was to usher in an Age of Gold, he flattered them by a pageant in Rome which stressed the ancient respect in which the Romans had held the Etruscans. It was customary for the countrymen of a pope to follow him to Rome and look for favour there. Alexander VI had attracted a crowd of Spaniards, Julius II a flock of suitors from Genoa and its hinterland. But contemporaries expressed amazement both at the number of Florentines to come to Rome and at the generosity with which Leo greeted them. The names of the men who looked to him form a roll call of the most prominent Florentine families: Albizzi, Capponi, Tornabuoni; his major-domo was a Neroni; he appointed Filippo Strozzi receiver-general of the papal exchequer; a Pazzi received a treasurership; Francesco Guicciardini became one of the Pope's most trusted administrators. For the first time a Medici was able to indulge in political patronage on a large scale, handing out sinecures in the papal chancery, military commissions and castellanships in the Papal States, with a freedom far beyond the means of Cosimo or Lorenzo. There were so many Florentines in Rome that Leo even founded a church for them, S. Giovanni de' Fiorentini, so many that they were blamed for the deplorable state of Vatican finance in his last years. 'The treasury of the Pope is empty', stated a Venetian ambassador in 1520, 'because he is so generous that he does not know how to keep back any money; and the Florentines do not leave him a *soldo*.' Leo was known to complain in private about his fellow-citizens' self-seeking, but when, after his death in 1521 and the brief pontificate of Adrian VI, Clement became pope in 1523, the pattern recommenced; 'all Florence hurries here,' a Bolognese envoy reported from Rome.

It is difficult to estimate how much Florence gained or lost financially from the link with Rome. Certainly papal diplomacy involved Florence in producing large sums of money to buy off threatening armies or buy admission to an alliance. Taxation throughout the period 1513–34 (the date of Clement's death) was heavy and resented. It is arguable that the greater part of the sums demanded from Florence were indirectly spent for its benefit, that while the Medici popes connived at the quashing of Florentine 'liberty' their diplomacy saved Florence's independence as a self-governing state. It is a problem that has hardly been investigated. When Leo shifted from an alliance with France to one with the Emperor Charles V after 1519 the extensive Florentine commercial links with France were damaged. With thirty Florentine banks established in Rome during his pontificate, however, it is clear that individuals benefitted. And when Rome was sacked in 1527 the Florentine Signoria (a packed body, it is true, but probably expressing a widely shared impression in this case) instructed their envoy in Venice to lard his doleful tale with the reflection that 'Rome was the marrow and heart of our city . . . lacking which we remain like a dead body.'

Clearer is the way in which the Medici, thanks to Leo and Clement, came to look increasingly like aristocrats and less like bankers and merchants. Lorenzo the Magnificent's marriage to the daughter of a Roman baron had started this tendency; his grooming of Giovanni to become a prince of the Church continued it. The marriages arranged for two of his daughters were uncontroversial but aimed at the 'best' Florentine families in terms of social status: Lucrezia was married to a Salviati, Contessina to a Ridolfi, both of them families more noted for lineage than for political weight. A third daughter, Maddalena, was married to a bastard, but not an inconsiderable one, for his father was Pope Innocent VIII. In terms of the international freemasonry among aristocrats, however, the Medici were still suspect. A German knight (and not a well-to-do one), Ulrich von Hutten, could refer to Leo X as a shopkeeper. When Leo's nephew Lorenzo became Duke of Urbino and seemed, with the Pope's backing, on the verge of making new conquests, the King of France angrily commented to a Ferrarese ambassador, 'he should remember that he is a merchant'. Nevertheless, Leo managed to marry Lorenzo into the blood royal of France in the person of Madeleine de la Tour, daughter of the Count of Auvergne. It was from this marriage that Caterina (Catherine de' Medici) was born.

Leo arranged for his younger brother Giuliano to marry Filiberta, daughter of the Duke of Savoy, a match that brought with it the title of Duke of Nemours. He made Maddalena's husband a count (of

Anguillara). Between them, Leo and Clement decked the mercantile family tree with two dukes, a count and four cardinals. So rapid an aristocratization of the family could not have been organized from Florence.

Leo adopted in the Vatican a style of living even more opulently and obviously designed to exemplify his princeship of the Church than had his predecessors. More and more Florentines from the upper class were exposed in the reigns of the Medici popes to the social atmosphere of a city where, in the virtual absence of a bourgeoisie, attention was focused on the style of life exemplified by barons and prelates. When the time came for a final Medicean restoration, Florence was prepared for a court both by a form of internal social evolution and by the example of Rome, and the Medici name had acquired impressive princely associations.

Florence without the Medici: 1494–1512

In Florence the change in 1494 was at first little more than a rejection of the Medici. With Charles marching towards Florence and a time of hazard and negotiation lying ahead, the regime, having squeezed Piero out, closed ranks. By the end of November Charles and his army had come and gone. On 2 December the bell of the Palace rang again, this time for a formal *Parlamento*. As usual, the agenda had been carefully prepared and assent assumed. On the surface the proposals were sweeping. They amounted to a complete satisfaction of popular demand: a return to the 'open' constitution as it had existed before Cosimo returned from exile in 1434. But the machinery which was to bring this about was designed to leave power in the hands of the men who had staffed the old regime, purged now of outright Medici supporters. A body of twenty *accoppiatori* was appointed to draw up new lists in preparation for a return to election by lot; while this was being done, they had power to appoint the government for the time being.

During the next few weeks, while the French army dropped further and further out of mind towards the south, Florence was loud with political debate. Outside the ruling class there was spreading disillusion. It appeared, one commentator wrote, that the expulsion of the Medici had been brought about 'not for the people but for preserving in power the same men who had been ruling before'. It was muttered that the people had rid themselves of one tyrant only to be saddled with twenty: the *accoppiatori*. It became clear that the old ideals of widely shared participation in government had merely been hibernating during the restrictive regimes of the past generations, and that those who wished to see a broader representation of the public in the government looked not only back to the days when the Councils of the People and of the Commune had had a real role to play, but across to the example of the Venetian Great Council, a legislative and elective body far larger than any organ of state that had existed in Florence. Nor was the debate about a broadened representation simply one between those who had become accustomed to government and those who had been excluded from it. Within the ruling class itself there were some, and soon many, who came to believe that their survival as a directing force depended on countenancing a dilution of their power, if only till the democratic fervour waned and the Medici stigma faded.

When the full weight of Savonarola's prestige and eloquence was applied to the liberal side of the debate, the issue was settled. The friar was not a Florentine; he came from Ferrara. But since he had become prior of S. Marco he had identified himself so firmly with the moral reform of the city, and with its inhabitants' conviction that God had appointed a 'special destiny' for it, that he was considered at least an honorary Florentine. He was one of the ambassadors chosen to negotiate with Charles VIII and, as it appeared that he had correctly prophesied the death of Lorenzo, the election of a 'wicked' pope, Alexander VI, and, most tellingly, the French invasion, he was revered as one to whom God vouchsafed visions of the future. And his appeal was extraordinarily broad: to humanists and painters and members of the ruling class as well as to the massive congregations who were always pleased to be scolded from the pulpit by visiting revivalists. The constitution that emerged towards the end of December has been dubbed 'Savonarolan'. Had it been only that, it would have collapsed as his influence dwindled in 1497 or with his execution (for heresy and treason) in 1498. He affected the degree of support it gained, possibly its timing; he was, for the last years of his life, its supreme propagandist; but he was not its originator.

The new constitution was essentially that of 1434, with one crucial innovation, designed to prevent the manipulations that had permittied domination by oligarchical groups. The innovation was the Great Council. Membership was granted to all those whose father's or grandfather's names had been drawn for the three major offices, and membership carried with it the automatic right to qualify for office in any of the organs of government. It was only when the records had been combed that it was realized quite how widely representative the Great Council was going to be: rather more than 3,000 strong. The contrast with the recent past could hardly have been more extreme: one out of every four or five males over the age of twenty-nine now had the chance of approving or turning down laws and tax proposals or being elected to a wide range of offices.

As such, the council became the supreme symbol of the city's rejection of the Medici. A special chamber, the *Sala del Consiglio*, for which Leonardo da Vinci and Michelangelo were later commissioned to paint frescoes, was built adjoining the Palace of the Signoria for its meetings. The Medici had hardly left when Donatello's *Judith* was brought from the via Larga and set up in front of the Palace with a new inscription as a warning to would-be tyrants. And it was very likely the symbolic force of the Great Council that attracted another statue of a tyrant-slayer. In 1504 Michelangelo's marble *David*, originally intended for the cathedral, was dragged in a great wooden cage from the cathedral workshop to the Palace, an operation that took four anxious days. Inside and out, the headquarters of government proclaimed Florence's rejection of sixty Medicean years. Similar in intention was the scheme, not carried out, to place statues of famous Florentines over all the city gates. From Dante, Petrarch and Boccaccio to Coluccio Salutati and Leonardo Bruno, they would have reminded visitors of the literary triumphs and republican sentiments of the pre-Medicean past.

By this time Piero was dead. Together with Giuliano, he had three times collected troops and attempted to force his way back, in 1496, 1497 and 1498. When Alexander VI's militant son Cesare Borgia was threatening Florence in 1501 and 1502, Piero was with his army. The attempt which came nearest to succeeding was a surprise attack in 1497, when Piero got near enough to speak to the defenders of one of the city gates. At last, when it was clear that the dozen or so of his strongest partisans within Florence had overestimated his popularity and that the citizens would not rise in his favour, and in addition, that Cesare was simply using him to exert diplomatic pressure against Florence, he joined the forces of the new King of France, Louis XII, in his attempt to defend Naples against the Spanish, who had intervened there after Charles VIII's conquest of the kingdom. At the battle of the Garigliano, in 1503, Piero was drowned while trying to evacuate some of the French artillery in a boat. From that moment his brothers gave up plotting against the state, devoting themselves instead to waiting on events and nourishing the Medicean fifth column within the city.

The palace in the via Larga remained empty. But Florence was not without members of the family in residence. Since Cosimo's death the sons of his brother Lorenzo, Francesco and Pierfrancesco, had lived quietly in the old family palace, next door to, but on bad terms with, Lorenzo the Magnificent. Nor, though the two branches lived on better terms a generation later, was there any real sympathy between Piero and his brothers and the two sons of Pierfrancesco, Lorenzo and Giovanni. After 1492 Piero brought the latent quarrel to life and, on the vaguest of charges, succeeded in having them exiled. When he in turn went into exile, they returned. Moderately successful business-men, and not without charm, they are mentioned here only because they decided to improve their fortunes by buying grain in the Romagna and selling it to Florence, or at least to act as middlemen in such purchases. It was in connection with such a deal that Giovanni was entertained in Forlì by its ruler, the widowed Caterina Sforza. And because he was strikingly handsome and Caterina was tired (her sub-jects whispered) of 'a cold bed', having arrived as a businessman he stayed on as a lover and, very soon, as a father. They were married shortly before the child was born. Within a few months Giovanni died of the family complaint, gout and its complications, leaving Caterina to bring up the young Giovanni. It was from her son's marriage that the future Duke Cosimo I was born. Genetically, the immediate stock of Pierfrancesco di Lorenzo played a crucial part in the history of the Medici; constitutionally they were of no account whatever.

The anti-Medicean constitution of December 1494 was not as straightforward as it looked. In theory it permitted the most widely representative government in Europe. In practice much depended on the functioning of the Great Council, who attended it, whom it elected to the executive and legislative bodies of the state, and whether it judged men and measures on their merits or with regard to party interests. Within a few months from its inception, it was clear that large numbers of qualified citizens did not want to attend council meetings which consumed time many could ill spare from shop or counting-house. Others who wished to attend could not because their taxes were in arrears. A quorum was set at 1,000 and it was often difficult to raise one in spite of heavy fines for non-attendance. And if many Florentines showed that they did not want the actual responsibilities of democracy, those who did attend showed a tendency to vote in elections for well-known men, and this favoured the wealthier and more experienced class.

It was a bias the chief families tried to emphasize by combining together to elect certain men and exclude others. This was an illegal practice, precisely the danger the medieval constitution with its rotation and lot and disqualification laws had tried to prevent. But in so large a body, party alignments were almost impossible to prevent, especially as one of the council's key functions was to pass or reject tax proposals and these, no matter how carefully devised, were bound to fall, or appear to fall, more heavily on one section of the community than on another. As a result, members of the same income and occupation groups tended to vote in blocks.

The drift back towards oligarchy was slight. It was perceptible enough, however, to keep alive among the families of the old regime the hope that their time might come once more. This was especially true when Savonarola's death had not only removed the man who stated that the Great Council expressed the will of God, but had allowed parties to regroup on more nakedly apparent class lines; while he had lived parties – at least those of the *frateschi*, his chief supporters, and the *arrabbiati*, his most savage opponents – had been determined by feelings for and against him which overrode class divisions. From 1498 there were two chief political groups: the whites (*bianchi*) who supported the new constitution and were predominantly of families which had been excluded from office before 1494, and the greys (*bigi*) who wanted to destroy it and whose ranks contained a number of outright Mediceans.

One last factor favoured a return to oligarchy: the *Pratiche*. Florence was continuously at war or in the midst of preparations for war. It was not until 1509, for instance, that Pisa (whose occupation by Charles VIII had been turned by its citizens into a full-scale rebellion against Florence upon his withdrawal from Italy) was at last reconquered. Signorie were faced with problems they did not feel competent to deal with on their own, problems of foreign policy, financial problems. It speaks much for anti-Medici feeling and the endurance of republican ideals that, when faced by perils graver than any the Florentines could remember, the city had turned to the least efficient of all forms of government, a quasi-democracy, and the least efficient of all forms of democracy, one based on a system that brought inexperienced men to positions of responsibility and made forward planning as difficult as possible. The *Pratiche* had been designed to offset these disadvantages. Naturally they were composed of men who had had experience, and this meant that the government listened to a steady stream of advice from members of the previous regime. As early as 1495 a diarist noted that 'the *bigi* were again called to the *Pratiche*, and . . . under the pretext of the great external danger, they were asked for their opinion as highly experienced men, so that they once more began to acquire political power.'

At these privileged and secret meetings there were, from time to time, discussions about further constitutional change. The advice, which varied from the interposition of a body like the Medicean Councils of One Hundred or Seventy between the three leading offices and the Great Council, to a suggestion that a temporary dictatorship should be established, showed the sort of criticism to which the new system's inefficiency was open, even if such advice were not followed. One change was made, however, and a significant one. In 1502 the two-monthly gonfalonierate of justice was transformed into an office tenable for life, and Piero Soderini was elected as its first incumbent. This was a second borrowing from Venetian constitutional practice, but it was also a tribute to the value of the continuity in fiscal and foreign affairs that had been provided by the Medici.

The establishment of the doge-like life gonfalonierate was, indeed, welcomed by the greater families as a sign that the constitution as a whole might begin to be amended. This did not happen. Soderini himself was a determined white. But in more indirect ways his appointment was in the end to favour those members of the greater families who were anxious to put the clock back, complete with a Medici to strike the hours.

Centuries of tradition had produced among the patrician families of Venice a mutual watchfulness which hindered any party attaching itself to a doge. But Soderini had been sponsored by a group of conservative, if anti-Medicean families, and as the years passed, he acquired the image of a party leader at least in the eyes of those who hoped for a Medici restoration and of those who merely wanted an impartial chairman to protect the interests and draw on the experience of the old guard as a whole. He was accused of influencing elections to foster his own policies and using chancery officials to the same effect; his use of Machiavelli on diplomatic and military business led the future author of *The Prince* to be dubbed Soderini's 'mannerino' or puppet. In 1510 his status appeared so threatening that a plot to assassinate him was hatched by a member of a pro-Medicean family, Prinzivalle della Stufa. It was discovered in time. Cardinal Giovanni de' Medici was accused of supporting the attempt and Florentines were forbidden to make any future contact with him, his brother or any other member of his family. It was an accusation he denied, but the episode both emphasized the polarization of the pro-Soderini and pro-Medici parties within Florence, and strengthened Soderini's refusal to listen to Julius II's urging the city to break its links with France; the Pope was seen as Giovanni's protector and, by inference, an accomplice of della Stufa.

The alliance confirmed with France after Piero's flight had been kept to. It was of use to Florentine trade north of the Alps; it had brought troops to help Florence against Pisa. It was also perilous. Florence was very much at the beck and call of a country loathed throughout Italy, and became diplomatically isolated. There were good reasons for allying with the Empire instead, good reasons for joining hands with the papacy, good reasons, even, for being a heavily armed neutral. Soderini, with great skill, and with the advantage of his continuing authority, kept Florence pro-French. During 1510–12 this policy became a turning-point in Florentine history. In the previous year an alliance fostered by Pope Julius II, in which the chief partners were France, Germany and Aragon, had set upon Venice and stripped her of the vast majority of her territories in the Lombard plain. Its very success appalled Julius. In 1510 he changed front and called upon the Italian states to combine against the monstrous occupation of Italian soil by what he now called foreign barbarians. Florence refused to join this league, or its formal version of 1511 by which Spain, Venice and the papacy sought colleagues in their attempt to drive the French back over the Alps. While the city, under the steady urging of Soderini, held aloof from this suggestion, war began. In 1512, outside Ravenna, a battle was won but the campaign lost by the French. Their general was killed. Loaded with spoils they retreated, first to their base in Milan and then – because the Swiss invaded the Milanese as allies of the league – back to France. Florence had now affronted a victorious pope who had a Spanish army at his side and who was determined to leave the French without their one ally in Italy. At a conference in Mantua the representatives of the league decided to invade Tuscany and bring down the 'Soderini' government. At this conference Julius II was represented by his legate, Cardinal Giovanni de' Medici.

As head of the family after Piero's death, Giovanni had prepared the way for a possible return in two ways: by revealing himself to visiting Florentines as a reasonable, approachable man with no obvious thirst for power, at least until his connection with the della Stufa plot, and by gaining the confidence of the Pope through his obvious ability in the handling of Church affairs. He had arranged the marriage of his niece Clarice to the son of one of the richest Florentines of the day, Filippo Strozzi, builder of the Strozzi palace. Marriage with the daughter of an enemy of the state was not only scandalous but carried with it the penalty of banishment, normally for twenty years or more. Strozzi was allowed to return to Florence after only three, an indication that some of the virulence of anti-Medicean feeling had died down. With an army to back them, a pope to bless them, and the expectancy of *bigi* support from within, the family seemed to have favourable auspices for their return.

More favourable, certainly, than those that had encouraged Piero to his attempts on the city in the previous decade. Piero had been a restless seeker of aid from others and had, moreover, proved his own ineptitude as a leader. From their base in Rome, Cardinal Giovanni and his brother Giuliano had acted as unofficial Florentine representatives, offering guidance to the labyrinthine Vatican bureaucracy and aiding those in search of financial or ecclesiastical favours. They were watched, and their visitors reported on, by Florence's official representatives, but their households, for patricians increasingly irritated by the special position of Soderini and what was seen as his overbearing conduct of foreign affairs, came to have something of the standing of a government in exile. Moreover, never having held political authority they had not compromised themselves by failing to exert it wisely.

All the same, had Soderini agreed to the league's chief demand, that Florence should break with France and join them, the Medici would in all probability have had to return to Rome. But he did not. The league's army crossed into Tuscany, took and sacked Prato and stayed there while the Florentines decided what action to take on the demands presented to them: join the league, depose Soderini and allow the descendants of Piero the Elder to return as private citizens. Through smuggled messages and surreptitious meetings, Giovanni and Giuliano were able to keep in touch with their supporters within the city. And the crisis brought into the open not only the *bigi*, or *palleschi* as they were now openly called, but the whole spectrum of upper-class opposition, comforted that, constitutionally, they were being asked to do no more than allow the Medici to settle back quietly into their long-empty palace. Argued with by many, even threatened with force by a few, Soderini judged the situation beyond his control and fled. On the evening of the same day, 1 September, Giuliano entered Florence.

Two weeks of financial and foreign policy negotiations with the army followed, and while these were going on the government was reconstructed in a way that shows on what lines the *non*-Medicean opponents of the constitution of 1494 had been thinking. The term of office of the gonfalonier was reduced to one year, and a new body was proposed, a form of Senate composed of eighty members elected by the Great Council from those who had formerly been ambassadors or gonfaloniers or members of the War Commission; a further fifty were then to be elected by these men. This council would thus be closely biased towards the upper class and it was to be given powers to approve all financial legislation and appoint to all the chief organs of state. The Great Council was entrusted with only one appointment, to the gonfaloniership. The relics of 1494 and 1502 were mere trimmings. It was a stark bid for power by a social, cultural and financial élite.

This plan assumed that while the Medici might join such a government they would not and could not attempt to control it, and to this position Giuliano, politically easy-going, and more concerned with his standing within his family than with the family's standing within the city, assented. But the pro-Mediceans wanted more power for themselves and they anxiously sent word to Giovanni and to his cousin Giulio, who had also come to keep an eye on what was happening in the city, suggesting that the family could never feel secure under a system which provided them with so little leverage, and which retained, even as little more than a symbol, that chief monument to republican liberty, the Great Council. The point was taken. On 14 September Giovanni rode into Florence and, encouraged by his presence and the approval of Giulio, the *palleschi* persuaded the Signoria to sound the bell for a *Parlamento*. Surrounded by soldiers from the league's army, the people in the piazza 'agreed' on 16 September to abolish the Great Council and appoint a *Balìa* to consider further changes.

The extent to which the majority of Florentines were prepared to bow themselves out of situations stage-managed by their betters, even after an eighteen-years' taste of comparative freedom, can be seen from the account of Luca Landucci, an apothecary and formerly a keen partisan of Savonarola:

The piazza was full of armed men, and all the streets and outlets from it were barred with men-at-arms, crying perpetually *Palle*. The palace itself was also filled with armed men, even up to the belfry; but some of the people who had entered the piazza voted that they were content with the *Parlamento* and the new government. God be praised! Everyone ought to be content with what Divine Providence permits because all states and forms of government are of the Lord, and if in these changes the people suffer some hardship, loss, costs or discomfort, we must consider that it is on account of our sins and with the object of some greater good.

When these changes emerged, the constitution looked very much as it had done in the time of Lorenzo the Magnificent, complete with Councils of Seventy and One Hundred, stripped of the Great Council, and with elections made by Signorie appointed by *accoppiatori* all of whom were proven Mediceans. As under Lorenzo, no Medici was actually written into the constitution. The familiar wheels turned, the machinery of bogus republicanism ticked over, Signorie and commissions changed membership, legislation was sent down to the councils for ratification. The difference from Laurentian Florence was one of tone rather than of form. Under Lorenzo there had been complaints that decisions were taken in the via Larga that should have been taken in the Palace of the Signoria. These recurred with added bitterness when Giovanni became pope in 1513 and the Medici palace itself came under orders from the Vatican. There was also the impression that there were always soldiers about, a breath of the atmosphere we identify with a police state. The native militia raised by the Soderini government was disbanded, large Medicean garrisons of mercenary troops were stationed in the countryside, armed guards controlled admission to the public buildings in Florence, and the hall built and decorated for the Great Council was partitioned into quarters for troops. Though the old armorial symbols of the Medici were replaced and proclamations issued ordering the return of all their property and chattels, and though every attempt was made to represent their return as a Restoration after an unfortunate lapse of civic common sense, the continuity had been broken. The new Medici brought with them a whiff of a world that did not take republics for granted.

Head of the family, as Lorenzo the Magnificent's eldest surviving son, was Cardinal Giovanni, aged thirty-seven in 1512. His cousin Giulio, illegitimate son of Lorenzo's brother Giuliano, was thirty-four. Giovanni's brother Giuliano was thirty-three: respectively they had been nineteen, sixteen and fifteen when they were sent into exile in

1494. Giovanni's nephew Lorenzo, on whom the family's leadership in the city was to devolve in the following year, was twenty and had left at the age of two. They were welcomed with verses linking them with the days of Cosimo, Piero the Elder and Lorenzo the Magnificent, especially the last and with his symbol the laurel; much play was made with rhyming 'Lauro' with 'restauro', much with the *broncone*, the stump of the laurel bush cut down in 1494 and now sending out new shoots. The day of Saints Cosmas and Damian, the Medici patron saints, once more became a public festival. But given their ages (especially with Giovanni's absence in Rome), what they could not remember, let alone restore, was the skilfully maintained balance of Laurentian days between family self-seeking and republican institutions. They could restore the pageantry of the past and enlist the arts to proclaim the return of the Golden Age. They could revive their family's prominence, but not re-create its role. Nor, had they been older, would this have been easy. The city's mood, too, had changed. 'Your forefathers, in maintaining their rule,' a supporter wrote to Giovanni from Florence, 'employed skill rather than force: you must use force rather than skill.' And the justice of this advice seemed proved with the discovery of an assassination plot in February 1513.

Its leaders, two young idealists fired with the idea of being Brutus to the new Caesars, were executed. Pierpaolo Boscoli and Agostino Capponi swore that they had no collaborators, but a list of names was discovered which suggested that they had, and the government rounded them up, interrogated them under torture and kept them in prison. Among them was Machiavelli. Undoubtedly innocent, he turned to the most sympathetic member of the threatened family with verses asking the younger man (Machiavelli was forty-four) to obtain his release.

> Giuliano, I have jesses on my legs
> And six hoists of the rope across my back;
> I won't relate my other miseries
> Because such torments poets never lack . . .

> What pained me most was, as I slept towards dawn,
> Hearing the chanted prayers for the dead.
> Well, let them rot! So long as you, kind sir,
> Break my vile bonds, and pity me instead.

His release followed, not because of his poem, but as the result of a general amnesty when, on 11 March, Giovanni succeeded Julius II as

Leo X and had to consider which member of the family to appoint as his representative in Florence.

In spite of the passivity expressed by Landucci there were many middle-class men who hoped that the days of the Great Council would come again, and an influential number of patricians grudged the shouldering aside of their Senate-based reform plan. The personality and bearing of the family's representative in Florence was therefore, especially after the discovery of the Boscoli plot, an important factor in maintaining their authority. Giuliano, who at first took Giovanni's place, was not only in title but by inclination a private citizen. Cultivated, somewhat moody and introspective, he had come to beguile his years of exile by devoting himself less to intrigue than to the pleasures of sex, luxury and the arts; Castiglione and Pietro Bembo were among his literary friends, he knew Raphael and Leonardo and the aged architect-scholar Fra Giocondo who was for a while in charge of the rebuilding of St Peter's. He had the figure to bear authority but lacked the will towards authoritarianism. He had shown this by supporting the Great Council, an 'error' corrected by Giovanni after the *Parlamento* of 16 December, and now he showed his easy-going approach to the Florentine political milieu by having his beard – a symbol in most of Italy of aristocratic birth – shaved off, a gesture of real ideological significance.

The gesture was not lost on Leo, who called him to Rome as early as April. While the pope's brothers-in-law, Jacopo Salviati (Lucrezia's husband) and Piero Ridolfi (Contessina's husband), acted as caretakers in Florence, Leo, Giulio, Giuliano and Lorenzo discussed the city's future with the more ardent Mediceans who had come to Rome to congratulate the Pope on his election.

By August the structure of the restoration was settled. Both church and state in Florence were to be stabilized by keystones carved and settled into place by Leo. He legitimized Giulio so that he could qualify for the highest clerical positions, appointed him archbishop of Florence and made him a cardinal. The determination, the personal ambition Lorenzo appeared to have inherited from Piero and from his implacable Orsini mother Alfonsina, led to his being promoted, in spite of his youth, to the control of state affairs.

Lorenzo did not shave his beard when he returned with Giulio. He did not attempt to be affable and he expected to be addressed cap in hand even by patricians. There were murmurs, angry entries in private journals, but no attempt to muster a revolt. The sham government, that of the Palace, and the real government, that of the via Larga, continued to function side by side. Leo had given Lorenzo clear instructions. He was to use constant vigilance to make sure that Mediceans remained in the majority on the chief commissions, especially those dealing with foreign affairs, internal security and administering the public debt. He was to work through influential men he could trust or through men with no following who would owe everything to his support. He was to obtain confidential reports on the loyalty of members of the government and keep in constant touch, through his chief secretary, with Rome. He was to do everything possible to placate the masses within Florence and in the surrounding countryside. But he was to represent force as well as skill. In May 1515 he obtained the reluctant consent of the Council of Seventy to his appointment as Captain-General of the armed forces of Florence and received his baton in the presence of a mounted guard of young courtier aristocrats. 'This Lorenzo has been made captain of the Florentines against their own laws,' reported the Venetian ambassador. 'He has become the ruler of Florence: he orders and is obeyed. They used to cast lots; no longer: what Lorenzo commands is done . . . So that the majority of Florentines have no taste for the power of the house of Medici.' The family intervened even in private lawsuits to obtain verdicts for pro-Mediceans. Steps were taken to exclude visiting preachers who by adopting the style of Savonarola might bring to mind his message. To be overheard speaking against the Medici was to run the risk of exile.

Lorenzo's determination to be the effective leader of the family had been apparent from 1512, when the rival festivities promoted by his convivial society, the *Broncone*, and Giuliano's, the *Diamante*, had been seen in terms of political competition. With Giovanni a pope and Giulio a cardinal, both therefore unable to have heirs, and with Giuliano a father, but unmarried, Lorenzo began to negotiate for a wife – negotiations that came to fruition only in 1518, when, with the cordial support of the French King, Francis I, he married Madeleine de la Tour d'Auvergne. Again, anxious to secure the duchy of Urbino for the Papal States, Leo had suggested that Giuliano should lead an army against its ruler and receive its investiture in his place. He refused on the grounds of the hospitality he had received there during his years of exile, hospitality whose nature we can recapture from the part he plays in the conversations commemorated by Castiglione in *The Courtier*. It was Lorenzo who took up the offer, becoming Duke of Urbino in 1516 and conquering the duchy in that and the following

year. Machiavelli had originally dedicated *The Prince* to Giuliano in
1513, when there were rumours that Leo intended to use him to increase
the Papal States by conquest. Now, after Giuliano's early death – at the
Badia of Fiesole after a long illness – and the conquest of Urbino,
Machiavelli changed the dedication and addressed the manuscript of
the conqueror's handbook to Lorenzo.

For by now Lorenzo had revealed himself as the sorcerer's apprentice.
He had challenged Leo's notion of the Medici return as a restoration
of the Laurentian golden age of cultural patronage and constitutional
harmony. By insisting on his military appointment, and by stopping
Leo's intention to qualify a larger number of potentially safe families
for entry to the Council of Seventy, he had staked a claim, if no more,
to found a line whose power would be more direct and openly acknowledged than Lorenzo the Magnificent's had been. And he challenged
Leo even more openly in foreign affairs, contradicting the Pope's distrust of France, planning – or at least he was widely believed to be
planning – an empire based on Florence but reaching down to independent Siena and across to papal Romagna. For the papacy was elective;
once cut down, that *broncone* could not provide its nepotic shelter any
longer. As Leo's Cesare Borgia, Lorenzo had to work fast in order to
consolidate his gains – the time denied Cesare by the sudden death of
Alexander VI when his conquests were still in mid-career.

It was, however, Lorenzo who predeceased his uncle. He died in May
1519. Of the relief felt in Florence at the news of Lorenzo's death
there is ample evidence. It is doubtful whether Leo had felt that Lorenzo
would break the leading strings he held, though he had been able to
stretch them. Lorenzo was a young man in a hurry, born to great expectations which he saw in the light of the generally accepted political
views of the day, those of courtiers looking up to a prince; and he had
found his courtiers. Leo had needed him, used him, suffered him –
reassured by knowing that Lorenzo's closest ministers, especially his
secretary, Goro Gheri, saw themselves in the last resort as the Pope's
servants, not the duke's. But he did not openly judge him. Both as an
exponent and a manipulator, ambition was a quality of which he was
something of a connoisseur.

The first Medici pope: Leo X, 1513–21

It was an attitude Giovanni had learned from his father. He had been
admitted into minor orders at the age of eight and was almost at once

made an apostolic protonotary by Sixtus IV at Lorenzo the Magnificent's request. From that moment he was addressed by his proud family as *Messere* and Lorenzo began a campaign of benefice-hunting for him. It is mentioned here as part of the atmosphere in which Giovanni grew up, an atmosphere in which bargaining for benefices, releasing poor livings to move on to better ones, the accumulation of private ecclesiastical empires, was conducted as though parishes, monasteries and cathedrals were like any other form of real estate. With little more to hope for from Sixtus and with pluralism under fire from some influential churchmen in Tuscany, Lorenzo had looked abroad, instructing the agents of the Medici bank and the diplomats sent out from Florence to keep their ears open for vacancies or for news of abbeys whose priors were ill or aged. Hearing that the cardinal of Rouen had died, Lorenzo wrote to Louis XI to ask for one of his benefices for his eight-year-old son. Louis offered instead the Benedictine abbey of Sainte Marie de Font-douce, near Saintes. A few months later Lorenzo heard that the archbishop of Aix was dead. He at once wrote to the Pope asking for the necessary licence for Giovanni to hold the see in *commendam*, that is, to have the title and income while the duties were carried out by substitutes; negotiations were in full swing when news came that the archbishop was, after all, still alive. These negotiations, at once followed by others, form a chapter of considerable importance in Lorenzo's life. Into them he put time, energy, and a characteristic blend of bullying and cajolement. Foiled in France after his success at Font-douce, Lorenzo dropped his caution and went for Italian benefices, with some success under Sixtus and with triumph under Innocent.* Not all were held together, the value of some hardly went beyond the name, but by the time Giovanni had finished his studies in canon law at Pisa and taken up his residence in Rome as the youngest member of the college of cardinals, his education in the ecclesiastical mores of his age was precociously advanced, and his youth amply compensated by his titles and influence.

On his father's death he had returned to Florence, leaving again with Piero and, like him, intriguing during the last years of the century for the military support needed to overturn the new republican govern-

---

* Among them were: a canonry in the Florentine cathedral; S. Antonio near Florence; S. Maria del Piano di Sovara; the parish church of Scarperia; the Vallombrosan abbeys of S. Piero in Moscheto and S. Salvatore in Vaiano; the abbey of SS. Giusto e Clemente in Volterra; the important abbeys of S. Michele at Passignano and S. Lorenzo at Coltibuono; the still richer abbey of Morimondo in the Milanese, and Montecassino, one of the most famous and strategically important abbeys in Italy; the parish church in Calenzano; S. Maria in Campidoglio – the list could be extended.

ment. When the first three attempts had failed, he set off on a long tour through Germany, the Low Countries and France, a tour motivated by a restlessness and curiosity rare at a time when few men travelled except on business or pilgrimage. Returning in 1500, he settled once more in Rome. His Madama palace became an echo of the Medici palace. He accumulated a collection of antiquities; he entertained scholars, artists and musicians. In behaviour, if not in physical appearance, he was already the chubby but calculating hedonist of Raphael's portrait, impressing the Florentines who came to Rome with his charm and the Pope with his shrewdness. As papal legate to Bologna and the Romagna, he was not only present at the league's defeat and France's pyrrhic victory at Ravenna, but taken prisoner, being lucky to escape as the French army retired northwards across the Po.

The regaining of his liberty was swiftly followed by the return to Florence of the family of which he was head and the crowning of his own career as a churchman. Spiritual elevation following so swiftly on dynastic restoration was surprising enough to give an air of authenticity to the remark fostered on him (by a Venetian ambassador four years later): 'Let us enjoy the papacy since God has given it to us.' The same source records that the remark was made to Giuliano – whom Leo abruptly removed from Florence when he appeared to be acting in a similar spirit.

All the same, Leo's enjoyment of his new dignity is amply documented. There was no gossip about love affairs either when he was cardinal or pope, but in other ways he indulged himself largely. Each October, traditionally a holiday month for the Vatican bureaucracy, he spent hunting, commonly from his castle-lodge at Magliano in the Roman Campagna. A lifelong passion, he retained it even when he became corpulent and had to wear spectacles at the kill to see where he was thrusting. He ate as hugely as he observed fast days with attention. Many of the accounts of his redoubtable and infectious *joie de vivre* centre on his dinners, his frank pleasure in the food, his delight in the impromptu verses of his more cultivated guests and the cavortings of his buffoons. Always a collector, he now bought what he wanted; always a friend of men of letters, he entertained them and rewarded their dedications with a not always discriminating liberality. To the Moorish traveller a-Hussan Ibn Muhammad al-Wazzani, presented to him in 1518 after his capture by corsairs, he gave not only a pension but his names, Giovanni Leone, and not the least of the Pope's memorials is the

History and Description of Africa which his protégé, commonly known as Leo Africanus, completed in 1526. Patronage of scholarship, the arts and letters was a family tradition: Leo pursued it as much, perhaps, for the pleasure of being able to do so as from a genuine interest in what he patronized. The humanists Pietro Bembo and Jacopo Sadoleto were among his secretaries. Cardinal Bibbiena (Bernardo Dovizi), author of the outstanding comedy *La Calandria*, was his treasurer general. His personal enthusiasms were rather for the drama, for pageants and for music – art forms which involved sociability and a certain diffusion of interest. But certainly his vision of the value of ancient literature and what could be done to enlarge men's knowledge of it was a large and noble one, untroubled by the possibility that there might be conflict between pagan wisdom and Christian faith.

In 1515 Filippo Beroaldo's edition of Tacitus' *Annals* was published in Rome with a letter of privilege protecting its copyright.

> Since God called us to the high dignity of the pontificate [wrote Leo], we have devoted ourselves to the government and extension of the Church, and, among other objects, we have conceived it to be our duty to foster especially literature and the fine arts: for from our earliest youth we have been thoroughly convinced that next to the knowledge and true worship of the Creator, nothing is better or more useful to mankind than such studies, which are not only an adornment and a standard of human life, but are also of service in every circumstance; in misfortune they console us, in prosperity they confer joy and honour, and without them man would be robbed of all social grace and culture. The security and the extension of these studies seem to demand two conditions: on the one hand, they require a sufficient number of learned and scholarly men, and, on the other, an unlimited supply of first-rate books.

This blithely confident letter was published not long after the Lateran council, under his own presidency, had published a bull drawing attention to the dangers inherent in the study of ancient literature. Candidates for the priesthood were enjoined to take a full university course in theology or canon law before they proceeded to study pagan authors, and universities were exhorted to guard against the erosion of Christian belief and behaviour that might follow from an uncritical examination of their ideas. Leo himself, trained almost from the cradle to be a prelate, had studied not theology, but canon law and spoken Latin – the subjects appropriate to the running of a diocese. This was on advice given to Lorenzo by Sixtus IV. His piety was taken for granted, and justly: he observed his devotions, and the papal master of ceremonies wrote approvingly in his journal of Leo's attention to all his ceremonial functions. Untroubled himself, his phrase about 'social grace and culture' suggests that he saw humanist studies as primarily an aspect of upper-class culture and a potential danger only when pursued by those without the steadying influence of a secure social background. Gentlemen, in these last pre-Reformation days, were not likely to be heretics.

He invited Greek scholars to Rome and sponsored a Greek college, though it soon foundered from lack of funds. He went about collecting manuscripts for the Vatican Library, especially texts hitherto unrepresented, in a mood not unlike his father's when benefice-hunting. He had agents examine libraries all over Europe but especially in Scandinavia and Germany, where the richest hauls of novelties were to be expected, and they were armed with letters promising rewards to those who sold their manuscripts or allowed them to be copied – and excommunication to those who did not. Leo knew the Tacitus manuscript that Beroaldo edited had been stolen from the Westphalian monastery of Corbie. He did not send it back, however, offering the monks instead a copy of the printed text together with a plenary indulgence for their church.

Leo was concerned for the monuments as well as for the literature of antiquity. A great part of the ruins of classical Rome were choked and hidden by vegetation and rubbish. Others, notably the Colosseum, were used as quarries for building material. The centre of Christendom was also the headquarters of the vandals. Even the popes themselves had been to blame. 'The new Rome', Raphael wrote to Leo, 'which we now see standing in all its beauty and grandeur, adorned with palaces, churches and other buildings, is built throughout with the lime obtained from ancient marbles.' Leo's interest, while it did not lead to the issuing of protection orders, did possibly help to slow the process of destruction. He approved the plan, sponsored by Raphael and Castiglione among others, to make an explanatory map of classical Rome; he encouraged excavations and insisted that no stone bearing an inscription should be destroyed, in the interest of furthering historical knowledge and 'the classical purity of the Latin language'. When new archaeological discoveries were made he identified himself with them, having the *navicella* placed in front of S. Maria in Domnica and installing the colossal statues of Nile and Tiber among the other antiquities in the Belvedere gardens, which he kept open to the public. At heart a collector rather than a preserver (he, too, used Roman marbles for St Peter's), Leo at least did something to make the Romans more aware of the value of their inheritance. And he continued another and more subtly influential process inaugurated by his predecessors, notably Sixtus IV: the gradual destruction of medieval Rome and the creation of broad streets and new palaces whose architecture, ignoring the Middle Ages, glowingly reflected something of the ideas that had shaped the battered survivors of the antique past.

Leo was not a man of powerful imagination; he was not himself a scholar, as Nicholas V had been; he did not have the creative insight that had enabled Julius II to challenge the imagination of Michelangelo. We owe to him Raphael's tapestries, the completion of the Stanza d'Eliodoro, the Stanza del Incendio and the paintings in the *loggie* of the Vatican, but Raphael's art owes nothing to Leo save the square feet he was asked to cover. Leo obtained nothing from Leonardo, who had come to Rome in 1513. He did not employ Fra Bartolommeo, or Sodoma or Sebastiano del Piombo, all of whom worked in Rome during his pontificate. Leo's real contribution to the culture of Rome, and thus of the Renaissance itself, was that he acted not as the inspirer of individuals but as a marvellously congenial host to the world of arts and letters. Under Leo, Rome resembled a vast country house where men foregather less for the personality of their host than for an atmosphere in which they can talk well, think freely and be sure to meet others who share their interests. If Rome became the cultural capital of Italy under Leo, it was less for what he did than for what he was.

Leo's critics have pointed to the fact that it was the selling of in-dulgences to pay for St Peter's that moved Luther to open criticism of the Church, and have also pointed to his attending a masque of Venus while Luther was explaining his anti-papal position at the Diet of Worms. But it is worth remembering that not one of the Italian states had seen the invasion of Charles VIII for the portent it was. There had been foreign armies in Italy before. There had been heretics before Luther. Leo set in motion the usual machinery of investigation just as the states had adopted the habitual defensive postures. In both spheres there was a similar failure of insight and communication but at least his Lateran Council promulgated reform decrees which, if they had been observed, would have disarmed Protestant criticism of the behaviour (if not of the function) of the clergy. Again, by the concordat of Bologna of 1516, Leo sacrificed certain papal interests to those of the King of France, and this has been seen as a grave miscalculation. But his predecessors had yielded far more to Ferdinand and Isabella of Spain. Yet again, he granted the title 'Defender of the Faith' to Henry VIII, soon to break altogether with Rome, and the irony of this reversal has been turned into a criticism. But at the same time he was bullied by French and Spanish monarchs to whom his predecessors had granted the titles 'most Christian' and 'Catholic'. As ruler of the Papal States and thus a secular prince competing with others, and as spiritual leader of Christendom, Leo was hardworking, tradition-bound, and unimaginative. The years of exile had made him suspicious and secretive, perhaps they had made him put too high a value on the aspect of papal life that was like a God-given extension of his ideal of private life. Apart from this last consideration, a judgment of Leo must involve a judgment of the system into which he was educated, of Lorenzo who initiated him into it, of Lorenzo's tutor Becchi who, as bishop of Arezzo, admitted him to minor orders, of Innocent VIII who covered a thirteen-year-old head with a red hat. Leo's fault is that his career sums up all that was typical and emphasized much that was excellent in clerical pre-Reformation Europe, and at no point rose superior to it.

He was not severely tested in the field of international relations. Since French armies had returned under their new King, Francis I, and repossessed the Milanese after the battle of Marignano in 1515, Italy was without large-scale wars until the year of Leo's death. Locally, he heeded the example of the popes of his childhood and youth, Sixtus IV and Alexander VI, who had used members of their families as the most trustworthy agents in extending the papacy's hold over territories in the Papal States. Dynastically he played strongly from a potentially losing hand. With no legitimate and marriageable member of the family left after 1519, he let it be known in Florence that Cardinal Giulio was to manage the family's political interests there, and sent a detachment of troops to make sure that the transition from Lorenzo's government should be given time; time, that is, to sustain the atmosphere of restoration which had become contaminated with the flavour of usurpation. Celibacy was a low card to play in a city of families, but it was, in the end, a winning one.

The Giulian compromise, 1519–23

At Lorenzo's funeral, when the citizens were obediently clad in mourning, one man appointed himself, unchallenged, a symbol of their inner relief: at the head of the grave procession of guild officials and government officers walked a young man carrying roses in his hand and dressed from head to foot in scarlet.

Lorenzo's successor as leader of the family interest in Florence was a man to whom scarlet was a working dress. Cardinal Giulio had played an increasing part in the city's affairs during Lorenzo's absences. He was accessible, modest in his style of life, living on the income from his benefices and taking nothing from the city – in notable contrast to Lorenzo's attitude: the city, for instance, had had to foot almost the whole cost of his conquest of Urbino. Giulio enlarged the number of families eligible for public office on the lines Leo had vainly suggested to Lorenzo. He took some of the sting out of the opposition to the regime by asking some of its critics to submit their suggestions in writing. Among them was Machiavelli, whose advice was that, since neither the head of the family, Leo, nor his deputy, Giulio, could have heirs, it would be wise to re-institute the Great Council but control appointments to it. Thus the Florentines would become accustomed once more to the functioning of an institution for which many of them pined, and ready to use it when the control of the city fell back into their hands. This proposal enabled Machiavelli to legislate for a republic while providing means to preserve Medici domination during the lifetime of his patrons – for Giulio had commissioned him to write his *Florentine History*. Giulio did nothing to implement this or other suggestions, content to release the tensions generated under Lorenzo into the thin air of discussion.

When Leo died in 1521, Giulio's name was canvassed in the College of Cardinals, but the choice fell eventually on the Fleming, Adrian VI. Giulio returned to Florence where in the following year he had to deal with the discovery of a threatened revolt, backed by Cardinal Soderini, on behalf of the exiles without, and the malcontents within, the city. Giulio dealt firmly, by execution and exile, with the conspirators and provided himself with a sizable armed guard under a professional captain, Alessandro Vitelli. Then once more he asked for suggestions, busied himself with raising the hopes of those who looked back to the constitution of 1494, flattering the aspirations of those who wanted Medicean domination, giving each the hope of triumph without having to resort to force, setting one against the other in squabbles that left him imperturbably in control. In one way his suavity of approach was successful. Neither the plotting of exiles nor the discontent within the walls came dangerously to a head. In another way it failed, for it prompted a ferment of discussion that boded ill were he not there to keep it, with his tact and his guards, within bounds. When, in 1523, Adrian died and the choice of the cardinals fell on Giulio and the Florentines watched him leave to reside permanently in Rome, the thought occurred to many that this voluntary and illustrious withdrawal could mean the end of one restoration, that of the Medici, and the beginning of another, that of the broadly based republic of 1494.

CHAPTER IV

The Principate Achieved

Clement VII, 1523–34

On 18 November 1523, the College of Cardinals elected a second descendant of Giovanni di Bicci de' Medici as pope, but not because he was a Medici. Giulio's victory over his rivals, among whom was Cardinal Wolsey, was due to three things. He had shown firmness and discretion as a politician in his handling of Florence, and as Leo's vice-chancellor and then as Adrian's right-hand man he had made a favourable impression in Rome; no one knew more about how the Church was run, no other cardinal's anterooms were more thronged by petitioners and ambassadors. In the second place, his candidacy was backed by the Habsburg Charles V who, already ruler of Burgundy, the Netherlands and Spain, had been elected Emperor of Germany in 1519 in succession to Maximilian. Third, through the multiplicity of his benefices, he was, of all the members of the conclave, the one with most to give away. He had rivals: the cardinals sympathetic to France were opposed to him, so were some of the older men who had resented the numerous additions to their numbers forced through by Leo X, so were those who had already voted against him in 1521 out of fear that the papacy might become, like Florence, Medici property. Only fate seemed to have a clear idea of the outcome: in drawing lots for the temporary cells erected in the Sistine chapel for the conclave, Giulio drew the one under Perugino's fresco showing Christ offering the keys to St Peter. The conclave lasted, scrutiny by scrutiny, for fifty days, one of the most fiercely combated elections of the Renaissance, but when it was over and Giulio emerged as Clement VII there was an almost unanimous feeling of relief and pleasure. Though the successor to St Peter could theoretically be of any nationality, the Italians, who formed a majority in the College of Cardinals, had fallen into the habit of expecting him to be one of them; Adrian's Flemishness had confirmed this prejudice. Popes for generations had lived as gentlemen, lavish in their patronage of art and letters, generous, if not always sumptuous, in the style they kept. Adrian, crabbed and puritanical, had brought a draught from the seminary into the most sophisticated court in Europe and the Romans had not liked it.

Clement was welcomed as a chastened Leo, a Leo with more experience of affairs and less Epicureanism, if less charm, a safer man for
more troubled times. Where Leo had been pious, Clement was devout.
As a patron he spent more cautiously but was more discriminating.
Raphael's *Transfiguration*, stylistically the most daring of his works, was
painted for Clement. He was one of the early supporters of Sebastiano
del Piombo, whose nickname records the office (affixer of lead seals –
piombi – to papal bulls) Giulio gave him when he became pope. The
dies for some of his coinage were engraved by Benvenuto Cellini and
one of his last acts was to commission Michelangelo to paint the *Last
Judgment* in the Sistine chapel. His patronage of letters was modest,
though by nature he was the most scholarly of his family; but he
retained Pietro Bembo, *arbiter elegantiarum* of the Italian literary scene,
as one of the papal secretaries, and he continued to build up the manuscript collections of the Vatican Library. Though the manuscripts were
to be housed in Rome, Clement made it clear that he was acting above
all as a Medici; one of the safe-conducts to be carried by his agents has
survived, and it calls on the secular and ecclesiastical authorities
throughout Europe to aid the good work begun by Cosimo and continued by Lorenzo the Magnificent and Giuliano (Clement's presumed
father) and by Leo. He was also a musician of such wide repute that a
professional, who shared the name Clement, was forced in self-defence
to invent the surname 'Not-the-Pope'.

Giulio's sympathy for scholarship and the arts was one of the minor
reasons for the popularity of his election. 'It seems', wrote that authority
on how aristocratic rulers should behave, Baldassare Castiglione, 'that
here everyone expects the best of the new pope.' But at a time when
the full bitterness of Charles V's rivalry with the Valois king of
France, Francis I, was making Italy yet again a battlefield, a pope
had to be above all a politician. 'He is a prudent and an intelligent
man,' a Venetian diplomat reported, 'but he makes up his mind
slowly and this leads to his following contradictory courses. He speaks
well and sees into everything but is very timid.' This opinion voiced at
the opening of his reign has become the judgment of posterity: desiring
neutrality but forced by their clamorous demands to choose between
supporting either France or the Empire, argued towards first one then
the other course by his two advisers, the pro-French Giberti and the
Imperialist Nicolas von Schönberg, Clement's irresolution became a
commonplace of diplomatic gossip and made the two monarchs even
more strenuous in the demands they made of him. There is a Machia-

vellianism of the intellect as well as of the moral sense: a ruler must sometimes give up the individual's luxury of allowing equal weight to both sides of a question, just as individual conscience must sometimes be sacrificed to the public interest. Though the spiritual leader of Christendom, Clement was prepared to deceive and to double-cross; he was able to silence conscience, but a counter-argument, never. Perhaps his illegitimate birth robbed him of some self-confidence. Perhaps the *Kleinstädterei* to which he had become accustomed in Florence limited his vision from Rome. But Clement is best understood in terms of the modern intellectual, better as an adviser than a leader, more qualified to analyse than to act.

Merely to list the problems that confronted Clement in the eleven years of his pontificate, however, is to suggest that the enormity of his task precluded success, especially for a ruler working from an impoverished treasury and on inadequate or faulty information. Apart from Habsburgs and Valois fighting for predominance in Italy, especially for control of Milan, they included Henry VIII bullying for his divorce; Suleiman leading his Turks into Hungary, defeating its king and threatening Vienna; Lutheranism spreading throughout the Empire and into Scandinavia; Zwingli lighting revolt against Rome in Switzerland. On those eleven years pressed the full weight of what were becoming the most pervasive spiritual and political crises Europe had experienced; one was linked to the other, and Clement was harnessed to both.

He did not manage to stop the sliding of parts of Europe into Protestantism or, in the case of England, out of communion with Rome. But it was with his encouragement that the forces were mounted – the reform of old religious orders, the creation of new ones – which were to inspire the Catholic counter-attack at mid-century. And surrounding the core of Lutheranism in the Old World was the enormous circumference of missionary activity which he sponsored in the New, from America to India. Spiritually, the pontificate was not without its splendours; politically, it was one of almost uninterrupted humiliation.

Two years after Clement's accession, an Imperial army not only defeated a French one at Pavia but took its king prisoner. Francis was forced to give up all the claims that had brought one French force after another into Milan and Naples. Charles V was to be unchallenged ruler of Naples and, through his puppet, Francesco Sforza II, unchallenged protector of Milan. As the ruler of two Italian states, Rome and Florence, Clement reacted as had his predecessors when one of the leading European powers threatened to deprive Italian rulers of their freedom of action; he joined the other side. Francis returned from his captivity in Spain in 1526, eager to break the terms of his surrender to which, he explained, he had agreed under duress. Between them, he and Clement arranged the adherence to the League of Cognac of Genoa, Milan, Venice, Rome – and, with Rome, of course, Florence – and began raising an army to run the Imperialists out of Italy.

But after this moment of decisiveness, Clement's nerve failed. There had probably never before been so widely shared a determination to free Italy from foreign control. On the other hand, alliances of Italian states had traditionally fallen to pieces. The peninsula was three centuries away from the spirit of the Risorgimento. The Pope, too historically conscious for the mood of the moment, distrusted his allies, let this be seen, and thus confused and weakened their common purpose. He looked forward ('he sees into everything'), but he saw there the consequences of defeat as well as of victory ('but is very timid'), and by doubling up his diplomacy he tried to placate Charles's wrath in advance and, detected in this, still further weakened the morale of the league. Charles, operating at long range, could neither control his army nor pay it. Clement, at the centre of the theatre of war, did not have the credibility to give the army of the league a sense of purpose, a cause to die for. There was no major confrontation. The Imperial army gravitated towards the loot to be found in Rome, its large Lutheran contingent (Charles's agents had not inquired into the faith behind the mercenary pikes) acting as a doctrinal flywheel within it; the league's army moved along behind as its irresolute shadow. In May 1527, the papal city was stormed and sacked. 'Hell', wrote an observer within a few days of the Imperialists' entry, 'has nothing to compare with the present state of Rome.' For a month Clement was besieged in his own castle of S. Angelo. Then came surrender and renewed prevarication.

As the conflict ground on, it became clear that Francis could not command enough resources to be even a background support to the papacy, let alone the architect of an outright victory over the manpower of Spain and Germany. In 1529 Clement changed sides openly. By the treaty of Barcelona he agreed to support the Emperor, albeit with the risk of appearing to be little more than his chaplain, and in return was promised help in the reintegration of the states of the Church and an army to clear a way back to Florence for Alessandro and Ippolito who, as we shall see, had succeeded him as caretakers of the family interest and been expelled on a new wave of republican energy not long after their guardian had been imprisoned in S. Angelo. A ritual significance was given to this agreement by Charles's pledging the hand of his illegitimate daughter Margaret to Alessandro. A bastard pope was thus to hope to ensure the continuity of Medicean rule in Florence through the betrothal of two bastards. No wonder the stabilizing shades of Cosimo and Lorenzo the Magnificent were to be so constantly evoked in future Medicean propaganda. Clement also agreed to give a deeper significance to the treaty itself by ratifying Charles's title through the solemn ceremony of Imperial coronation.

This ceremony, even more definitely than the sack of Rome, marked a turning-point in the history of Italy and of the Medici. It was a symbol of the acceptance of political helplessness. Charles chose to be crowned in Bologna rather than Rome, and Clement, with pathetic ingenuity, engaged a team of decorators to make the interior of S. Petronio resemble that of St Peter's as nearly as possible. It was attended by representatives of all those Italian states whose weakness Charles had demonstrated, and with becoming reverence. It implied that independence of outside domination was a thing of the past and that if the princes of Milan and Mantua were prepared, as they were, to become courtiers of the Emperor, Italy was now so changed that the Florentines would eventually be prepared to become courtiers of the Medici. And so it turned out, though only after a last struggle whose violence helped cauterize their republicanism.

The Medici bastards and the Last Republic, 1523–30

When Giulio left Florence for Rome, he left a vacuum at the heart of the Medicean system of political control. This system had come to be based on three principles: retaining the republican constitution but controlling elections to its chief components, notably the Signoria and the War and Public Order Commissions; maintaining professional armed guards within the city and a militia force in the surrounding countryside composed of peasants who, in return for some tax exemptions and the privilege of carrying arms, and because of their antipathy to the patricians who had taxed them so heavily in the past, would support the regime were it threatened; and, lastly, through flattery, the securing of appointments and other favours, encouraging a form of clientage, a personal dependence on the Medici which drew men away from their traditional family and party loyalties.

Each principle called for leadership, but in Giulio's absence what leader could be found? The available cast was as follows: Giuliano's bastard son Ippolito, aged thirteen, Lorenzo's four-year-old daughter Caterina, and Alessandro, also about thirteen, given out by Giulio as Lorenzo's bastard but widely rumoured to be his own. Not an impressive list, but a sufficient number of patricians desirous of maintaining the *status quo*, plus a more general feeling that a link with another Medici pope would be to the economic and political benefit of the city, led to its acceptance. Ippolito was installed in the Medici palace as the family's leading representative. Alessandro moved into the Medici villa at Poggio a Caiano.

Though the age restrictions were waived to enable Ippolito to take public offices, he was, of course, little more than a puppet. As successor to himself as archbishop, Clement appointed his young kinsman Cardinal Ridolfi to advise on clerical matters. For administrative business Ippolito inherited the personal bureaucracy of the Medici palace, centred on Lorenzo's and Giulio's loyal and efficient secretary Goro Gheri. Politically he was virtually under the tutelage of Clement's own representative in the city, the cardinal of Cortona, Silvio Passerini. Thus the vacuum was filled. For the moment, at least, the pro-Medicean party and the more conservative of those families who hovered irresolutely about its fringe were satisfied. But the leadership, on which the system depended, was divided and precariously popular. Ippolito, centre of the clientage relationships, speedily gave himself the airs of a spoiled and haughty princeling. Passerini, labouring under the disadvantage of coming from one of Florence's subject cities, was an abrupt, secretive, dried-up man as incapable of soothing opposition as he was of veiling the fact that Florentine policy was determined more rigidly from Rome than it had been under Leo. The stability of this unattractive *ménage* would depend on how the Florentines judged the advantages of the Roman connection.

Awareness of this, as well as irrepressible family pride, led Clement to use the frail influence of cultural patronage to stress the continuity between the present Florentine regime and that of the great and by now greatly mourned fifteenth-century members of the family. He and Leo had commissioned frescoes for Poggio a Caiano. One of them, Franciabigio's *Triumphant Return of Cicero to the Campidoglio*, was a reference to Cosimo's return from exile in 1434; it was on his own return from exile that Cicero had been granted the appellation *pater patriae*. Andrea del Sarto painted there a fresco of *The Tribute Presented to Julius Caesar in Egypt*, whose detail recalled the gifts of zoological *curiosa* (including a giraffe) made to Lorenzo the Magnificent by the sultan of Egypt. Leo had commissioned Michelangelo to design a façade for the 'family' church in Florence, S. Lorenzo, but the project had been allowed to lapse. Clement did not revive it. By tradition a church façade could not carry actual portraits. It could celebrate a family through an inscription, as Bernardo Rucellai was commemorated on the façade of S. Maria Novella, but Clement wanted something more personal, something that would, this time with the authority of marble, buttress the authority of his own kinsmen by associating them with the cultural and civic distinction of their ancestors. So Michelangelo was invited instead to press ahead with an earlier project to construct a new sacristy in S. Lorenzo which would contain monuments to Alessandro's and Ippolito's presumed fathers, Lorenzo and Giuliano, and to *their* illustrious forebear Lorenzo the Magnificent. Michelangelo began the statue of Lorenzo the younger in 1525. Then the project faltered. Funds were not forthcoming from Rome. The Florentines were being taxed to such an extent that it was hazardous to ask them to pay for Medici monuments as well as for Medici policies.

For already the value of the Roman connection was in doubt. Clement's hesitating support of the Habsburg campaigns in northern Italy up to 1525, then of French policies after Francis I's defeat at Pavia and more openly after his return from captivity in Spain in 1526, cost money for which the Pope turned unhesitatingly to Florence. Though the return to a pro-French policy was a return to a Florentine tradition, it was not tradition but protection that the Florentines now wanted, and the armies raised by the Papal-French league seemed no match for the formidable build-up of troops organized by the Imperialists. In addition, though patricians were dutifully being fed into the constitutional machine they had less and less to do there apart from passing Florentine money to Rome.

A month before the sack of Rome a mere rumour was enough to show how insecure the Medicean regime had become. The Imperial army was moving from Romagna towards Tuscany. Passerini and Ippolito rode out to greet the commander of the league army, encamped at Barberino, some twenty miles away, but as they had not chosen to inform the government of their diplomatic gesture the rumour quickly spread that they had fled the city. So much credence was lent to this hoped-for explanation, and so militant the glee of the anti-Medicean citizens, that the Signoria was pressured into proclaiming a return to the republican constitution of 1512.

This reversal was short-lived. Passerini was only two miles outside the walls when the news reached him, and he at once turned back with a large escort of horsemen. The effect of their appearance in the approaches to the Palace of the Signoria, and the sound of their arquebuses discharged into the air, changed the mood of the demonstrators so abruptly that, as one observer put it, mouths that opened to say 'Popolo!' shouted 'Palle!' instead. Passerini's escort then attacked the Palace itself in a skirmish during which Michelangelo's *David* had an arm broken by a stone dropped from the roof. The Friday Rebellion (*Tumulto di Venerdì*), as it came to be called, was a failure. Behind Passerini was a whole army.

But it was a dress rehearsal, a training in roles, for the revolution that was almost bound to come if the league suffered any serious reverse or if Clement himself were to suffer a diplomatic defeat. Among the chief supporters of the Medici were many who, in spite of heavy taxation, were largely influenced by the advantage to their businesses of the link with Rome; if that were to break, a major cause of their loyalty would snap as well. Then came the sack: Clement locked in his own strongroom, the Castel S. Angelo, the league's army impotent to help, Rome's population practically halved by slaughter and flight, its business life suspended, its banks pillaged. Within days the reaction came from Florence, this time meditated and surprisingly calm. It was represented to Passerini in firm and not discourteous terms that the temper of the city was such that it would be best were he to withdraw, taking his wards with him. With Clement powerless, he was compelled to agree; and with an escort provided this time by the Signoria, he, Ippolito and Alessandro rode out through tense, but on the whole quiet, crowds towards another Medicean sojourn in the political wilderness.

As after the previous expulsion of the Medici in 1494, there were two views as to how the city should be governed. Either control should be in the hands of an oligarchy, a small self-perpetuating group of patrician families who would share power among themselves for the common political, and their own economic, advantage, or the suffrage should be extended more widely, more democratically. Those who had engineered the Friday Rebellion as well as those who had dispatched Passerini favoured the former alternative. They included patricians who had never wanted even the appearance of a principate, and those Mediceans who had disliked either the personalities of the past regime or subordination to Rome, or both. After 1494 the partisans of a 'democratic' constitution had, after a short oligarchical interregnum, come out on top, and, supported by the politicized evangelism of Savonarola, created democracy's guarantee, the Great Council. That body had been abolished in 1512. Not long ago: but since then pre-occupation with the actual state of current affairs during years of constant crisis had shortened men's historical perspective. In 1494 many of them had been moved by vague if splendid notions of Florence's greatness in the remote days of the medieval commune. Now they saw the Great Council not only as a convenient party instrument but as a glorious tradition, part of the Florentine way of life. And not much more than a month after Passerini's withdrawal the oligarchs were forced to concede to popular demand – and adapt their policies to dominating the Council, as they had, after all, managed to do with some success in the days of Savonarola and Soderini.

While the city, with held breath, waited helplessly if not hopelessly for the resolution of the French-Papal-Imperialist conflict, its recoil to the mood of 1494 intensified. Savonarola became once more a name to conjure with, the old party names – *piagnoni, arrabbiati, bigi* – came back into currency. Christ was once more proclaimed King of Florence. Class conflict became more open. But from June 1529, when Clement's support of Charles V under the treaty of Barcelona was known, and still more from October when the city was actually invested by an Imperial army, the shared sense of crisis meant that class antagonism was a luxury that had to be concealed in the interest of patriotic solidarity. Arguments for efficiency were brushed aside. As in 1494, emergency spelled democracy, and it can be seen as the glory as well as the fate of republican Florence that a constitution which favoured paralysis was again imposed at a time that called for urgent decisiveness.

Not surprisingly, feeling against the Medici and their known or sus-pected supporters mounted throughout the three years 1527 to 1530. Unlikable he may have been, but Passerini was no craven. Part of the tension felt as he left was due to the fact that before surrendering he had driven a bargain: no one was to be punished retrospectively for support given to the regime since 1512. He left behind him, then, a Medicean party protected by treaty. The Medici's quitting the city had been followed by a wave of vandalism of their coats of arms. This symbolic revenge was soon followed by a breach of the agreement with Passerini, for tax laws were introduced which permitted retaliatory measures against the adherents of the late regime. Each new danger to the city, rumoured or real, produced more symbolic destruction. More shields with the *palle* were destroyed; there is scarcely one existing today that antedates the Last Republic. It was proposed that the inscription to Cosimo *pater patriae* should be erased, even that the Medici palace be destroyed. Careggi was burned, Castello was saved only by chance, plans were laid to burn Poggio a Caiano, but by that time the Imperial army was too close for this to be practicable. A special commission was set up to supervise the imprisonment of Medici partisans and, as the siege tightened, anyone who bore the Medici name, however apolitical, however young, was put under guard. Maria Salviati and her son Cosimo, later to be Grand Duke, fled from their home in Trebbio to Venice. Ottaviano de' Medici, Alessandro's ex-guardian at Poggio a Caiano, a distant relative but married to Maria's sister, was imprisoned. The child Caterina, daughter of Lorenzo, Duke of Urbino, and later to be Queen of France, was brought into the city and immured in the convent of S. Lucia as a hostage. There were suggestions that she should be killed or held up on the walls as a target for the cannon of the Imperial army. These threats came from extremists and were discountenanced by the government, but the current of anti-Medicean feeling was stronger than it had been after the flight of Piero and was sustained by a puritanical legislation that deliberately recalled the days of Savonarola, and that represented a complete rebuttal of the way of life the Medici stood for. The carnival was suppressed, the *palio* horse-races were forbidden, the laws against gambling tightened, new sumptuary laws were passed against extravagant dress and lavish entertaining. A book censorship was instituted. As far as it could be done with prisons and ordinances, a clean break was made with both Medici men and Medici manners.

Though the walls, in part refortified under the supervision of Michelangelo, withstood both cannon and assault, losses from plague and privation and in skirmishes and raids outside the city led the government to capitulate on 12 August 1530 to the huge army that encircled it, after ten traumatic months of siege.

The peace settlement and the first Medici duke, 1530–37

The surrender was made to the Imperial commander, Ferdinando da Gonzaga, and the terms stipulated that a new form of government 'was to be arranged and instituted by his Imperial Majesty within the next four months, always providing that the city's liberty be maintained.' The events of the two years that followed form a commentary on the contradictions enshrined in this formula. Liberty meant self-determination, a republican government without a hereditary leader. This the Emperor would not, and, under the treaty of Barcelona, could not allow. Both he and Clement, who confirmed the agreement of 12 August, were determined to ensure continuity in Florentine foreign policy by installing the Medici as hereditary rulers, pledged to support the Habsburgs. Where Charles and Clement differed was as to how this should be done. Charles would have waved the wand of an Imperial fiat over the defeated republic. Clement, knowing the complex antagonisms within the Florentine body politic, preferred to introduce the notion of formal rule for his family with the maximum of assent. His plan – and he showed a skill in pursuing it far superior to his skill in international affairs – was to persuade Florence to ask for what he was in any case determined to force on it.

Meanwhile, the familiar ritual took place. A *Parlamento* was called. Known Mediceans were allowed through the papal troops lining the Piazza approaches, were assumed to be a quorum of the Florentine people, and were asked to approve the appointment of a *Balìa* which for form's sake included the gonfalonier but was otherwise, as always, packed. Ottaviano de' Medici was one of them. The Great Council was once more abolished, the constitutional clock turned back to 1527 – but with no mention of the Medici until in February 1531, at the urging of Clement's new representative, von Schönberg, Archbishop of Capua, special legislation was passed affirming Alessandro's right to sit on all the organs of government regardless of his age. The meaning of what von Schönberg had in mind became clearer a few months later when Alessandro, who had been with his future father-in-law in Brussels, entered the city and delivered Charles's decision, dated the previous October.

Florence, the Emperor had written, was to retain its republican constitution (that of 1512–27), but Alessandro was to be the head (*capo*) of its government and should sit as such on all its deliberative bodies. Nothing was said about a succession. The *capo* title was calculatedly vague. The decision was velvet, but Charles knew that the gristle beneath it would be sensed. Alessandro was already a duke in his own right – of Penne, a gift from the Emperor. He was soon to be, by marriage, one of Charles's family. The legitimization of under-age Medici to public office had been voted at intervals since the entry on to the political scene of the youthful Lorenzo the Magnificent and repeated for Ippolito: it could thus be represented as just within the 'liberty' mentioned in the surrender terms, but it also carried some implication of hereditary right. Logically the next step was to make Alessandro duke and vest the title in his heirs.

Logic, yes, but self-interest and fear affected the constitutional choice as never before. The siege had lasted only ten months, but its effects were traumatic in the sense that only two previous events in Florentine history had been: the great plague of 1348–49 and the Ciompi revolt of 1378. It combined the shock of both these events. From disease, famine and battle casualties the population had been reduced by at least a third. The venom felt by the workers and shopkeepers for their betters had veered from concentrating on those believed to be pro-Medicean towards the privileged group as a whole. Against a background of loss and misery the siege ended with class set against class. Then, as the exiles returned, reclaiming secular and Church property which had been confiscated and redistributed, the tension within the vengeful and embittered patricians increased: it was estimated, late in 1530, that two-thirds of them were anti-Medicean. Yet nearly all, by experience or hearsay, had come to fear the mob, many of both parties had suffered losses which, in the short term at least, could only be ·made good by salaried offices. The attractiveness of the social and economic shelter offered by a principate had never seemed so inclusive or so urgent.

Clement let another two months pass and then began – as he had done when he was still Cardinal Giulio – to ask some of the 'safer' members of the Florentine aristocracy for their opinion: how could the security of the Medici best be ensured, bearing in mind the interests of the city, its peace and prosperity? This was in fact an indication to the group accustomed to a dominant role within the city that they should re-think, with urgency, their own position. This group had been in charge, at least of internal affairs, since the end of the siege, and by exilings, hangings and imprisonments had still further alienated the popular party with a brutality that would be difficult to live down. With enemies within, exiles without, and the Medici an anomalous and foreboding presence, which was the safer course: to remain an oligarchy embattled against prince and people, or to become courtiers? It was a choice that had hovered over them since 1512; it was now one that they must make. It was a crisis confronting a class, and whereas the city as a whole had reacted to crisis by becoming constitutionally open, the aristocracy, though with many mental reservations, took the opposite course. In April 1532 Clement was sure enough of his ground to persuade the *Balìa* (which was still in being) to appoint a reform commission of twelve – a sort of sub-*Balìa* – to make proposals for a re-casting of the constitution, and to make sure that its members included those whose opinions had been in accord with his own desires, among them Francesco Guicciardini, Roberto Acciaiuoli and Francesco Vettori. It was this body that at last, in a decision of 27 April, wrote the Medici into Florence's constitution as its hereditary rulers.

The Signoria was abolished, and with it the gonfaloniership. In its place were to be four councillors (*consiglieri*), elected for three-month terms of office. This 'Supreme Magistracy' was to be responsible to a senatorial body of forty-eight citizens (chosen by the reform commission), who would legislate on all matters concerning foreign policy, finance and security, and appoint the officials who sat on the chief commissions, those of war, public security, the *monte*, and also the governors of the key towns of the Florentine possessions in Tuscany (the *dominio*): Pisa, Arezzo, Pistoia, Prato, Volterra, Cortona. The senators would also appoint ambassadors. In addition there was, for form's sake, to be a larger council of two hundred. Membership was for life, but its functions were restricted to dealing with matters of secondary importance arising from the *dominio*: complaints of injustice from individuals, petitions against taxes from communities. To give an added standing, however, to this council, a proportion of the membership of the chief commissions was to belong to it. Perpetual chairman of the four councillors was to be Alessandro, 'who henceforth is to be called the Duke of the Florentine republic', and this position was to be inherited by his son or, failing a male heir, his next of kin. There was, of course, an element of compromise in this scheme. Alessandro became duke; no political move of importance could be initiated without his presence. On the other hand, it was an attempt to limit the 'unofficial' government which earlier Medici had used to bypass the formal constitutional structure, and it meant that the duke's measures would need the cooperation and assent of the four and the forty-eight, who were drawn from the city's leading families. And while the title of duke did move the patricians towards the status of courtiers, the decision of 27 April protected them from popular pressure by abolishing the difference between major and minor guilds, thus ensuring for all practical purposes that the multitude of offices in the city and the *dominio* still filled from the guilds would come to be held by those most akin in social tone to the aristocracy.

The first Medici duke was then about twenty years old. The date of his birth was probably 1512, but it is uncertain. So, as we have seen, is his parentage. His mother was a servant girl of the Medici in Rome called Simonetta, but there is no proven indication who his father was: the choice still lies open as between Lorenzo, Duke of Urbino, and, somewhat more probably, the young Giulio before he became cardinal and pope. Though (again, probably) Alessandro was a few months younger than Ippolito and less experienced in affairs, Clement chose him because Ippolito was a cleric already, indeed, a cardinal, and could have no legitimate heir. He had been disliked for playing the peevish prince-ling before 1527 and had revealed a restless and unstable character thereafter – he had, for instance, rioted incognito with a gang of like-minded teenagers through the streets of Bologna at the time of Charles's coronation. Clement's decision aroused his furious resentment. He appealed to the Emperor, he mixed with the growing crowd of Floren-tine exiles and tried to persuade the Pope to release him from holy orders so that he could become their martial leader. Clement diverted him from this purpose by appointing him legate to a crusading army assembling in Hungary shortly after the reformed constitution had been announced. Grumbling, Ippolito set off with sword and shield. But his intrigues recommenced on his return and culminated in a plot to blow Alessandro up with an infernal machine beneath his bed. Not long after the discovery of this plan, Ippolito died, comfortingly near to his mistress, Giulia Gonzaga, but so suddenly that Alessandro was suspected (unjustly) by the exiles of having arranged for him to be poisoned. This was in August 1535. Clement had died in the previous year. Full responsibility for his family's position now lay with the Duke.

Alessandro's character was in some respects not unlike that of his cousin, the bravo-aristocrat in cardinal's clothing. He shared Ippolito's taste for going about incognito. Sexually the most voracious of his family, his rank reinforced his *beau-laid* charm so effectively that a rising toll of seduced daughters, wives and nuns not only scandalized the ex-Savonarolan middle class but alienated men he could ill afford to offend, and it was appropriate that the trap that led to his assassination was baited with a woman. But he was also, in an informal and eccentric way, a skilled politician. He was careful to keep on good terms with the majority of his well-to-do supporters, but as often by dropping in on them without notice as by invitations to the Medici palace. He made a point of listening in person, at set times, to complaints from the poor; not only the fact that he did this was commented upon (and favourably), but also the genuineness of his interest in the stories of unpaid dowries and contested inheritances that were poured out to him. This trait, and tales of his spontaneous generosity when meeting instances of peasant misery on his rides in the country, have prompted his biographers to see the effect of his mother's plebeian blood. It is hardly necessary to resort to theories of heredity, however, to accept the fact that an appetite for women, an interest in low life, and a calculating passion for absolute power can inhabit one personality. On the other hand, Alessandro's character is notably divergent from those of his forebears, wherever his paternity lay, save for his interest in the arts. Thanks to this, we have three portraits of him, one by Bronzino, one by Pontormo and one by Vasari.

Vasari explained the iconography of his painting in a letter to Ottaviano de' Medici. The stool on which Alessandro sits is round, to show his unending dominion. The human figures who decorate the stool's legs represent the Florentine people, who need neither arms nor legs themselves, for they exist to obey, not to act of their own volition. Underneath the stool is the shadowy figure of Volubility, from whose bridled mouth run the bonds which wrap round the term-like extremities of the 'Florentines'. 'This', Vasari wrote, 'is to show that this unstable people are bound and steadied by the fortress that has been built, and' – he tactfully added – 'by the love that his subjects bear towards His Excellency.' The fortress was the Fortezza da Basso, the largest historical monument in Florence and one of the most crucial to an understanding of the sixteenth-century Medici, for it is an indication that the stabilizing of their rule through the reformed constitution of 1532 was not enough: it needed the stony corroboration of a citadel and its guns.

One of Alessandro's first actions had been to order the great bell, the *vacca*, to be removed from the tower of the Palace of the Signoria as a sign that there would be no further *Parlamenti*, no more changes of regime. The Medici arms were placed once more in the Palace and over the little fort at the Porta alla Giustizia. The Duke impounded all weapons belonging to citizens; he even had those hung in churches as votive offerings taken down and confiscated. Yet with the tower silenced and the citizens disarmed, Alessandro still did not feel secure. In addition to having a garrison of Spanish troops under the command of Alessandro Vitelli, he revived the civilian militia of the *dominio* and had it put on a war footing. These measures had a twofold cause. Very heavy, and therefore very unpopular, taxes had to be raised to restore the financial and material damage caused by the siege and to pay a war indemnity to the Emperor, which had been one of the surrender terms;

outside the city the exiles were conspiring with an increasing vigour to raise military support. And the more frequently Alessandro found it necessary to act harshly, the more confident the exiles became that the citizens would be galled into revolt if they could depend on outside support. In 1534 Ippolito wrote to Charles V, begging to be allowed to replace Alessandro and thus save Florence from a tyranny which had become universally hateful. Many of the chief families, he reported, would welcome this substitution – and he named the Salviati, the Rucellai, the Strozzi, the Pazzi and the Ridolfi. With a little military aid, he pointed out, the exiles could storm the defences, still weakened from the siege, and expel Alessandro before he had time to appeal for aid to France. Then citizens and exiles would work tranquilly together under Ippolito to make Florence a really useful and profitable ally of the Emperor.

In the main, this was wishful thinking. Moreover, the other leading exiles misconceived Charles's intentions when they complained, as work began on the Fortezza da Basso, that 'a great fortress was being built with the blood of that unhappy people, as a prison and slaughter-house for the distressed citizens'. The Emperor was not concerned to disarm Alessandro but to strengthen him; he even made the fort's completion a condition of the Duke's betrothal to his daughter Margaret being confirmed by marriage. Building went on with all the more urgency when Clement's death in September 1534 meant that one of the new regime's props had fallen away. By early December enough had been done to enable a garrison to take up their quarters there. The ceremony of their installation was carried out with great pomp and attended by all the civic dignitaries, secular and ecclesiastical. At its conclusion, the standards of the Medici and the Emperor were broken out over the ramparts; Paolantonio da Parma, the castellan, swore an oath to preserve the fortress for the Duke and, were the Duke to die, to hand over its keys and reveal the password only to Charles or his representative. From this the significance of the Fortezza da Basso is clear; it was a guarantee that the succession to Alessandro was to be decided not by the Florentine people but by the Emperor.

Henceforward the connection between the Fortezza and Medicean tyranny became a republican dogma. As one contemporary historian put it, the Medici determined 'to place on the necks of the Florentines a yoke of a kind never experienced before; a citadel, whereby the citizens lost all hope of ever living in freedom.' And similar views were expressed by other writers who were antagonistic to the Medici.

Florence now not only resembled constitutionally but physically looked like other princely states – Milan, Naples, Mantua or Ferrara – where the ruler's citadel could be armed against his subjects as well as against attack from strangers.

The Fortezza da Basso has tended to hide in its shadow the more positive aspects of Alessandro's rule: his interest in the economic welfare of the towns of the *dominio*; his fostering in Florence of crafts which had been hard hit by the dislocation of commerce during the siege and by the plague which accompanied it; his extremely shrewd choice of a new class of administrators, drawn from the countryside and unfettered by local family allegiances, of whom the most valuable to him, and to his successor, was Francesco Campana. His accomplishments have been obscured even more effectively by the lurid circumstances of his death, at the hand not of an army of exiles but of his most intimate companion, Lorenzino, son of Pierfrancesco de' Medici the Younger.

Great-great-grandson of Lorenzo, Cosimo *pater patriae*'s brother, Lorenzino was poor, proud and self-woundingly ambitious. It was a grievance that he was related to a pope and was not favoured by him, a source of bitterness that a young bastard bearing his own name and only two years his senior should be taken up by an emperor and given Florence to rule. He hobnobbed with exiles and added their grievances to his own. He drew from the humanist culture which surrounded him in the years he spent in Rome especially the story of Brutus, and he brooded, as had the young Boscoli in 1513, on the baleful glamour that surrounds the slayer of a tyrant. Like other men whose sense of desperation is kept active by the belief that somewhere, at some time, a deed will be done that will compel admiration, Lorenzino had a hectic charm which recommended him to Alessandro, who saw in him an ideal lieutenant for his seamier pastimes and failed to see either the rancour or the sense of purpose the relationship fostered. Lorenzino thus became courtier to his victim, a relationship which gave a psychotic edge to his resentment.

Thanks to the progress of the Fortezza, Charles had permitted the marriage between Margaret and Alessandro to take place. It made little difference to the Duke's pursuit of women. In January 1537 his objective was Caterina, the beautiful and hitherto faithful wife of Leonardo Ginori. On 5 January, Lorenzino announced that he thought her ready to yield and Alessandro agreed to wait alone, without guards, while she was brought to him in secret. Meanwhile the Duke took off his sword and, waiting, fell asleep. When he woke it was to find Lorenzino and a hired assassin standing over him. From accounts that are, for obvious reasons, hard to trust, it appears that the assassin wounded Alessandro mortally but that Lorenzino had to hold him steady while the death blow was given, and that Alessandro bit some of Lorenzino's fingers to the bone before the last thrust killed him. At least, those who saw Lorenzino riding out of the city to safety reported that one hand was covered by a bloodied bandage.

After but five years the principle of hereditary Medici rule was yet again put in doubt. Alessandro and Margaret had not had a child. He left one illegitimate son, Giulio, who was too young to be considered as his successor. Two years previously, Charles had turned Milan into an Imperial viceroyalty on the death of Francesco Sforza without an heir. It was possible that he would do the same to Florence, possible that Francis I would now take the opportunity to avenge himself on Charles by aiding the exiles – their party strengthened by the adherence of one of Florence's wealthiest and most respected citizens, Filippo Strozzi – to return and re-shape Florence into a satellite of France. There was also the possibility that Clement's successor Paul III, as intent on establishing his own family, the Farnese, in a position of political power as Leo and Clement had been for theirs, would intervene in their interest. He had already done all he could to break Alessandro's betrothal to Margaret and to persuade Charles to marry her instead to his own nephew, Ottavio. Now, unless the Florentines made up their minds quickly, they might be pressured into accepting Ottavio as their ruler under the colour of preserving the political–financial axis Rome-Florence, an axis that held out some promise of independence from Charles and had always involved profitable business with the Curia.

Only a speedy decision could, in fact, prevent Florence's fate being decided from any of these directions. But if there were three external dangers that called for speed, there were three internal factions which acted as a brake: the still vocal popular party which looked back to the heroism of the siege itself and the Savonarolan time that had preceded it; the oligarchy, weakened by banishments but still hoping for a constitution controlled by themselves; and the Medici-Imperialist party of Alessandro's court.

In the hectic debates that followed, the lead was taken by Cardinal Cybo, who was not only Charles's representative but a Medici himself through his mother Maddalena, Leo X's sister. The news of the assassination was kept secret to prevent the popular party from making trouble, and the decisions were limited to a circle drawn, above all, from those who had sat on the reform commission of 1532. Their decision was to nominate as Alessandro's successor the son of the *condottiere* Giovanni de' Medici, nicknamed 'of the black bands' (*delle bande nere*), but with the compromise title not of duke but of 'head and leader of the government of the city of Florence'. This son was Cosimo, then just turned eighteen.

Cosimo I: the creation of a Tuscan territorial state, 1537–74

The youth thus plucked from political obscurity was connected with both lines of descent from Giovanni di Bicci; his mother, Maria Salviati, was half a Medici of the line of Cosimo *pater patriae* (after whom he was named at the wish of his godfather, Leo X); his father was a descendant of Cosimo's brother Lorenzo. A professional soldier, his father had never played a part in Florentine affairs; this was all to the good, as nothing dimmed the reputation he had gained as a folk hero by his military exploits and his tragically early death from wounds. Killed fighting the armies that had moved on to sack Rome and then encircled Florence, he was the one Medici to be looked on with favour by the popular party, and it was hoped that his son would be greeted with something at least approaching tolerance.

Cosimo himself was virtually an unknown quantity to the Florentines, though his mother had done her best to keep him in the public eye by sending him with a tutor and a few servants to pay his respects, as the unprotected son of a famous father, to the Doge of Venice, to Clement VII and to the Emperor himself. From her home at Trebbio, Maria had also been careful to arouse the interest of Alessandro, and the Duke, not averse to the company of a lively youth who was a legitimate but undangerous member of the family, took him up. They went hunting together. Alessandro took him to Naples to greet Charles V on his return from the conquest of Tunis from the Moors. As Charles was also greeted there by the exiles, it can have done the bastard Duke no harm to be seen together with Giovanni's son. But there was never any hint that Cosimo was in Alessandro's political confidence. This again was all to the good from the point of view of the wary alliance between Cosimo's would-be guardians: aristocrats like Guicciardini and Vettori looked to his inexperience to allow them to keep control within their own group; Cybo looked for little interference to his brief for yoking Florence more firmly than ever to the Empire.

Cosimo was soon to reveal that he answered to none of these expectations. Outside Florence, no Italian of rank could see the charm of extending participation in government to shopkeepers. The popular party in Florence looked back to 1494 to 1512, and to the 'democratic' fervour of the siege, but Cosimo was not born until 1519, was only eleven in 1530; the Great Council and all it stood for was without any emotional appeal for him. Nor could he share the conviction of the oligarchical party that the city's interests were best served by themselves in cooperation with a mainly titular head of government. The passion underlying that view was also based on experience he had not shared. With no mercantile knowledge, brought up somewhat austerely, a soldier's son, he had no instinctive feeling for the blend of business sense and cultural refinement that characterized Guicciardini and his associates. Raised in a Tuscan village he did not share both parties' assumption that the countryside existed to be exploited by the city of Florence. It was easier for him to share the views of Cybo's group, of men like the bureaucrat Francesco Campana and the garrison commander Alessandro Vitelli whom he had met through his comradeship with the murdered duke.

He was given time to consider his stance because the immediate problem was an external one posed by the exiles. With the help of the Farnese they intrigued for support in Pisa and Pistoia, where anti-Medicean parties took up arms, and in July their troops assembled at the hill fortress of Montemurlo in the hills a few miles north of Prato, where they were routed by a Florentine army stiffened by the Spanish troops commanded by Vitelli. The leading exiles were taken prisoner to Florence, summarily judged and executed. Montemurlo also destroyed the morale of those Florentines who were related to exiles and had formed a potential fifth column within the city. Though Vitelli had won the battle, Cosimo, who had been in close touch with its preparations, was given the credit for saving the city from another wave of vengeance and confiscations. Secure and respected, he was thenceforward able to devote himself to the four major themes of his reign: the easing of the duchy away from Imperial control, the closer integration of Florence and the *dominio*, the detachment of government from the class historically responsible for it, and the glorification of the house of Medici.

Young as he was, his precociously independent and authoritarian personality was helped by what was almost a law of politics: the history of the past hundred years had demonstrated that, given the social and political composition of Florence, to insert a Medici in it was at once, or almost at once, to escalate his powers. It was a sort of political chemistry; a piece of Medici, however insignificant, when introduced into the unstable solution of civic rivalries either swelled to a dominating block or produced an explosion. In July Cosimo had been represented by an Imperial commander. In September he received the ratification of his succession as Alessandro's kinsman and the title of duke from Charles V himself. Without any compensating reliance on the oligarchs who had supported his election, he set himself to discredit Charles's representatives in Florence, first Cybo and then Vitelli, in the Emperor's eyes. One by one they were withdrawn, leaving Cosimo master of his own government.

In 1543, taking advantage of Charles's need for money for yet another war with France, he paid a heavy sum in return for the withdrawal of the Imperial garrisons from the Fortezza da Basso and the citadel of Leghorn and their formal cession to him. From that moment the Emperor lost his last physical hold over Cosimo's freedom of action in Tuscany and was forced to exert pressure through the usual diplomatic channels used by heads of state. The duke spelled out his new independence in instructions to his ambassador to the king of France in 1545. Tell him, he wrote, 'that we are a ruler who accepts the authority of no one apart from God and, but solely on account of our gratitude for benefits received, the Emperor . . . to whom we have never paid tribute nor offered vassalage – unlike the duke of Ferrara who pays homage to the Pope.'

It was, however, the independence of a pigmy from a giant, and was aided by accidents, now Charles's need of cash, now his fear that were Florence to become so obviously an Imperial satellite as were Milan and Naples the other Italian states, notably Venice and the papacy, would combine against him. Cosimo therefore accompanied his withdrawal from Spanish-Imperial control with overtures to France, represented to Charles as purely commercial negotiations, and with more open and diplomatically more persistent overtures to the papacy. He persuaded the Farnese pope, Paul III, to become reconciled to the new situation in Florence, and on his death, Cosimo's new friendship with the other members of the Farnese family helped to secure the election of their joint candidate Giovanni Maria del Monte as Julius III (1550–55). By constantly working through his agents or through cardinals who supported his own predominantly neutralist views, he was able to help bring about the election of another pope who was neither pro-French nor pro-Spanish: Giovanni Angelo Medici, who took the name Pius IV. Though no more than a Medici in name (he came from a family of lawyers and soldiers in the Milanese), in gratitude as well as by conviction he was almost fully Medicean in his policies.

Twice dominated by Rome, Florence now reversed the roles and set a precedent Cosimo's successors were to follow with conspicuous if not continuous success. At the same time Cosimo took pains to make the duchy as strong as possible. He continued militia reforms begun by Alessandro, he improved or built new fortifications at Pisa, Pistoia, Arezzo and elsewhere, guarding passes and pegging down frontiers with new fortress towns like Terra del Sole, towards Forlì, and Sasso di Simone, towards Urbino, and within Florence he built the bastioned trace that formed a hypotenuse inside the south-west triangle of the old city wall and was the work of (among others) Baccio Bandinelli and Benvenuto Cellini. He built a small but powerful fleet of war galleys and from 1548 turned Portoferraio on Elba (which he leased from the Appiani of Piombino, its nominal rulers) into a strongly fortified naval base with a new name, Cosmopoli. In all these military preparations he took an active and informed interest that justified the paintings he commissioned to show him discussing fortifications with his engineers or consulting with his captains. Long journeys through his dominions, moreover, which became almost an annual feature of his reign, enabled him to keep a close eye on the public works that were going forward.

As Tuscany became more heavily armoured, Cosimo had to step increasingly warily in his relations with Charles V and, after 1555, his successor as King of Spain, Philip II. Spain, as a Venetian ambassador put it, 'will not allow a creation of its own to expand of its own volition'. Yet Cosimo was determined to expand. He bought or bullied his way into a number of little, but strategically useful, fiefs like Caprigliola and Corlaga in the Lunigiana, inland from La Spezia. He wanted to protect the Tyrrhenian Sea not only from Turkish pirate raids but from French and Spanish navies, for Spanish and French rivalry clashed there as on the north-west mainland of Italy. His foothold on Elba caused alarm. When he was offered Corsica by the islanders in return for the protection of his galleys, Spain firmly warned him off and he had to refuse. He also, and for the same reason, had to refrain from taking over Piombino. Now prodding, now yielding, Cosimo, as the result of a tireless diplomatic activity, slowly established the geographical limits within which he could operate as an increasingly absolutist territorial prince, sacrificing the acquisition of further territory as the price of being able to strengthen what he already owned.

By 1554 he had a state not much larger than the one he had found, but far more powerful in terms of his unchallenged rule throughout it, its defensive strength, and the men and cash he could raise from it. He wanted both to consolidate and to expand, and his expansive policy was, in the main, checked. But a by-product of this failure was an enhanced freedom of action and an enhanced prestige, an advance of status from that of near-satellite to an ally to be handled with some care and respect even by a superpower such as Spain. And from this there came to follow an acquisition that was notable in size as well as being of thrillingly urgent concern to the Florentines: Siena.

From 1495 to 1509 Florence had plunged itself into political isolation from the rest of Italy in order to gain French support for the reconquest of Pisa, at least as much for historical as for economic reasons: its harbour was silted, its trade in decline, but it had become a symbol of Florence's leadership in Tuscany. Just as bitterly charged with historical associations was Siena, which had long been a symbol of resistance to this leadership. At the same time that Charles V had installed a garrison in Florence after the siege to ensure its Imperial orientation, he had installed another in Siena for the same purpose. Siena remained a republic and a restless one, constantly changing the social complexion of its government and veering now to a pro-Imperial diplomacy, now, in spite of the presence of Spanish troops, to a pro-French one. A pinprick in times of peace, the loyalty of a place of such considerable strategic importance was a matter of real concern to Spain and France in time of war. In 1552, the Sienese, resenting the building of a citadel on Charles's orders to control them more firmly, revolted with a fury that expelled the Spanish garrison, and declared for France.

Charles at once called on Cosimo to supply the army of reconquest he himself could not spare from his wars in Germany. But the duke was not prepared simply to be used by the Emperor; he wanted Siena for himself, not a pat on the back for regaining it for his great ally. 'You are to point out', he wrote to a Florentine ambassador in Rome, the great distributing centre for diplomatic rumours and attitudes, 'that I am no feudatory of his Caesarian Majesty . . . nor am I bound to be friend of his friend and enemy of his enemy more than I choose.' At the same time he let it be known to the papacy and the Sienese that he was negotiating a secret non-aggression pact with France, thus lulling their suspicions that he would act in support of Charles; he released this news through an agent whom he carefully kept unaware that he was at the same time exploring terms by which he would feel able to act on Charles's behalf. This was diplomatic double-dealing at its most literal, and both its aspects were successful.

He waited until Charles's need of him had become acute enough for bargaining to take place; he mobilized covertly but on a large scale, and his attack, early in 1554, took the Sienese by surprise. Prolonged by French support to the Sienese, the war dragged on for a year, however, before the city was starved into surrender, and two more years elapsed before terms between Cosimo and the Emperor had been haggled into shape. Cosimo's subordinate place in the alliance appeared in the concessions he was compelled to grant: permanent Spanish garrisons in Siena's southern dependencies, Orbetello, Talamone, Porto Ercole, Monte Argentaro and S. Stefano; a promise to respect the independence (really the Spanish clientage) of Piombino and Elba apart from Portoferraio; and a cash payment. But what he gained would have been unthinkable in the early years of his rule: hereditary dominion over Siena, though as an Imperial feudatory, with the title *Dux Senarum*. The significance of this southward extension of the *dominio* was not lost on Italians, who recognized the importance of Cosimo's gains. By controlling Arezzo, Cosimo was already master of one of the three chief central and western routes connecting north Italy with the Papal States and Naples; Siena now gave him control of a second, and Grosseto, a Sienese dependency, of the third – at least as far as Orbetello. When Cosimo went to visit the Pope in 1560 he was greeted, noted an observer, 'not as a duke, not even as a king, but as an emperor'.

Though exaggerated, the remark is not unrevealing. Cosimo was far less Florence-centred than earlier members of his family and he measured himself against his contemporary rulers rather than against what had been expected of him by the Florentines. One of his earliest actions was to write to the chief magistrates of the subject cities in Tuscany appealing for their support and promising his personal interest. He did more than any of his predecessors had done to make Florence into visibly a 'Medicean' city, but he was very much a prince of the sixteenth century, thinking in terms of a state rather than a city, and thinking of that not only in strategic but in economic and administrative terms. He broke the city's monopoly of making silk and wool cloths, encouraging both industries elsewhere in Tuscany. He encouraged local initiative in the extraction of minerals. He set up a sugar refinery at Pisa. By encouraging drainage and land reclamation schemes he opened the way to wealth to men from Pietrasanta and Pisa to

Arezzo who had hitherto been discouraged by the exploitative and jealous attitude of the capital. And this Tuscanization of the economy not only eroded the plutocratic exclusiveness of the Florentine patriciate but threw up new, successful and non-Florentine families from whom Cosimo could draw loyal recruits to his bureaucracy. It also, through the granting of licences, the return on subsidies, the control of prices and of the volume of exports and imports, above all through the massive purchase of barren but reclaimable lands masquerading as hunting reserves, gave Cosimo a personal income superior to those of the patricians who had once seen themselves as his tutors, and an image of princely extravagance that distanced him from them in another way.

Simultaneously, by weakening the autonomous legal systems that had existed in many of Florence's subject cities, and by using an increasing number of men drawn from his own bureaucracy as his resident representatives, he diminished the administrative contrasts between one city and another and made more uniform the relationship between each of them and Florence. Differences remained. What was a misdemeanour in one city might be treated as a crime if committed in another. Concessions negotiated in the past as territories fell to Florence were in some cases – the incidence of the salt tax is an example – still held to. Or again, when Cosimo's privy council came to consider a problem relating to Pistoia, its members, without moving from their places, had to move that they were, for the time being, the privy council of Pistoia. But if the new strata of legal and economic enactments retained traces of the past in fossil form, and if the government of the 'new state' of Siena retained many of its old practices under its new master, a number of administrative innovations, like Cosimo's plans for the relief of orphans and paupers, were applied to all areas alike. A historical vista of piecemeal conquest and individual bargains was overlaid by a unifying statism. It was in every way appropriate that the title he eventually cajoled from Pope Pius V in 1569 and persuaded Philip II to ratify, was that of Grand Duke, not of Florence, but of Tuscany. And within months of gaining it he ordered annual surveys to be carried out along the Tuscan frontiers to make sure that no erosion of his domains was taking place.

Cosimo I: politician and patron

Cosimo could not have pursued a diplomacy aimed towards independence from foreign control unless at the same time he had made his political power increasingly independent of the checks imposed on ducal initiative by the constitution of 1532, which still remained in force. The complex continuity of his negotiations, the forced peasant labour which built his fortifications, the network of spies and informers, the heavy taxation needed to support his armies and carry through the war against Siena: all depended on his not remaining the glorified chairman of the body of four councillors, not deferent to the initiative of the senatorial Council of Forty-eight, not reliant on the approval of the Council of Two Hundred.

If his flair for diplomacy could not have been foreseen in 1537, neither could his mounting passion for the desk-work of government. He saw politics as an activity to be pursued in the ruler's study, with information flowing in and orders flowing out, and a corps of alert and knowledgeable men available for consultation in a nearby room. That government could not work as simply as this, he knew. But this was his ideal. That he could come near to it was due to the fact that he was not a Medici of the stamp of a Cosimo *pater patriae* or a Lorenzo the Magnificent, and that times had changed in favour of closet government and the social satisfactions of a court. He was careful, in his preoccupied and somewhat charmless way, to remain on good terms with the families whose representatives staffed the councils. But he put his trust in the men assembled by Alessandro, notably Campana, accepting them first as his teachers and then, as he grew into his position, using them and certain unquestioning adherents among the patriciate, as sounding-boards for what were increasingly his own suggestions. From this inner group, which came to include a growing number of men from the Florentine middle class and from other parts of Tuscany, came the ambassadors and the provincial governors and the permanent secretariat.

The hub of substantive government was the Privy Council or *Pratica Secreta*, a consultative body honouring in its name an old institution, the *Pratica*, and admitting by the qualifying word 'secret' its new extra-constitutional function. Here military, diplomatic and financial legislation was planned; here the delicate relationship between Church and State was reviewed, the integration of the *dominio* discussed. The *Pratica Secreta* met frequently, often daily when Cosimo was in Florence, and always at the duke's bidding.

To this controlling hub was belted the official machinery via the four councillors drawn for three months at a time from the forty-eight and with a nominee of the duke's as permanent chairman. It was they who were responsible for taking executive action on laws passed by the forty-eight, a Senate which soon came to be composed of ex-councillors, men who had become aware of what measures would please or offend the duke. Under the familiar plea of urgency, the four councillors could be asked to approve ducal measures without their going before the councils, though this was formally a contravention of the constitutional law of 1532. The councillors, moreover – called with their chairman the supreme magistracy – had the power to pass into law any measure that had been rejected three times by the two hundred. A clear picture of how far Cosimo's rule had acquired an autocratic tone is given in a memorandum addressed to him in 1561 by his secretary, acting as *locum tenens* during one of Cosimo's tours in the *dominio*. 'The decrees passed by the supreme magistracy, be they in the form of law or general provision, are done so only with your approval and must be obeyed by all magistrates. It is not necessary that they be passed in the Senate, although I do this with those that seem most important.'

Still closer links between Cosimo and the conciliar structure were provided by a small corps of legal experts called auditors. Appointed by the duke, three of them were of outstanding importance in making the semi-republican constitution of 1532 serve the purposes of autocracy. The fiscal auditor sat *ex officio* with the four councillors, ostensibly to help them give a watertight legal shape to financial measures, but also to reinforce the contact with the duke's will, already represented by their chairman. Similarly, the auditor *della riformagione* sat with the forty-eight and the two hundred, not only to give advice on points of law and on drafting procedures, but to represent the duke's point of view to these bodies and to report their discussions to him. A third, the auditor *della giurisdizione*, was responsible for scrutinizing all papal legislation in order to guard against any infringement of the duke's sovereign rights over the Church in Tuscany, especially with regard to appointments, property and actions against laymen in Church courts.

As far as crimes against public order were concerned – treason, the fomenting of disorder or the spreading of rumours calculated to bring discredit to the regime, correspondence with exiles, and so forth – the responsible magistracy was that of the Security Commission (*Otto di Guardia e Balìa*). Like the supreme magistracy, this had a rotating membership drawn from the two councils, and again Cosimo had been able to bring an organ whose powers dated back to the republican period under his own control through the auditor system. Finally, like Alessandro, Cosimo let it be known that he possessed an equitable jurisdiction in his own person, which all his subjects could approach either directly or after dissatisfaction with a judgment of the courts; in this way he was able to temper justice with mercy for the poor and learn much about the intimate affairs of the well-to-do. In either case a subtle increase in his political power was involved.

All this reorganization was carried out openly. It was accompanied, however, by the secret engagement of a staff of spies and informers whose job it was to watch the remaining exiles, to track down those who had been involved in the Montemurlo attack and had not been brought to justice and to alert Cosimo to any signs of conspiracy in the city or the *dominio*. Every monastery was said to contain an informer, every church, square and street. His word alone could condemn a man to the *secrete*, the political prisons which allowed no visitors and seldom opened to release their inmates. Unlawful assembly was a capital offence, even whispered criticism a crime. Throughout Tuscany men learned to check their impulse to discuss politics with a 'God save me from the duke's *secrete*.'

Cosimo's authoritarianism was the result of a determination to protect the regime from the revolutions of the generations before he became its head, and his person from another Lorenzino, but it was also the consequence of his personality. He called for statistical surveys, population returns, copies of army muster rolls and stores. Even the constant use he made of the *Pratica Secreta* did not conceal his desire to run the government himself. His comment on Vasari's first design for a painting dealing with the capture of Siena catches this tone very clearly: 'The group of councillors which you have placed about our person, where you represent us in the act of deliberating upon the campaign against Siena, is not in the least necessary as we acted entirely alone in the matter. You can fill up the places of these councillors with figures representing Silence and some other Virtues.'

This advance by the duke to the centre of policy-making, administration and justice could not have been made without a corresponding retreat on the part of the patriciate. This retreat was already well under way as early as 1540, when Cosimo moved his own household and staff into the Palace of the Signoria, leaving the Medici palace for the reception of distinguished visitors. The substance and the form now worked side by side, the decisions of the one being echoed by the rubber stamps of the other. The veterans of the groups which had striven since the first return of the Medici in 1512 to keep government centred within an oligarchy were dying, Vettori in 1539, Guicciardini in 1540. The rest of the patriciate recognized that Montemurlo had cast a shadow on the loyalty of their class as a whole. Among emperors, kings and popes, ducal authority seemed more appropriate – especially after the failures of 1512 and 1530 – than government by committee. Above all, a prince could protect them from the classes they had long exploited and recently persecuted. The retreat from policy-making, then, was in the main a voluntary one.

A Venetian ambassador has left a clear and – from other evidence – convincing portrait of Cosimo at the height of his powers, aged forty-two, in 1561:

His physique is unusually large, very sturdy and strong. His expression is gracious but he can make himself terrible when he wishes. In toil or in taking exercise he is indefatigable and delights in recreations that call for agility, strength or dexterity, having no rival in lifting weights, handling weapons, tournaments or ball games, and in other similar pastimes, from which he derives great pleasure. And in these, as in fishing and swimming, he doffs all his authority and dignity, and jokes with easy familiarity with all around him, wanting to be treated with equal informality without any special marks of respect. But apart from these recreations, he recognizes no one, however familiar or well known to him, nor is there anyone bold enough to presume to make the slightest advance to him; he relapses at once into a habitual severity, so much so that there is a proverb in the city to the effect that the duke puts authority on and off when he pleases [*si disduca e s'induca quando vuole*], changing between a private individual and a prince. But this happens only among his associates, with others he is never familiar and keeps himself aloof save when business makes this impossible.

This prince has a very lively and quick intelligence, and one well adapted for every subject. He has an extremely retentive memory for though he has memoranda concerning income, expenses, troops and munitions in every place, he remembers it all . . . And he remembers everyone by name, and if he sees a stranger he has not seen before he wants to know who he is and what he does . . . And if anyone comes to him with a petition who had been in his presence before on a different errand, he remembers him and tells him what he asked of him even twenty years before: a great gift in any man, but most of all in a prince.

In affairs of government he has a sound judgment and never

changes his mind, he is resolute in his statecraft and has shown himself ingenious and valorous in war . . . and if he were a soldier, as was his father Giovanni de' Medici, who was so great and famous a captain, he would accomplish great things. Peace has brought him such advantages, however, that he has no thought of breaking it.

This prince holds the skilful in all professions in great respect and takes pleasure in all the branches of study, and much enjoys sculpture and painting, and continually employs excellent men in both arts to make things rare and worthy of the times . . . He delights in jewels, statues and ancient medals and has so many antiquities that it is a marvel. And he has the history of his times written in Latin and Tuscan and pays excellent men to write commentaries on his life in both languages. So with painting, sculpture, print and imperishable paper he will be eternal and glorious after his death as he is happy and fortunate in life. And God will continue these qualities for him to the end, since, as it is said, this prince shares the same astrological constellation as Octavius Augustus and the Emperor Charles V.

But what makes his name most worthy of praise is his exemplary continence . . . there is no hint that he has anything to do with anyone but the duchess his wife since he became prince . . . And as far as his household is concerned he does not live in truth like a prince, in the exquisite grandeur employed by other princes or dukes; he lives rather as an outstanding family man, eating always with his wife and children at a moderately plain table . . . And when he goes through the city or into the country his wife and children and household accompany him, and always with a guard of Germans, a company of light cavalry and a hundred arquebusiers.

For all his simple ways, Cosimo was extremely touchy on the score of his dignity – a fight to establish the ceremonial precedence of his ambassadors over those of his fellow duke of Ferrara lasted from 1541 to 1567 – but had much more of the autocrat than of the aristocrat about him. His letters were blunt to the point of rudeness. Though his court had the trappings of aristocratic life, down to jesters and dwarfs, he lived within it simply, letting it be seen that ceremony was to him a duty rather than a pleasure.

His marriage at the age of twenty to Eleanor of Toledo followed Charles V's suggestion that he should marry one of the daughters of his viceroy in Naples, Don Pedro de Toledo. But at least he was given his choice among them and the marriage, as the ambassador's portrait suggests, turned out to be a happy, and thanks to the regularity with which she produced child after child, a politically stabilizing one. Eleanor's death in 1562, following the tragically early deaths of two of their sons, Giovanni and Garzia, from malaria, left Cosimo severely shaken. He handed over more and more of state affairs to his eldest son Francesco – in 1564, indeed, he formally abdicated, though he continued to direct the state from the background – and lived a fairly austere private life tempered by two successive mistresses, Leonora degli Albizzi and Camilla Martelli. When he eventually married Camilla he tried to anticipate the criticisms of his son and of his fellow princes. Though a commoner, he wrote to Francesco, 'she is a lady and a worthy one'. It is as though he were apologizing for allowing his unease amid the aristocratic values he manipulated so skilfully to come at last into the open. He was the last Medici to show a flicker of the family's bourgeois origin, and then only under the pressure of loss, age and infirmity; in his last years he was partially paralysed.

It was in these years of seclusion that the antagonism which could not express itself in political opposition found an outlet in the circulation of scandal. He was rumoured to have committed incest with his daughters Maria and Lucrezia, to have stabbed his son Garzia to death under his mother's eyes, to have caused her death through the horror of the scene. These and other alarming stories – all subsequently shown to have been false – obscured the real tragedy of the years between retiring in favour of Francesco and his death, at the early age of fifty-four; years of pathetically dependent womanizing, of senile fits of rage and sobbing, of relapses into sheer childishness.

His incapacity was particularly grievous because he had always been so active. The long tours in the *dominio*, on which he dragged his family and household, had exhausted them but left him untired. An enthusiastic hunter in the Italian manner of everything from wild boars to robins, he was grateful for the Medici heritage of villas and maintained the tradition of improving them from time to time, a tradition his son Francesco followed eagerly. He improved the Medicean monuments in Florence more deliberately, for these were in the public eye. It was above all in Florence that he set out to ensure that he would be 'eternal and glorious after his death'. He commissioned Pontormo to paint the choir of S. Lorenzo, and paid for Bronzino's huge fresco of the martyrdom of S. Lorenzo in the left aisle. Before leaving the Medici palace in 1540 he set on foot a search for the objects that had been pillaged from it in 1527 and restored it to its original condition.

Though in no sense a literary scholar (his tastes were practical and scientific – botany, zoology, chemistry), he continued not only to fill gaps in the Medici library caused by its moves to Rome and back but added new manuscripts. And he continued this homage to his ancestors by building up Lorenzo the Magnificent's collection of coins and medals. Entirely in the Medici tradition was his order to the Florentine resident diplomatic agent in Constantinople: 'Do your best to procure as many Roman, Greek and Egyptian medals as you can, of gold, silver or other metals and send them all here to us; use all possible diligence in your search, for these as also for Greek manuscripts.' In the same way he added to the family collection of antique sculpture, most notably perhaps through the *Arrotino* (now in the Uffizi) which Vasari had notified him in 1558 as being for sale in Rome.

But Cosimo's homage to his ancestors went much further than this. The Poggio frescoes had already used paint to cover up the crack of 1494–1512 and Ottaviano had bridged that of 1527–30 by commissioning one of Vasari's strongest works, his posthumous portrait of Lorenzo the Magnificent. Cosimo took this hint and made it into a cult, commissioning from Pontormo a companion portrait of the first Cosimo – with the *broncone* playing a prominent role in the design – and turning the Palace of the Signoria into a pictorial genealogy of his forebears. The architect in charge of the alterations that made this combination of fortress, town hall and office block into a princely home was Vasari. Vasari, too, was largely in charge of its decoration, acting with the advice of learned programme devisers like Cosimo Bartoli and Vincenzo Borghini, and doing nothing without consulting the Duke himself through memoranda on which Cosimo would dash his comments.

When the structural alterations were complete in 1558, the first 'Medicean' room to be decorated was devoted to the memory of Cosimo *pater patriae*. He was shown returning in triumph from exile, passing judgment on Brunelleschi's design for S. Lorenzo, conversing with scholars – scenes that are interpolated by representations of his virtues: shrewdness, diligence, prudence, and strength of character. Next year it was the turn of Lorenzo the Magnificent to be commemorated, his prowess in war and statecraft being balanced by his interest in learning. Meanwhile, the large room dedicated to Leo X was going forward, containing busts of Giuliano and Lorenzo, son and grandson of Lorenzo the Magnificent, and dominated by one of the most impressive paintings of the entire series, showing the Pope presiding over the College of Cardinals. Another room was devoted to scenes from the life of

Clement VII: the coronation of the Emperor at Bologna, Florence under siege. Here, too, are portrayed key moments in the life of Alessandro: his investiture with the ducal title, his marriage to the Emperor's daughter. Yet another room concentrated on the deeds and lineage of Cosimo's father, Giovanni *delle bande nere*.

This same theme, praise of his ancestors, was pushed home also in the pageants organized for Cosimo. For the celebration of Francesco's marriage with the Habsburg archduchess Joanna of Austria in 1565, for instance, a series of elaborate stage settings greeted the procession as it wound its way from Porta al Prato to the Palace of the Signoria. One of these was a simulacrum of a classical amphitheatre, dedicated to the glory of the house of Medici – the wedding party encountered it immediately after a triumphal arch dedicated to the house of Austria. Cosimo, Lorenzo, Leo, the younger Giuliano and Lorenzo, Clement, Alessandro, Giovanni *delle bande nere*, were all represented here.

So was Duke Cosimo. But his statue was no more than a prelude to the procession's encounter in the via dei Gondi with a triumphal arch entirely devoted to the major events and admirable qualities of his reign. Paintings showed the war of Siena, Cosimo receiving petitioners, sitting in judgment, organizing the militia. Statues celebrated his constancy, fortitude, wisdom in the conduct of affairs, his vigilance, prudence, generosity and moderation. And there was more to come. At the procession's end, in the courtyard of the Palace and on the walls of the Salone dei Cinquecento (as it is now called), there were paintings of Cosimo's building projects, his fortifications and his possessions. Here, as on the arch, were references to Cosimo's birthsign, Capricorn, stressed because it was to remind onlookers of the birthsign of Cosimo's favourite spiritual ancestor, the Emperor Augustus.

Publicity was an aspect of power, and Cosimo sought it where he could. He continued the interest Lorenzo the Magnificent had taken in Pisa; he patronized its university, improved its water supply and stimulated its shipbuilding industry. And at mid-century this was commemorated in Pierino da Vinci's superb marble relief *Cosimo I as Patron of Pisa*. He paid more historians to write what he hoped would be flattering versions of his reign than did Charles V or Francis I. He founded the Florentine Academy in 1540, largely to purify the Tuscan tongue, and to republish its classics and broadcast its virtues. To genuine literary interests of his own, Cosimo added, by political instinct, an element of propaganda, and under his sponsorship rules were forced through which guaranteed that members of the Academy would not dare to wander from the territory of philology to that of politics. In this respect, as in its constitutional changes, the reign of Cosimo I is a sketch towards the history of European absolutism as it was to culminate in the eighteenth century. But again, Cosimo was leading men prepared to be led. In the previous generation Machiavelli had accepted a Medici stipend to write his *Florentine History* and had groaned at the problem of squaring what he wanted to say with what Clement VII wanted to hear. No such conflict was experienced by Paolo Giovio, Scipione Ammirato or the other historians paid by Cosimo. The Platonic Academy of Lorenzo the Magnificent had had no ruler, no constitution, no formal membership; nor had the comparable Academies elsewhere in the previous century. By the middle of the sixteenth century, however, scholars and men of letters were institutionalizing themselves into what amounted to masonic lodges for intellectuals in many parts of Italy.

Another cultural rein was taken into the ducal hand in 1563 when Cosimo became president of the newly instituted *Accademia del Disegno* in Florence. With a membership of some seventy painters, sculptors and architects, with Vasari, Bronzino and Bartolommeo Ammanati among the chief organizers, this was the first academy of art to be established in Europe. It had formal rules and was governed by six consuls. It is likely that a majority of its members had already worked for Cosimo. For the Palace alone, he had commissioned sculpture from Bandinelli, Romolo Ferruzzi, Battista del Tasso, Sansovino, Cellini and Ammirato, and paintings or tapestry designs from Vasari, Bachiacca, Ridolfo Ghirlandaio, Bronzino, Pontormo and Francesco Salviati. Even larger teams ran up the plaster statues and the canvases used for festival and ceremonial purposes. Vasari had already painted the Duke giving orders to a whole circle of sculptors and architects.

After the markedly divergent styles that had characterized art in Florence in the first generation of the sixteenth century, a fairly widely shared style emerged, relying more on gesture than anatomy, on the interrelationships of figures rather than on a realization of the space that enclosed them, a decoratively potent but intellectually unstrenuous form of mannerism that not too misleadingly can be called the style of Cosimo I. And it is possible that it did indeed owe much to the group projects sponsored by the Duke. But, once again, Cosimo did not call the Academy and his headship of it into being; the initiative came from the artists themselves. When in 1564 the Academy planned an elaborate funeral service for Michelangelo, the most ferociously independent of artists, they petitioned that it should be held in the Medicean church of S. Lorenzo (though he was to be buried in S. Croce), and they did their utmost to identify the ceremony with the duke Michelangelo had consistently refused to serve, in spite of repeated invitations. The rein was slipped into Cosimo's hand by painters who wanted the precise opposite of the demeaning guild system to which by law they had to belong. From this law Cosimo released them in 1571, thus breaking one more link with the republican past from which both prince and painter wanted to escape.

Cosimo's exploitation of the counterpoint between the Florentines' willingness to accept his leadership and his deliberate inflation of the image of that leadership was vainglorious, but it was shrewd. He did succeed in glamorizing the Medici name and without alienating the great majority of those over whom the glamour was cast. The fifteenth-century Medici had let others praise them. Raphael's Leonine frescoes in the Vatican had put the Pope in a safely anachronistic historical context: Leo X's face on top of his fifth-century namesake's body. Vasari's portrait of Alessandro had sounded the new note but Cosimo was the first Medici consistently to blow his own trumpet and systematically to exalt his own rule. From Bronzino, sycophantically proud to serve 'the heavenly house of Medici', he ordered portraits of himself and Eleanor, and of their children. Bandinelli portrayed him in marble, Cellini in bronze. He had a set of twelve medals engraved by Pier Paolo Galeotti, with his head on one side and the notable aspects of his rule on the other. He commissioned one of the finest of all Renaissance carved gems: a large white onyx showing him and his family under a winged figure of Fame. The peak of this self-laudation was reached in 1564. In that year he cut down the space Vasari had tactlessly proposed to allot in the Palazzo Vecchio to representation of republican institutions like the militia *gonfaloni* and the guilds. In a world dominated by Habsburgs, one of whom – and a legitimate one – was about to become joined to his family, there was prestige to be gained from portraying his ancestors selectively, not as bankers but as statesmen and patrons of the arts; there was nothing to gain from emphasizing their commercial background. More significant still was his changing the figure of Florence in glory, which Vasari had prepared as the centrepiece of the new ceiling of the Salone dei Cinquecento, to another figure in glory – himself. For with this gesture he subordinated the whole history of Florence, its founding, its conquests, its cultural achievements, to his own fame.

CHAPTER V

Grand-Ducal Tuscany

Francesco (1574–87) and Ferdinando I (1587–1609)

On Cosimo I's death in 1574 Francesco succeeded him without a murmur of protest in Florence. Having already been accepted as regent for ten years he had merely to invite the Senate of forty-eight to 'elect' him, and two days after Cosimo's death they did. Yet this was not enough. In the eyes of princely Europe the Medici were still *parvenus*. The title of grand duke had been awarded only five years previously and by a pope; its validity had been but grudgingly acknowledged by the two great chieftains – Philip II of Spain and Maximilian II of Austria – of a world which still, on the topmost of its herald-patrolled slopes, thought in feudal terms. Like other *parvenus*, Francesco had recourse to display, and planned for Cosimo a funeral that would compensate by its opulent dignity for the newness of the grand-ducal image.

Cosimo died on 21 April. To give time for heads of state to attend and preparations to be made, the funeral was announced for 17 May. Meanwhile, the body was embalmed and an effigy prepared for the lying-in-state in the Palace of the Signoria, dressed in robes of state, crowned and sceptred, its waxen hands and face modelled by Giambologna. The notion of the lifelike effigy and its message, 'the king never dies', was borrowed from the funeral ceremonies of the kings of France. The pageantry employed for the procession to S. Lorenzo and the stage-management of the service itself were modelled on the elaborate funeral commemoration of Charles V, organized in Brussels by Philip II in 1558. For propaganda purposes, Francesco was turning France and Spain into the sponsors of his rank by means of iconographical borrowings.

The object of the Emperor's commemoration service had been to glorify his rank, his conquests and his possessions, and to identify his heir with them. Akin, and knowingly, to the apotheosis ceremonies of the emperors of ancient Rome, which elevated the departed ruler into a godlike genius presiding over his successor's reign, it was designed to glamorize the living with the halo of the dead. It was a model that perfectly suited Francesco's needs. It was the anti-symbol of republicanism and it was an allegory of hereditary succession. So he wore a penitent's costume similar to that worn by Philip; Buontalenti built a *baldacchino* for S. Lorenzo which resembled the one used in Brussels; and Francesco followed that example in having it decked with the titles and insignia of the defunct and the emblems of his subject territories. Borghini was once more called upon to provide a programme; the team that had worked on Michelangelo's funeral was remobilized. A small army of painters and carpenters transformed S. Lorenzo into a mausoleum, in which skulls and skeletons alternated with allusions to Cosimo's achievements in peace and war. Glorified in life by Vasari in the Salone del Cinquecento, Cosimo was now glorified in death before the assembled emissaries from the towns and cities of Tuscany and from other Italian states. The funeral's message was backed by earnest diplomatic pressure on Spain and Austria. In the following year Philip invested Francesco with the Sienese territories Cosimo had held from him as a fief, and in 1576 the Emperor Maximilian solemnly confirmed his right to the title of grand duke.

This influence from beyond the grave was to characterize all the public aspects of Francesco's career. Though he was thirty-three on Cosimo's death he never emerged from the shadow of his father's long reign or acquired a political *persona* of his own. Nominally regent since 1564, he had been in reality a reluctant apprentice, and showed little interest in improving on the administrative and economic policies he learned in that capacity. From his early twenties Cosimo had had to reprimand him for his moody retreat from public life, for burying himself in laboratories and workshops by day and taking solitary walks about the city by night. He totally, almost defiantly, lacked his father's confident and genial, if occasionally savage mastery, his flair for combining a patriarchal style of private life with a rigid control of public affairs. To protect himself from the exposure Cosimo accepted with such ease he insisted on a formality, a rigid decorum that obviated the need for spontaneity, and within the fabric of the city he built boltholes and skyways where he could keep himself apart: the windowless *studiolo*, the tribuna in the Uffizi, the Vasarian corridor above the Ponte Vecchio. Cosimo had taken a close interest in technology, especially in connection with shipbuilding, metallurgy and irrigation. Francesco, too, was drawn to applied science, experimenting with the effect of heat on crystals, new forms of porcelain, even the manufacture of time bombs. His interest in crystals and semi-precious stones led him to become the founder of one of Florence's most enduringly prosperous luxury crafts, work in *pietra dura*, but this interest, and the stimulus he gave to the glass, porcelain and coral-cutting industries started by Cosimo, arose rather from their relevance to his private study of chemistry, especially in its alchemical guise, than from a hard-headed desire to steer a private taste towards the public good.

In 1570 he commissioned Vasari, in consultation with Borghini, to decorate a small room opening off his bedroom in the Palace of the Signoria. The theme was to be the relationship between science and nature, worked out with reference to the four elements, earth, air, fire and water. The team employed, which included Bronzino and Allori among the painters, Giambologna and Ammanati among the sculptors, not only produced the most beautiful room in late Renaissance Florence but, in its nervous intricacy as well as its celebration of man's Promethean power to comprehend and put nature to work, a valid symbol of Francesco's state of mind. In this *studiolo*, in cupboards concealed by paintings, he intended to house his collections of ingenious, rare and precious objects. There, by day or night, he could come to brood over his minerals and glass under the sign of fire and the protection of Apollo and Vulcan; his goldsmith's work under the sign of earth and the earth deities, Pluto and Ops; crystals and cut gems under Juno and Zephyr, deities of air; pearls and curiosities from rivers and the sea under the deities of water, Galatea and Venus Anadyomene. There were paintings showing knowledge put to use, as when fire melted bronze into guns, but it was, above all, a place for solitary musing, or to show to a few friends and favoured visitors.

In general, indeed, he had learned what ought to be done, but did not care to do it. His subjects approached him not in person but by slipping their petitions into a slit beside the stylistically enigmatic door inserted for him in the Uffizi by Buontalenti, who also made a peephole through which he could watch public audiences unobserved. The letters of foreign ambassadors were filled with glum references to his inaccessibility, whether in the city itself or in one of his closely-guarded villa retreats. Ignorance of what the grand duke was doing with much of his time led to rumours of orgies, of depraved banquets with liquors distilled by himself and weirdly spiced exotic foods, of self-medication with fire and ice and powdered gems. Our knowledge of what he did in his city retreats is less dependent on rumour. Most of his time was spent in the workshops and laboratories originally established by Cosimo in the Palace of the Signoria and which were transferred first to the Boboli then to the Uffizi. There, in addition to metallurgical experiments, he carried on pharmaceutical work, including research on poisons that necessitated a supply of thousands of scorpions, and attempts to find the secret of perpetual motion.

Indifferent to the routine of government, he found little in his family life to draw him away from solitude. He had little or no affection for his wife Joanna, the daughter of Ferdinand I of Habsburg. It was, of course, a purely political match, but not even the pleasures of companionship followed from it: she was plain, stupid, uncultivated and demanding. It was the first of what was to be a long series of disastrous Medici marriages. He was on bad terms with his brother Ferdinando, the Cardinal, who in any case spent most of his time in Rome. Isabella, the most lively and talented of his sisters, was murdered by her husband, the Duke of Bracciano, for her adultery. His brother Piero murdered his wife on the same pretext. Both crimes were ignored by Francesco on the grounds that they were simply matters of protecting family honour. His illegitimate (by Leonora degli Albizzi) brother Giovanni, whose earliest ambition was to be a soldier, was still growing up; he left to begin his martial career in Flanders in the year of Francesco's death.

Melancholic, a prey to outbursts of violent temper, Francesco knew how to obtain obedience if not how to rule. He totally lacked Cosimo's coolly architectonic approach to government, but it was his impatience that forced forward the building of the new fortified port of Leghorn in the teeth of a European economic recession. He was capable of such a naïveté as to assure Mohammed Pasha that Turkish merchants could use the port, in spite of the galleys of the crusading Order of S. Stefano that were docked there, on the pretext that these galleys belonged to an independent order founded by his father for whose vows (though he had taken them himself) he was in no way responsible! In foreign affairs he seized the thickest of the threads of Cosimo's policy, amity with Spain, but left the subtler ones that had counteracted the dependence this involved – flirtations with France, Austria and the anti-Spanish Italian states – to be woven by his diplomats, who, in the absence of clear directions to the contrary, continued to operate as though Cosimo were still alive. The grand duke's originality showed itself most clearly at the benches of his laboratories, in his patronage of the arts, and in bed. Nothing is more dreary in the historiography of the Medici than the literature dealing with the family's 'secret history', for nothing that happens in private and behind closed doors, from Cosimo I's incest to Cosimo III's homosexuality, can be proved, though, as in the former case, it can sometimes be almost disproved. Every period of security is a period of scandal. The security of the grand-ducal period has produced a view of it seen through eyes reddened by long and usually vain peering through keyholes. In the case of Francesco, however, attention to scandal is not altogether unjustified. He is best known for his long liaison with Bianca Capello. Like his other obsession, alchemy, it was essentially a private concern, but it had its public and knowable aspects even before, on Joanna's death, he married her.

At the age of fifteen, already considered extraordinarily beautiful, Bianca had eloped from an aristocratic home in Venice with a young Florentine who was little more than a bank clerk. Piero Buonaventuri had hardly smuggled her across the lagoon when the alarm was raised; by the time the couple reached Florence the Venetian government had declared Piero an outlaw and demanded that the couple should be returned for punishment. This was in 1563. Cosimo could not ignore the Venetian demands, but the couple were legally married; he was impressed by Bianca's energetic refusal to return to her parents, and he agreed to do nothing as long as they lived quietly in the Buonaventuri house facing S. Marco. Cramped in this voluntary confinement, Bianca was haunted by the possibility of Piero's assassination by agents of the Capello family, and of being abducted herself and immured for life, as her father had sworn, in a nunnery. Her awakening from infatuation to the realization that her husband was poor and obscure came at a time when she was ready for both protection and romance. The young Francesco offered both, and blindly. Neither his promotion to the regency nor his marriage affected their liaison. Though he knew that the luckless Piero, looking elsewhere for love, had become involved in a feud of the sort that could lead to assassination, he did nothing. When Piero was indeed stabbed to death, he took no action against the murderers but installed Bianca more publicly than ever in the Rucellai Gardens on the via della Scala, which he bought for her, and where Buontalenti built a house which became an acknowledged second court. Living in luxury, not without some influence as his unofficial consort, Bianca was nevertheless totally dependent on Francesco. Her expedients to keep his sense of responsibility to her alive went so far as the staging of a false pregnancy and the production of another's baby as her own. Such a melodrama, which Francesco detected and forgave, was unnecessary. Two months after Joanna's death in 1578, Bianca became Grand Duchess of Tuscany.

From that year, with both Bianca and his alchemical experiments at hand in the Pitti, Francesco shrank more into the background of public affairs than ever. He even lost the very considerable interest he had shown in the arts. Like Cosimo he had continued to commission public statuary. Giambologna's *Rape of the Sabines* joined the *Perseus* and Donatello's *Judith* in the Loggia dei Lanzi. He was quick to turn the genius of his youthful drawing master, Buontalenti, to account as military engineer, architect, deviser of pageants and firework displays, even as a decorator of porcelain. His patronage of painters seems to have been more dutiful than enthusiastic, but he carried on the decoration of the Salone del Cinquecento, which had been left unfinished on his father's death, and sustained the propaganda of its programme by commissioning Jacopo Ligozzi, his court painter, to depict Cosimo's election as duke by the Florentine Senate. But his real interest was in the curious and the bizarre, in the nascent taste for grotto architecture in which natural and sculptural forms teasingly interpenetrated, and in garden statuary conceived either as the freezing of an episode from real life into a *genre* subject in stone or as the shaping of some heaved-up aspect of nature itself. It is as though the transmutation of one substance into another in the heat of his crucibles led to an affection for the conundrums posed by the relationship between nature and art.

Francesco added to the family collection of villas – he bought Lapeggi and the villa Magìa del Quarata, and treated them as places to decorate rather than to hunt from. His favourite was Pratolino, which he had Buontalenti rebuild; and in its grounds Giambologna's giant figure of the Apennines, squatting among stalactites, water oozing over its shoulders, represents one aspect of his taste for art's collaboration with, not mastery of, natural substances. Even more extreme was his licensing Giambologna to thrust Michelangelo's unfinished slaves into the angles of a grotto in the Boboli Gardens as though to plunge them back into the pre-art chaos of rock fragments, shells and stalactites from which the other figures there are shaped. He also gathered the greater part of the family's paintings and antiquities together and launched them on their long accumulative career as a collection.

Psychologically, this was a turning-point in the history of Medici patronage. To assemble works of art in galleries, as Francesco did in the Uffizi, is to notice gaps, to think historically, to approach painters rather than wait to be approached by them – as Francesco approached Barrocci, whom he knew only by reputation. The remarkable range of the Medici collection that hangs now in the Uffizi and the Pitti is due in great part to the policy of deliberate choice introduced by Francesco.

The grand duke had seven children, but no heir. The first six were girls, the seventh, Filippo, died when he was five. The marriage with Bianca was barren. His last years were made all the more depressed by the knowledge that he would be succeeded not by a child of his own but by the brother he disliked, Ferdinando.

The Cardinal was thirty-eight when Francesco died in 1587. With the tastes neither of a student nor of a solitary, he was more suited to the leadership of a state than Francesco had been, and by keeping lavish open house to visiting diplomats and taking an active part in ecclesiastical affairs while he was in Rome, he had acquired a knowledge of public affairs as a churchman which Francesco had not troubled to acquire as a duke. Soon after his succession he was described by the Venetian ambassador in Florence as a man who liked pleasure and ceremony, who was not ambitious to extend his state nor particularly energetic as an administrator, but who had the economic interest of his subjects at heart and was determined to maintain the dignity of his court and 'to enjoy the greatness of his rank and the beauty of his state'.

Events bore out this assessment. Ferdinando quickly gathered the reins of policy from the hands of ministers and ambassadors into which Francesco had let them fall. Such a policy could not, even when directed most firmly, be called 'absolutist' in any very meaningful way. Cosimo I, with the advice of his jurists, had underwritten an attitude to the law which made equality before it paramount, and neither he nor his successors cared to bend it to their own short-term interest in issues or in individuals. Nor, in practice, was government efficient enough directly to reflect a sole will, let alone carry its expression into action without more delay or compromise than the term 'absolutist' readily admits. When an agent for Duke Francis Stephen of Lorraine came to report after the death of Gian Gastone, the last Medici grand duke, he wrote in dismay that 'the government of this place is a chaos almost impossible to disentangle; it is a mixture of aristocracy, democracy and monarchy.' There was platitude behind this, and some misunderstanding, but from Cosimo I to Gian Gastone, the Medici had put up with some blurring of their authority by the vested interests of institutional tradition and the demands of their leading citizens.

In economic affairs much of Ferdinando's attention was taken up with Leghorn, but he initiated large-scale drainage and road building projects in southern Tuscany to make the great marshes there cultivatable, more healthful, and attractive to farmers. To support the silk industry he ordered that mulberry trees should be planted along the roads leading from Florence to Pistoia and Pisa. His long career in the

Church in no way inhibited his new career as a statesman. 'Use bribes freely', he instructed his ambassador in Spain, 'to ferret out accurately the secrets that can be of service to our house. . . . The chief ministers and those who are wealthy are of course very hard to corrupt, but they have inferiors under them who can be won over.' Cheerfully accepting the need to produce an heir, he renounced his cardinal's hat and in 1589 married Christine of Lorraine, a niece of Catherine de' Medici. This alliance with a French house was not only the first move in a policy of modifying Florence's dependence upon Spain but strikingly successful in achieving its main purpose. An heir, Cosimo, was born within a year and eight more children followed in rapid succession. In 1600 Ferdinando arranged the marriage of Francesco's youngest daughter, Maria, to Henry IV, a move so much in contrast to the inert policy of the previous reign that the Spanish reaction was to build a new fortress on Elba.

It was indeed a move that took Ferdinando further than he had intended. Henry showed no sign of honouring his Medici bargain by protecting Tuscany from Spanish demands for money and diplomatic servitude. In 1608, therefore, after long negotiations, the ex-cardinal arranged a third match, between his heir Cosimo and the Archduchess Maria Maddelena of Austria, with the aim of placating Spain (whose queen was Maddelena's sister) while taking advantage of the conflicts of interest between the Habsburgs of Spain and of Austria. And the elaborate pageantry designed to welcome Maddelena to Florence was designed to draw attention to the importance of this third element in the balance of forces upon which Tuscan independence relied.

Ferdinando's concern for Tuscany was widely various. In Florence he founded what was probably the first convalescent home in Europe, designed to complete the rehabilitation of patients discharged from hospitals. He sponsored an expedition to the Amazon to explore the possibility of Tuscan colonization in Brazil. He took an interest in the University of Pisa and appointed the twenty-five-year-old Galileo to the chair of mathematics there. In the Piazza della Signoria he added Giambologna's *Hercules and the Centaur* to the Loggia dei Lanzi, and commissioned from him the equestrian statue of Cosimo I, specifying for the reliefs on its plinth the by now almost mandatory references to the legitimacy of grand-ducal rule over Tuscany: the Florentine Senate's acceptance of Cosimo as duke, his coronation as grand duke, and the triumph over Siena. He commissioned the equestrian statue of himself which was begun by Giambologna and finished by Pietro Tacca and which stands in the Piazza SS. Annunziata. He also started construction of the most controversial of Medici monuments in Florence: the chapel of the princes in S. Lorenzo.

The idea of building a mausoleum suited in its solemnity and splendour to the family's new dignity had been first mooted by Cosimo I. Vasari had produced a design, but the plan was dropped on Cosimo's death. With either this plan in mind or another of which there is no record, Francesco began to collect the marbles and the semi-precious stones, chalcedony, sardonyx, jaspers and agates, with which they were to be inlaid. In 1604 the foundation stone was at last laid after a competition in which his brother Giovanni's plans were preferred to Buontalenti's, and work began on what was to be at once the most opulent memorial to the dead of a princely house in Italy and the most portentous specimen of *pietra dura* work in the world.

Ferdinando's concern that Florence as a whole should remain a monument to the Medici prompted him to pass legislation against the export of works of art without a grand-ducal licence. He had been an avid collector of antiquities in Rome, buying widely and conducting excavations of his own. Some of the finest of his acquisitions – among them the Venus de' Medici – he left in the new Villa Medici in Rome, but he added many of them to the sculpture gallery in the Uffizi. To the family's collection of Tuscan villas he added Petraia, the Ambrogiana at Montelupo and, loveliest of all, Artimino.

Easy-going, shrewd and imaginative, Ferdinando succeeded, without loss to his geniality, in restoring the vigour of Cosimo's reign. Having founded a mausoleum that was to turn out to be the costliest building project ever embarked on by a Medici, he declared in his will that he was to be buried without fuss and that the normal expenses for a grand-ducal funeral were to be set aside as a trust for poor children in Florence and Siena. And in that same will, conscious of having restored order after the incumbency of his brother, he warned his successor to leave well alone, to maintain a respectful but guarded stance towards Spain, to maintain the present level of taxes 'because it is necessary for a prince to be rich', but to raise new ones only if a defensive war made it necessary and to cancel them as soon as the danger had passed.

Court and constitution

The machinery of government went on running through Francesco's reign on the momentum imparted to it by Cosimo, and enough was left for Ferdinando to restore its thrust without real strain. The momentum derived principally from the bureaucracy established by Alessandro and extended by Cosimo, the permanent officials, secretaries, *auditori* and judges, whose powers and competence sufficed to keep the administration moving so long as no crisis required the taking of decisions that would shift it in a different direction. Cosimo had relied heavily – and in legal appointments exclusively – on men from outside the Florentine patriciate, men from Prato, Volterra or Fano without vested interests in the capital, and loyal to him and a system of government seen through his eyes rather than to the tradition represented by the councils and magistracies, with their rotating membership. Some of these men he ennobled, thus qualifying them for election to bodies such as the Senate, and in this way he was able to insert his own point of view into the deliberations of organs of state dominated by patrician families, the Guicciardini, Strozzi, Salviati, Ridolfi and their like. And the chief bureaucrats, powerful and alien as many of them were, were not the faceless members of a secret inner regime. Secretaries and *auditori* sat regularly at meetings of the patrician councils, they built or bought palaces in the city, they intermarried with patrician families, on the many religious holidays which brought government business to a halt they walked, were indeed, compelled by law to walk, in processions among the representatives of patrician families and the guilds.

In the interest of their own security as a class and of assuring continuity and strength in the conduct of foreign affairs, the patriciate had released their control of the formation of policy. They accepted the notion of the principate, of hereditary rule; some were even to grant the principle that the Medici ruled by divine right. But this does not mean that the political history of Florence could henceforth be written in terms of grand dukes and bureaucrats. 'Liberty', that old republican watchword, had shifted its significance from liberty to participate in government to liberty to be left alone in security. A court had produced courtiers. But if patricians served the state on different terms, they continued to serve it. To steer Florence in its new constitutional direction Alessandro and Cosimo had policed the route with as many outsiders as they thought necessary; in Cosimo's case, as many, perhaps, as he dared. Once the route was established, however, its hired guardians were progressively called off. Under Ferdinando, more responsibility for routine administrative affairs was given back to the old republican magistracies that Cosimo had tethered with red tape:

the *Otto di Pratica*, the Conservors of the Laws, the Public Debt Commission, the Twelve Good Men, and the rest. No longer ghosts of the past, hovering apologetically among the bodies directly expressing ducal power, freed from the taint of the automatic rubber stamp, these offices brought a renewed interest and prestige to the hundreds of men from the patrician class who served on them each year. By Ferdinando's death, one-third of the key permanent positions in the central government were held by patricians, and it was a proportion that was to grow. Similarly, the numbers of patricians employed on embassies abroad and as governors of Tuscan cities increased. By 1609, a process of re-education, part voluntary, part enforced, had allowed the survivors of the old cast to play a changed, but in many respects reassuringly familiar, role on the wider stage of the new Tuscany.

Meanwhile, as partial compensation for their dependence on him, Cosimo had begun escalating their status. He turned his title into a fount of honours by founding in 1562 the crusading Order of the Knights of S. Stefano, membership of which brought prestige – reflecting that of similar orders in Spain and the Empire – and was functional, for the knights were pledged to take part, or pay others to take part, in galley warfare against the Turks. He and his successors lavished money on the headquarters of the Order in Pisa, the Palazzo dei Cavalieri, and on the fabric and furnishings of its nearby church, and the Order served at least as much to propitiate leading families in the *dominio* as in Florence itself. To the same effect, a number of fiefs were given or sold to men upon whose support the dukes wished to rely, though not so freely as to run the risk of creating a potentially separate neo-feudal class.

The grand dukes, again, were careful to accentuate the princely ritual of the court, where etiquette on the Spanish model was stressed: who could remain covered in the grand duke's presence, who could take his hand in greeting, what order of precedence should be observed at meals or when listening to concerts – trivia which would have alienated rather than intrigued the Florentines had not the grand dukes, like themselves, retained an active interest in business and trade. For they remained bankers, though through intermediaries. They speculated in grain, financed interloping voyages by Dutch and English captains into Spanish waters and traded with galleys of their own. They stressed public ceremonial and were quick to detect and complain of slights to their dignity on the part of foreign powers, but none of them was in the fullest sense a public figure: within the potentate was, never fully at ease, something of the scholar-merchant. For all its wealth, for all its copying of foreign manners and the magnificence of its cultural accoutrements, the grand-ducal court remained incorrigibly provincial. This robbed the contrast with the pre-ducal past of some of its sting. Foreigners were prone to sniff at grand dukes who sold their own wine, but the Florentines found this a homely and a reassuring trait.

On the other hand, like the monarchs of the north, the grand dukes reserved hunting grounds for themselves – in the seventeenth century the Cascine became a ducal chase – and moved about among a number of sumptuous country residences. Partly to follow this example, and partly because land was a reassuringly safe investment, the Florentine aristocracy followed suit. The seventeenth century was to be the great age of the Tuscan villa, and if the men who used them were rather sharper with their stewards and more knowledgeable about pruning than were their opposite numbers in France, they were but following the example of their rulers. Within Florence it was also a great age of palace building. Special legislation was passed in favour of anyone who wished to enlarge his house and turn a merchant's home into an aristocrat's residence. And though well-connected Florentines never became as court-centred as did their opposite numbers north of the Alps, it was an indication how far the leadership of the court at the Pitti Palace was accepted that the Oltr'Arno became the most fashionable district and the via Maggio its most exclusive street; S. Spirito had always been a wealthy quarter, but the majority of the great houses there date from grand-ducal times.

The climax of a process so often referred to in these pages, the transformation of a republican patriciate into a courtier caste, must be seen in realistically Florentine terms. It was not a taming of political opponents by turning them into ornaments, or of economic rivals by tempting them to become drones. Perhaps it is fitting at last to call the patricians aristocrats, but if they defined their rank with reference to their relationship with the grand dukes as well as to their forebears, marriage alliances, civic offices and wealth, they continued to be business and family men first and foremost. If something approaching a flight from commerce and finance to the land can be observed, this reflects the state of the market rather than an appetite for a new sort of status. We are talking of an intellectual adjustment, not a radically changed style of life. And the adjustment was most pronounced in the purely intellectual pursuits of aristocrats who subordinated their leisure time to the conventions of academies under ducal patronage, and in the writings of professional intellectuals, classical scholars, literary men, historians, who now, almost to a man, subsisted on ducal pensions. After three centuries, the Florentine body politic could no longer be likened, as Dante had phrased it, to a sick woman tossing and turning on a bed of pain. Embattled factions; constitutional experiments; political speculation and controversy; these were now stilled into an almost unquestioning conformity. There was no longer any need to envy the stability of Venice. There was discontent, and the network of spies remained on the payroll to detect it, but the old-style militant exile had given way to the apolitical émigré, and when agitation did from time to time become widely vocal it was in the form of shouts for bread and for work, not for a return of the republic.

The existence of a grand-ducal court was associated with but hardly conditioned this acceptance of the *status quo*. Socially, it functioned intermittently. The great majority of aristocrats and their wives entered the Pitti only on widely spaced special occasions, concerts or weddings. These, as in Cosimo I's day, were elaborate affairs. Over 6,000 ducats were spent on confectionery alone at Ferdinando's marriage to Christine of Lorraine. One of the entertainments designed for Maria's marriage to Henry IV cost 60,000. But these occasions were planned less to indoctrinate the Florentines than to impress the other princes of Italy and the ambassadors of the great European dynasts.

And just as Francesco had borrowed from the funeral ceremony of Charles V, he and Ferdinando copied and, in turn, influenced the theatrical festivities that were so much in vogue in the great courts of Europe: gorgeously mounted plays, dramatic pieces interspersed with musical interludes, masques, tournaments, river pageants and horse ballets. A large room was set aside for theatrical entertainments in the Pitti; in 1586 Buontalenti constructed a theatre within the Uffizi with seating for between three and four thousand spectators and a stage area designed for the complex machinery that made spectacular transformations possible: the opening of a mountain, the descent of gods in clouds of glory, the metamorphosis of Florence into Olympus.

For whereas the iconography of Medici-sponsored art continued to stress the family, the great ancestors, the legitimacy of its rule and its glory, the content of the theatre festivals was predominantly mythological. But publicized throughout Europe by engravings and the eyewitness accounts of diplomats in residence at the Tuscan court and foreign visitors, the image was spread of a court life thoroughly familiar with the visual *lingua franca* of monarchical Europe, a language overwhelmingly freighted with classical allusions. For home consumption, the greatness of the family, for dispersal abroad, wealth and modishness: these were two aspects of a propaganda made all the more effective by the genuine interest of the grand dukes in the technology and the artistry, as well as in the publicity value, of the pageantry they sponsored.

In the year before his death, Ferdinando's plan for Cosimo's wedding to Maria Maddelena of Austria had as its centrepiece the most grandiose river festival ever staged in Florence: the seizure by Jason of the Golden Fleece, which involved boats disguised as sea monsters and birds as well as an artificial island whence the captured fleece was conveyed to the bride. In addition to weddings and state visits by foreign princes, carnival time was celebrated each year with pageants and equestrian ballets, sometimes in the grounds of the Pitti, sometimes in Piazza S. Croce, for while only gentlemen were invited to watch and participate (along with professional actors and singers) in the entertainments that took place indoors, the wedding celebrations included open-air spectacles that could be watched by everybody, from street corner, river bank or grandstand, and the carnival festivities were devised with the populace in mind. It was only with the grand dukes that the Medici can be said to have adopted a policy of *circenses* to offset the rising price of bread – caused (at least in part) by their monopoly of grain distribution.

The 'system' of Cosimo I had survived the assault and plotting of exiles, the pressure of other powers. Under Francesco it survived an equally searching trial: that of neglect. Under Ferdinando it was seen to be not only effective but popular. In 1600 the Venetian ambassador noted that although governmental initiative was firmly in the control of the grand duke and his chosen advisers, the citizens played their part so willingly in the magistracies within Florence and the elective posts – captain, *podestà*, chamberlain, controller of customs – in Tuscany that the regime could now expect more faithful service from its own subjects than from foreigners.

The Medicean city

Florentine society was thus becoming Mediceanized, and, in the main willingly; its leisure diverted by Medicean festivities, its ambitious men absorbed by the Medicean bureaucracy, its intellectuals glad to come together under Medicean sponsorship, its upper class aristocratized on Medicean lines, its eyes caught by new Medicean buildings, statues, fountains and paintings.

Numerically, Florence was not a leader among the cities of Italy. By the beginning of Cosimo I's reign its population had been reduced by war, plague, exile and misery to 50,000. By the mid-century there were 60,000, by 1600 some 75,000 inhabitants, a figure still trailing behind those for Milan, Venice, Rome, Naples and Palermo. Within a city of this size, quite small physical changes were significant, large ones of compulsive interest.

Only one change was compelling in the most literal sense, the Belevedere fortress, built in 1590–95, which looked across to the Fortezza da Basso as the second jaw of a vice squeezing the principate on the people. Apart from the church of S. Pier Scheraggio and its attendant slums, destroyed to let the Uffizi march down to the Arno, no monument of republican days was demolished. A project of Bandinelli's to classicize the façade of the Palazzo Vecchio was rejected; it was enough that its interior decoration celebrated the new race of princes. The Loggia dei Lanzi was untouched, though the interior, where the priors had received visiting embassies, became a sculpture gallery. The chapel of the princes, a monument to the Medici designed by a Medici, was tactfully based on the ground plan of the Baptistery. No new streets were driven through the urban fabric of Soderini's or Machiavelli's day (though mention of either of them was anathema). Political aspiration may have been diverted into new routes, but no architectural vistas were created to regiment the eye at the risk of alienating the owners of property. Tax exemptions, indeed, encouraged the completion of palaces started in republican times but left unfinished. Specific laws allowed the retention or addition of personal coats of arms, private houses were allowed to call attention to themselves by stuccoing and painting their façades with the arabesques made popular by Buontalenti's work for Bianca Capello. Pride in descent, symbolized by the craze for genealogy, self-esteem based on continuity of possession: these politically safe forms of nostalgia were encouraged by the grand dukes both in Florence itself and throughout Tuscany.

Cosimo I had identified himself with public works that were for the advantage of the city as a whole, such as the repaving of the Piazza della Signoria, the construction of Ammanati's Ponte della Trinita across the Arno, and the creation of the Lungarni Corsini and Acciaiuoli. The aerial corridor connecting the Uffizi with the Pitti was a reflection of Francesco's obsession with privacy and it contrasts with Cosimo's less daring and more educative treatment of the public and processional route across the river to the Pitti. In the Piazza Santa Trinita he placed a column commemorating the defeat of the exiles' army at Montemurlo and topped it with a figure of Justice. On the other side of the river, in Piazza San Felice, he erected another column, this time celebrating the defeat of the Sienese, and he planned to surmount it with a figure of peace. And as well as showing visitors to the Pitti, whose superb inner courtyard was begun in 1558, that he was strong enough to bring the benefits of justice and peace through victory over domestic and foreign rivals by land, he drew attention to his ability to defend Tuscany from the sea. He took great pains over the fountain of Neptune in the Piazza della Signoria, holding two separate competitions for the design until he was satisfied with that of Ammanati, and having water piped all the way from a spring by the Porta S. Niccolò via the Ponte alle Grazie.

Cosimo kept images of his own face withindoors, save in connection with the temporary structures erected for specific festivities. Ferdinando was secure enough to be less reticent. Thanks to him, Cosimo's bronze figure sits in the Piazza della Signoria, frozen to the back of one of those horses he hunted so tirelessly and dictated so many orders from. Ferdinando's own equestrian statue, more frankly an expression of power, was placed in the centre of the Piazza Santissima Annunziata, whereas Cosimo's was tucked away to one side. And Ferdinando paid for, or allowed others to commission, busts of himself, Francesco and Cosimo (some twenty of a larger number survive) on street corners, on the façades of palaces, and within arcades (like those of the hospitals of S. Paolo and the Innocenti) open to the public view. In the vaulting of the latter he got Poccetti to paint Cosimo's foundation of the fortifications at Portoferraio on Elba, his coronation as grand duke, his institution of the Order of S. Stefano and of the Academy of Design. Because the building is a charitable one, Cosimo's actions are associated with the theological virtues, faith, hope and charity, but most important is the cardinal – and political – virtue, Justice. The scheme is conventional enough. More significant is that, like the reliefs on the equestrian statue of Cosimo, it takes the moments symbolizing the Medicean grip on military, political, social and intellectual life into the open. Some of Ferdinando's monuments to his family have offended the taste of posterity. None is known to have galled the susceptibilities of his contemporaries.

The economy

Apart from the chapel of the princes, the volume of the grand dukes' artistic projects showed a restraint that bore little relation to their income. Just what this amounted to is uncertain: it has not been investigated. Thanks to the identification of state fiscal and commercial policy with the personal direction of the grand dukes it is perhaps beyond investigation. If Lorenzo the Magnificent put his hand in the communal till to repay private moneys disbursed in the public interest there was at least a clear distinction between what belonged to the Medici and what belonged to the state. When the state became constitutionally identified with the Medici the distinction became blurred. Cosimo and his successors used the 'comandata' or apportionment of peasant labour services for their own land reclamation or building schemes (the construction of Artimino, for example) as well as for roads and fortifications. They appropriated the right to control the salt monopoly and the extraction of minerals. It is reasonably safe to assume that in terms of dues, chattels, property and the return on capital invested in loans, industry, commerce and agriculture, Francesco and, still more, Ferdinando were wealthier than any of their predecessors, including Cosimo *pater patriae*.

In 1589 and 1601 the Arno flooded. Ferdinando walked through the devastated district of Santa Croce organizing the distribution of grain for bread. This action brought him immense popularity. 'It brought tears to my eyes,' wrote the pensioned scholar and historian Scipione Ammirato. It was an action later to join those Medicean moments that were to form part of the family's pictorial hagiography. But as the chief purchaser of grain in his dominions he was selling to others at a price largely fixed by himself as well as giving away grain to the poor. And if rumour was correct in saying that he recouped himself for his gift from the state loan bank, this was not unreasonable: he was the chief investor in its bonds, which yielded a tranquil five and a half per cent.

As far as the return on investment was concerned, the fortunes of the grand dukes altered with those of the Tuscan economy as a whole. Cosimo I died in a country that was probably more prosperous than it had ever been. War had crippled France and the Low Countries, the chief competitors in the silk and wool manufactures; Florentine banks had prospered, mainly through their branches in Rome, Venice, Lyons and, less securely, Antwerp. Florentine merchants (including the grand dukes) were exploiting the demand for manufactured goods among the colonists of Spanish America just as – Bardi, Cavalcanti and Alberti among them – they were demonstrating a flair for profit, no less acute than in republican days, from Madrid and Lisbon to Cracow and Lwow. Constitutional changes had had little effect on the economic pursuits of the patriciate, certainly less than international events which closed a market here and opened another somewhere else, or recessions, booms, loan demands or mass defaultings, whose causes lay outside the dominions of the grand dukes. A *Pratica Secreta*, an intermittently splendid court at the Pitti: these and other phenomena of a princely regime had their effect. But while opportunities existed for the tradi-tional patrician pursuit of profit, they were less important than the wool and silk industries at home, trade in commodities and banking activity abroad. Political continuity, the expectation that identical political enthusiasms would flow from father to son, had slackened from the days of Piero de' Medici the younger, but the expectation that a son would continue the economic pursuits of his parent remained as strong as ever until the advent in the seventeenth century of a real and indefinitely prolonged recession, a recession unresponsive alike to risk, diversification or a policy of wait and see.

After a period of fairly steady economic expansion after the consoli-dation of Cosimo's position in the city, a decline occurred under Fran-cesco, to be followed by a renewed up-turn during Fernando's reign. The prolonged recession did not occur until the 1620s.

Though the first decline appears to have coincided with a period of slack between two periods of forceful government, the blame cannot be attributed to Francesco. The major causes of recession were beyond the control of an age that had no overall view of European prices and ex-change values. Though partly vitiated by their own interests as mer-chants and price-fixers, the policies of the grand dukes were not unenlightened in terms of Tuscany itself, being geared to the protection of local enterprise from foreign competition and the satisfaction of local interests by a multitude of tolls on internal transport. But at a time when the balance of trade was operating against the Mediterranean countries and the great need was for free capital for investment outside Italy, the treatment of Tuscany as a watertight economic unit was a mistaken one. And its effects were worsened by the high cost of Medici diplomacy, the maintenance of a large staff, the purchasing of in-formation with lavish bribes, many cash subsidies to allies in lieu of direct military involvement, splendid ceremonies for propaganda pur-poses and extravagantly costly marriage connections: Maria took to

Henry IV a dowry of 600,000 florins at a time when the total population of Tuscany was some three-quarters of a million, and when 1,000 florins was an annual income to be envied.

Inevitably taxes increased, capital accumulation became even more difficult and, even if the gap between the extremes of income narrowed, the difference between rich and poor became more absolute, the poor more drastically affected by food shortages, such as those that followed a cluster of poor harvests between 1590 and 1607. Rising wages for craftsmen, builders and weavers probably meant that though these declined in terms of food prices, the decline was not so steep as in many other parts of Europe. Hardest hit were agricultural labourers, whose wages lagged behind the rising price of wheat (again, a European phenomenon), and who drifted in ever-growing numbers to the food hand-outs and cheap lodgings organized by the authorities in Florence.

Throughout Francesco's reign three phenomena, all caused by economic recession, could be observed: new palaces were built by families priced out of trade or banking and putting their capital into buildings instead; the extension of farm houses and the building of villas by those distrustful of commerce but with enough capital to produce wheat and other produce fetching high prices; beggars in every piazza and beside the doors of every church, beggars whose numbers hardly changed as a period of partial recovery from the end of the century made it easier again for the well-to-do to make larger profits.

However, there was a more cheerful continuity: the evolution of Leghorn into one of the great Italian ports. The arts would have flourished without the Medici: they were but one source of patronage among many. But if dynasties are to be remembered for what they create, rather than for what they change or improve, then Leghorn is the true monument to the grand dukes. Leghorn was developed from a handy anchorage and a few hovels into a busy metropolis, in part, it is true, because it had a good harbour, but largely because from Cosimo I onwards one grand duke after another lavished money and care on it. Even the harbour had to be transformed by huge man-made moles, and transport across the town's marshy hinterland to be improved by the driving of a canal cross-country to Pisa. The harbour was a starting-point, but Leghorn is essentially an artefact, a phenomenon with no parallel until the recent development of Marghera on the Venetian lagoon.

Again, this is a continuity that started with Cosimo I, though the site still had less than a thousand inhabitants at his death. He did, however, foresee the site's importance as a substitute for Porto Pisano, which had become silted up in its turn, as Pisa had become in the mid-fifteenth century. It was he who constructed the canal. But it was Francesco and Ferdinando I who built the city behind the port and attracted settlers to its wide streets and to the protection of its bastioned *enceinte*. By 1600 it had a population of 5,000 and it continued to grow throughout the century. This influx was the result of legislation that was enlightened, temerarious, indeed, for its day. In 1592 Ferdinando declared Leghorn to be a place of sanctuary to all seeking work whether heretics or condemned criminals, and offered a house to whoever could put down one-third of the purchase price, the remainder to be paid in instalments. In the next year an exemption of twenty-five years from taxes and complete freedom of trade in perpetuity were guaranteed to merchants of any nation, from east or west, Spaniards, Portuguese, Greeks, Germans, Italians, Jews, Turks, Armenians, Persians and others, who would settle there. These measures were completed by the declaring of Leghorn to be a free port. By the end of the reign these measures had been so successful that France, Venice, Ragusa, Genoa, Holland, Portugal and Sweden were all represented by consuls there.

Though Buontalenti designed its cathedral and the grand dukes had a palace which they visited regularly in order to preserve a momentum in driving the public works forward – quays, land reclamation, warehouses – Leghorn remained a severely utilitarian city. The larger merchants did not settle there: the crime rate was high, the atmosphere malarial; they operated through agents, and if the money was made at Leghorn, it was counted in Pisa or in Florence itself. Its growth was helped by religious persecutions that attracted Jews from Spain, Catholics from England, Protestants from France, and by 'closed-shop' practices that drove merchants from Genoa and Ragusa. But if the creation of an international free port was opportune, the grand dukes took the opportunity and improved upon it. The unloveliest of their creations was also the most useful and the most original, though it is possible that once Leghorn became a free port the economic advantages to foreign merchants outweighed those to Tuscany itself.

Tuscan economic history during the reigns of Francesco and Ferdinando is still at a state when conclusions must be tentative. The influence of non-Tuscan factors have to be taken into account, and each of these presents its own complications. If Florentine trade in Antwerp, for instance, more or less ceased with the closing of the city as a market in 1585 so did the Portuguese pepper trade there; but this was then diverted to Germany through Leghorn. Then there is the complication arising from the grand dukes' personal ventures. Ferdinando's marble statue on the waterfront at Leghorn bestrides Turkish captives. The bronze of his equestrian statue in Piazza Santissima Annunziata came from captured Turkish guns. But the galleys of S. Stefano were sent against the infidel as pirates rather than as crusaders, and the loot brought back from successful 'Tuscan' raids was sold in the name and for the coffers of the grand duke. But at least some of these ventures paved a way for others to follow, diplomacy creating openings that individuals would have found difficult to establish on their own. As in other respects, the styles of the brothers differed. Francesco was not slow to accept an advantage when it was positively offered, as when Philip II, wishing to escape from the Genoese bankers who were responsible for transferring funds to pay the Spanish armies in Flanders, offered him the concession. Ferdinando, however, frequently took the initiative, opening new markets or buying unfamiliar commodities in England, Morocco and Persia. His plan to search for gold in the Orinoco came to nothing, but that he should think of it suggests that when the picture becomes clearer, his contribution to the improved state of the economy may be seen to compare with the new sense of duty and direction he gave to the administration of Tuscany.

Independence and security

It was customary for foreign powers to enlist one of the more influential cardinals as protector of their interests at the papal court. Ferdinando had acted for Spain, and the information he received in this capacity enabled him to judge the gravity of the blow dealt by England against the Armada of 1588. On succeeding Francesco in the following year, he took advantage of Spain's weakness to negotiate for a French wife, let it be known that Tuscany would no longer automatically supply Spain with loans which had seldom been repaid in the past, and demanded that Philip II should give up his claim to the overlordship of Siena and its territories, maintaining only the right to keep garrisons in the *presidii*. Success on all these fronts brought Florence an independence in foreign affairs it had not known since the days of Lorenzo the Magnificent, and a greater security of control over Tuscany than Cosimo I had enjoyed.

His aim was to please all and offend none, not an easy course to pursue at a time when axes or client relationships were the rule in international affairs. To still the pendulum which swung the other nominally independent Italian states (like Venice) now towards Spain-Austria, now to France, Ferdinando exploited his contacts in Rome.

Though he had been forced to withdraw from orders in order to marry when he became grand duke, he had the influence still – and much more money and power to back it – to intervene in successive conclaves. He strove first to obtain pontiffs who would support his move towards France, and then, anxious lest he had gone too far in that direction and wanting to swing cautiously back towards Spain, he intrigued to help the Spanish cardinals bring about the election of a remote member of his own family, Alessandro de' Medici, as Leo XI in 1605. 'He is entirely ours', wrote Ferdinando's agent in Rome, 'and will do more for us than any pope has formerly done.' Leo died less than a month later, but the same combination of pressures produced another pro-Spanish and pro-Medicean pope, Paul V.

There was a price to pay for using Rome as a fulcrum for the levers of foreign policy. And there was a poetic justice in the form it took: the flooding of the ex-churchman Ferdinando's territories with land-hungry and non-taxpaying religious orders and the filling of monasteries and convents with non-productive fugitives from Tuscany's potential work force. The freight of nuns carried by the capital alone approached 5,000. Whereas Cosimo I had treated church appointments and property (a number of churches and monasteries were erased by his fortifications) with unbending *étatisme*, Ferdinando genuflected. He could complain. 'In sixty or seventy years the nuns will have swallowed everything', he prophesied to the archbishop of Florence. But the bargain had to be honoured: ecclesiastical influence in Tuscany in return for political pressure on the Vatican.

Ferdinando bulks large in Tuscan history chiefly because he dominated a small stage. But he had the energy and sense of purpose to stretch back through the dishevelment of his brother's reign to catch and twist together the ends of policy left loose when Cosimo died. He brought a long period of experiment to an end. He proved that an enlarged Tuscany could be made secure and independent, and that though the 150,000-odd inhabitants of the 'new' *dominio* of Siena were administered by a purely personal bureaucracy that bypassed the old councils and magistracies, that the whole state could be governed strongly from Florence with a degree of uniformity remarkable for the time. On the other hand, by edging the state out of the more dangerous currents of international affairs he set it drifting into a backwater.

THE MEDICI QUEENS OF FRANCE

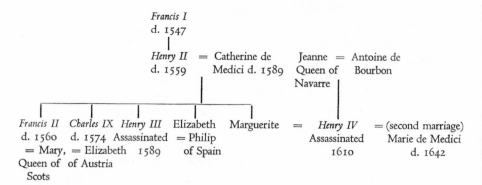

Francis I
d. 1547

|

Henry II = Catherine de   Jeanne = Antoine de
d. 1559   Medici d. 1589   Queen of   Bourbon
Navarre

Francis II   *Charles IX*   *Henry III*   Elizabeth   Marguerite = *Henry IV* = (second marriage)
d. 1560   d. 1574   Assassinated   = Philip   Assassinated   Marie de Medici
= Mary,   = Elizabeth   1589   of Spain   1610   d. 1642
Queen of   of Austria
Scots

The French perspective: Catherine and Marie

Interesting as were the characters and careers of the two Medici queens,
they are of no importance to an understanding of the fortunes of
Florence. All the same, to see how female members of the family com-
ported themselves in positions of power and to emphasize the smallness
of the ducal stage, it is worth turning briefly from Tuscany to France.

Apart from Leo X and Clement VII, no Medici played such a conspicuous role in European affairs as did Caterina, daughter of Lorenzo,
Duke of Urbino, and Maria, youngest daughter of Grand Duke Francesco. As widows of French kings and regents for their children, they
were involved with the leadership of the second greatest power in
Europe for thirty-seven years, Catherine from 1559 to 1589, Marie
from 1610 to 1617; while the grand dukes ruled over a reasonably
tranquil population of some three-quarters of a million, they were
intermittently responsible for a country of fifteen millions which was
going through the greatest crisis it had experienced since the Hundred
Years' War.

Between the careers of the two queens there were certain similarities.
Both found their husbands firmly attached to mistresses whose influence
they had to accept. Both women became regents because their husbands
met violent deaths in middle age: Henry II died from a wound
received in a tournament, Henry IV was stabbed. Both women had to
overcome what in aristocratic French eyes was the stigma of their birth;
Catherine, wrote the duchesse de Guise, came from a family of 'trades-
men who are not fit to call themselves our servants'. Maria was dubbed
a 'fat she-banker'. Both discovered in themselves a passion for power

when the occasion arose for them to exert authority. But from the way in which they faced the problems of the office they had in common, the regency, it can be seen how superficial these similarities were.

It was in France that the theory of absolute rule had been expressed most clearly. But the power exerted by French kings was in practice limited: they had neither the military force nor the bureaucratic machinery to press their subjects hard, nor, in fact, did they have the will to emulate the powers attributed to them by absolutist theory. They respected the rights and privileges accumulated through the centuries by the nobility and towns as long as these did not prevent the crown from drawing an adequate income from the country and pursuing a foreign policy of its own choosing. What gave France the appearance of being an absolutist power in the eyes of foreign observers was the sentiment of loyalty to the crown, which was expressed more openly in France than in other European states, and which was as important a factor in giving freedom of action to its monarchs as the administrative structure itself.

But this loyalty was not available to a woman ruling on behalf of her son. France was centralized as much by emotion as by institutions; it was easy for the nobility to shrug off a regent's orders and to relapse into a state of 'medieval' independence by saying that the child-king would not have approved had he been of age. A queen-mother could only compensate for this lack of emotional appeal by the efficiency she induced in the administrative organs making for unity, and by the dexterity she brought to handling the nobles as individuals. It was in these areas that Catherine acted with something often approaching genius and Marie revealed herself to be normally irresponsible and sometimes positively a fool.

Francis had contracted the marriage between Henry and Catherine because, since the battle of Pavia in 1525 at which his army was defeated and he himself carried off a prisoner to Spain, he had looked for ways of neutralizing the pope's pro-Spanish policy. By 1531, when the contract was signed, this policy had already given Clement the army which forced his family back into Florence, and it was now gravely compromising his diplomatic freedom of action. The political import of the match was thus congenial to both the king and the pope, and the dowry of 100,000 gold *écus* which Clement promised was welcome to a monarch in perpetual financial straits. Clement was careful not to give the French any claims to the personal or territorial possessions that Catherine inherited from her father: he bought them from her for another 30,000 *écus*. She went to France rich but with no means of disturbing the family's position in Italy. Clement also promised political assistance to Francis's plans for the reconquest of the duchy of Milan. This clause was secret, and it is difficult to believe that either party could have taken very seriously a move that would have reopened large-scale war with Charles V. More directly tempting was Clement's undertaking to give to Catherine (and thus to Henry) the Florentine ports of Pisa and Leghorn and the papal cities of Reggio and Modena. Nothing had been done to implement this promise – so bizarre against the background of Florentine struggles after 1494 to get the two ports back from the French – when Clement died in the year following the marriage.

The change in scale as we move from Tuscany to France is reflected in the amount that has been written about Catherine – far more than about any other member of the Medici family – and the enormous bulk of her correspondence, from which some 7,000 letters have survived. She and her court became the object of an avid, Europe-wide curiosity. The one she joined as a young bride of fourteen may have lacked the polish of some of the small courts of Italy – Castiglione's portrait of the court of Urbino in *The Courtier* was read in France as a model to be aspired to – but under Francis I it had become the centre of a lively culture and a brilliant, if rough and ready, society. The King's liking for pretty faces, moreover, had made it, for a woman, the most competitive of European courts; the fact that Catherine, who was not pretty, not a Frenchwoman, and not of unexceptionable birth, was able in time not only to dominate but to maintain something of its brilliance throughout so many troubled years, is a tribute as much to her character as to her position.

As she fattened, pregnancy by pregnancy, she became a commanding, if not a physically appealing figure, tall and stout, with shrewd, rather bulging eyes, a heavy nose and a full mouth. Her public manner was marked by a persistent cordiality that was none the less effective for being almost certainly deliberate. She had learned to please as a way of adapting to a new, sometimes hostile, and often miserable environment, and the art of pleasing became part of her art of ruling. And it was only in its indiscriminateness that this cordiality was forced. She was by nature cheerful and resilient. Physically large rather than strong, her nervous energy saw her through difficult childbirths and the host of misunderstood minor ailments that led so many of the women of that age to spend much of their time in bed. Francis I had gone out of his way to commend her skill as a horsewoman and she continued to hunt as regularly as she could. She has been credited with the invention of the sidesaddle. She was a stout enough trencherwoman to have been given the credit of enriching the dishes of France with the culinary methods of Italy. This toughness showed in the concentration she brought to affairs of state and her omnivorous interest in the details of government, an interest to which her vast correspondence bears abundant witness. 'You feed on this labour', the future Henry IV was to say to her, 'and you would not be able to live for long without it.'

The change is also one of pace. Three months before his death in 1559, Henry II had signed the Treaty of Cateau-Cambrésis which had adjusted the differences outstanding between Valois and Habsburg and announced the conclusion of French attempts to claim territory in Italy. The comparative tranquillity that then settled on the peninsula, and the concurrent shift in economic and political interest away from the Mediterranean to the Atlantic powers, inaugurated 'the forgotten centuries' of Italian history. But for France the end of conquests and defeats abroad was the beginning of domestic catastrophe.

Henry II had already appointed Catherine his deputy when absent on campaigns. During the fleeting reign of her eldest son, Francis II, she learned much but could do little. At fifteen, he was legally of age. His feelings were totally surrendered to his wife, the young Mary, Queen of Scots, his wits to his two uncles, Francis, duke of Guise, and his brother the cardinal of Lorraine. But on his death, when her third son Charles became king at the age of ten (the second had died in infancy), Catherine had seen how fissured, almost tri-partite, France had become, how necessary it was to balance the 'empires' of the three great noble clans, the Guises, the Montmorencys and the Bourbons, and to save politics from the infection of militant Huguenot and Catholic fervour; without waiting for legal endorsement she assumed the regency.

Three years later, in 1563, Charles was declared of age. Delicate in health and averse to grappling with affairs of state as he was, Catherine became more active than ever in trying to preserve the independence of the crown. Her policy invoked a spirit of reasonableness and reconciliation which, in an age of fanaticism, seemed insincere or self-interested and earned her the nickname 'Madam Serpent'. Goaded at last to extremes, she became a partisan in religion and a plotter in politics and is remembered if for nothing else by her implication in the Massacre of St Bartholomew's Day in 1572 and its 3,000 victims.

Two years later, on Charles's death, she prepared herself to shape yet another unpromising son, Henry III, deeply unreliable and a slave to his own curious pleasures, into a king of whom Francis I would have been proud. In 1586, however, another civil war broke out (the fourth she had witnessed), and when she died in 1589 it was only months before Henry was assassinated.

Working on so large a stage, in such passionate and confused times and with such recalcitrant material (her sons), Catherine cannot be summarily judged. But it can be said that she failed to see past individuals to the nature of the causes that motivated them. She presents with almost mythic force the image of a woman whose intensity of will and keenness of intelligence are turned into disastrous courses by a lack of imagination. But this is not because she was a foreigner.

Half-French by birth, Catherine was to become wholly French by experience and, indeed, by inclination. Fifty-five out of her sixty-nine years were passed in France, and her girlhood was unsettled and passed in an obscurity which has left few traces. Her mother, Madeleine de la Tour d'Auvergne, died fifteen days after her birth. Five days later the death of the duke of Urbino left her an orphan. Under the guardianship of Giulio, later Clement VII, and in the care of her aunt, Clarice Strozzi, she grew up first in Rome and then, from 1525, when she was six, in Florence. From 1527 to 1530, treated, as we have seen, as a hostage by the parties that had ousted the Medici, she was guarded first by the nuns of the Murate and then – their loyalty to the republican regime being suspect – by those of the convent of S. Lucia. When the siege came to an end and the Medici returned to Florence, Clarice was dead and, resuming his guardianship, Clement VII brought Catherine to Rome. At eleven she was old enough to be diplomatically negotiable. The Pope received bids from the dukes of Ferrara, Mantua, Vaudemont and Richmond (Henry VIII's illegitimate son), from the King of Scotland, James V, on his own behalf, and the King of France on behalf of his second son Henry. Catherine herself was rumoured to be infatuated with the dashing Cardinal Ippolito de' Medici who, rumour continued, was contemplating leaving the Church in order to marry her. The gossip was loud enough for Clement to send her back to Florence, once more to the custody of an aunt, this time Maria Salviati, mother of the future Cosimo I. Little more than a year later Catherine was on her way to France.

Apart from eighteen months in Rome as a plain, clever and energetic eleven-year-old, Catherine's Italian years were spent in convents or in the households of aunts. It is difficult to sympathize with the assumption – frequently met with among her biographers – that the character and policies of the veteran regent can be best understood if she is thought of as a Florentine. She was, rather, an anti-Florentine. While her gratitude to the nuns of the Murate led her to make gifts to their order and to keep in touch with its head throughout her career, her chief loyalty was to her Strozzi aunt, and as Henry II's wife she extended all the favour in her power to the exiled enemies of Florence's ruler. Piero Strozzi became a marshal of France; Leone, captain-general of the French galley-fleet; Lorenzo, bishop of Béziers. When Piero was appointed captain of the forces defending Siena against Cosimo I, Catherine left no doubt in her husband's mind that, though a Medici, she was fiercely on the side of the Sienese. It was French policy to keep Siena out of Florentine hands. Catherine never put her countrymen's interests above those of her adopted land.

Machiavelli dedicated *The Prince* to Catherine's father. But it would be rash to accept the suggestion that she was 'Machiavelli's pupil', or that light is thrown on her actions by seeing her as 'this careful student of Machiavelli'. There is no evidence that Catherine ever read *The Prince* or any other of the Florentine's works. If she appeared to act in terms of Machiavellian dicta, it was because, in her attempts to buttress the crown against the noble families which sought to dominate it, and to prevent France from breaking down into confessional as well as territorial blocks, she was forced to use guile, to pursue self-contradictory policies and to be ruthless rather than just if her concept of the commonweal so prompted her. Catherine's 'Machiavellianism' needs no explanation outside the nature of the role she was forced to play and the temperament she brought to it.

She retained some memories of Italian art. In 1541 she wrote to Pope Paul III asking for a portrait by Sebastiano del Piombo she had seen hanging in Cardinal Ippolito's rooms. She wrote asking Michelangelo to make an equestrian statue of Henry II (he deputed the commission to his pupil Daniele da Volterra, who had finished only the horse at his death). She commissioned Primaticcio to design a mausoleum for the tombs of herself and her husband. She welcomed Italian *Commedia dell' Arte* troupes to court. Urged by Pietro Ramus (one of the victims of St Bartholomew's Day) to imitate the example of Cosimo and Lorenzo the Magnificent, whose libraries were in the capital and thus readily available to men of letters, she had the French royal library brought from Fontainebleau to the Louvre. But, overwhelmingly, the very wide patronage she extended to painters, sculptors, architects, jewellers and poets was given to Frenchmen. The Italian element is explicable simply in terms of the extent to which the culture she found in France was already Italianized.

These early years at Fontainebleau, during which Catherine was conditioned towards becoming a Frenchwoman, were all the more formative because of the interest shown in her by Francis I. He concealed his disappointment when the political help he had calculated on receiving from Clement VII as a consequence of the marriage failed to materialize. He welcomed her company on his hunting expeditions. He consoled her and promised to support her when the years went by without her becoming pregnant and it began to be murmured that her marriage should be dissolved. He became more and more a substitute for the father she had never known. It was this that finally plucked Catherine free from her roots in Italy. A mixture of awe and gratitude underlay this attraction of a young woman of comparatively undistinguished birth towards the intensely glamorous figure of the greatest of the Valois kings. It was her feeling for her father-in-law as well as for her husband that made Catherine so fanatical a respecter of the royal dignity. And if some echoes of Francis's policies remained to be picked up at the century's end by Henry IV, it was because the less able monarchs who intervened were subject to the influence of the daughter of an Italian princeling who became *plus royaliste que le roi*.

Had Catherine been a queen rather than a queen-mother, there is little doubt that she would have been as formidably effective a monarch as was her English contemporary, Elizabeth I. Ironically, she had less power, that is, power legally vested in her, than did her distant relation, Henry IV's second wife Marie de Medici. Aged fourteen on Catherine's death, Marie was made regent for her young son Louis XIII when Henry was assassinated in 1610, and retained this office for seven years. She was formally a ruler for a longer period than Catherine had been, and in quieter circumstances, for Henry IV had left a country more united, and more firmly centralized than had Henry II. Her failure is all the more glaring against a knowledge of the qualities Catherine would have brought to this opportunity.

Catherine linked the name Medici indissolubly to the history of France although, almost as soon as she was married to a Frenchman, she ceased to think as an Italian. Marie was little more than a fretful and ambitious passenger within a country she had little desire to understand.

Born in 1575, she was of mixed parentage, Habsburg on the side of her mother, Joanna of Austria, Italian through the grand duke Francesco, her father. But her background was entirely Tuscan: she was twenty-six when marriage took her from the Pitti to the Louvre. Little is known about her childhood save that from the age of five she was in effect an orphan. Her mother died then. Two months later her father married Bianca Capello and went to live with her at Pratolino, leaving his children in the care of a staff of governesses and palace officials. Marie herself was to throw some light on the jealous consciousness of rank she displayed in later life when she referred to the humiliation she suffered from having a 'bourgeois widow' as a stepmother. By the age of nine she was alone; her brother Filippo died in 1582, in 1584 her sister Anna died and her eldest sister Eleanora went to live with her husband in Mantua. When in 1587 she came under the protection of her uncle, Ferdinando I, she showed no affection for him or for his wife, and wrote only scolding letters to them once she had gone to France. Just as Catherine had been at heart anti-Medicean, so was Marie, though for a more trivial – unpolitical at least – and pathetic reason.

In her loneliness she attached herself with what became a passionate and uncritical dependence to a child who was brought to live in Palazzo Pitti as a playmate for her. Intelligent and lively, Leonora Dori, the daughter of Marie's wet-nurse, was still described simply as Marie's maid when she went with her mistress to France in 1600, but long years as the too-long-unmarried princess's only *confidante* had given her an ominous hold over the new queen's mind, a hold that became even stronger when Marie found that she had come to love a man who constantly betrayed her.

Her marriage to Henry IV, was of course, a mercenary one, as Catherine's had been. The Protestant had had to fight a long and expensive war to compel the Catholic League and its headquarters, the city of Paris itself (even though he thought it 'worth a Mass') to accept his sovereignty. He inherited debts that had been accumulating since the beginning of the civil wars. His previous marriage, to Marguerite of Valois, had proved childless, and husband and wife had agreed to grant one another full freedom to pursue their own affairs. As early as 1592 Henry had heard that Marie would be worth 1,000,000 *scudi*, but in mid-campaign and ecstatically involved with Gabrielle d'Estrées, he had let the matter drop. At the end of the century, however, his ambassadors in Tuscany and Rome took the matter up again. The

Pope promised an annulment of his existing marriage. The grand duke Ferdinando was eager to buy France's diplomatic support against Spain but not, it turned out after much acrimonious bargaining, for a higher figure than 600,000 florins; Henry was reminded that Ferdinando had already lent him large sums which were still owing, as were the loans advanced to Charles IX by Cosimo I. At the urging of Sully, his finance minister and right-hand man in the laborious task of putting France's affairs in order, the king agreed; it was, after all, the biggest dowry any queen of France had brought with her.

There followed ten stormy years. Henry was nearly twice Marie's age in 1600. Gabrielle d'Estrées had died shortly before, but her place had been swiftly taken by Henriette d'Entraigues. Wife and mistress gave birth to their first children within weeks of one another, and the children that followed them on both sides of the blanket were brought up in the Louvre together. Henry's affection for the pink and white, and plump (her features showed little of her Italian blood) wife who presented him with six children was genuine enough for him to enjoy this double *ménage*; after one of the violent quarrels to which it led, he went so far as to say that if she were not his wife he would have given a fortune to have her as a mistress. But there was more than jealousy between them. Their temperaments were opposed. Henry's character was expansive, impulsive and affectionate, but he was mean with money. Marie's was inward-turning and suspicious, but she was instinctively generous. Beyond that, however, was Marie's unwillingness to identify herself with anything to do with France except its artists and the power she was waiting to be hers.

After St Bartholomew's Day, Henry had conceived a loathing for Catherine and, with her, all Italians. It was one of the reasons why he had so long lost interest in the Medici marriage. Marie's own instincts, backed by Ferdinando's concern about the new environment she would encounter in her mid-twenties, led to her bringing to France a sizable corps of Florentines. She at once tried to thrust them into some of the jealously guarded positions in the royal household. The corps as originally suggested had been cut down in the face of Henry's fury (recouched in more tactful terms by his ambassador to the grand-ducal court), but it was still large enough to enrage him afresh on Marie's arrival. Catherine's presence in France had attracted exiles like the Strozzi, and families seeking financial advantage, like the Gondi. But at least they had never constituted an insulating layer between the Queen and her natural French advisers and ministers. But Marie never mastered French, and throughout her marriage and throughout her regency never put her trust fully in a Frenchman.

In the party she brought from Florence was Concino Concini, the son of an Italian of good birth who had been made a knight of the order of S. Stefano by the grand duke Francesco. Freed for the first time from the heavy etiquette of the Tuscan court, Marie found his company delightful on the long journey to Paris. So did Leonora, who married him, and Marie bent all her energies to advancing their fortunes and relying on their counsel in the face of the French nobility. She obtained for Concini the title Maréchal d'Ancre and, when she became regent, so loaded him – largely for the sake of his wife – with properties and pensions that it is hardly an abuse of the cliché to say that he became the best-hated man in France.

Some part of this excessive loyalty can be traced, no doubt, to the circumstances of Marie's youth, some to an optimistically mistaken understanding of Henry's own change of front to Concini; he came to appreciate his wit and urbanity as a gaming companion, no more. Mostly, however, it sprang from defects of character so alarmingly at odds with the role she wished to play that no sketch of Marie's career can avoid a note of pathos: inability to concentrate, quickness to take offence, inordinate vanity, infirmity of judgment, luxurious self-indulgence, a hectoring insistence on the respect due to her position. These were all qualities that closed her mind to a steady appraisal of where her duty – and thus her fortune – really lay, and reduced her to the status of a termagant who could be used by others as a ready malcontent but could make no impact unmistakably and creatively her own.

Above all, however, she was ambitious – in one of her tantrums with Henry she had called for the precedents defining the rights of a queen-regent – and this, allied to her extravagance and her love of display, made her an impressive patron of the arts. Interested only in the details of her personal adornment or those of her immediate surroundings, jewellery and tapestries, she was sufficiently absorbed in her fame to bring Frans Pourbus the younger from Mantua to paint her portrait over and over again, to entrust the noblest architect of his age, Salomon de Brosse, to build the Luxembourg for her, and to bring Rubens to decorate its two long galleries with the greatest examples of baroque painting in France – their subject: her husband and herself. Pourbus and Rubens were foreigners of whom she knew only by repute. From her birthplace she commissioned an equestrian statue of Henry IV by

Giambologna and overcame her repugnance to her family enough to write asking to be sent plans of the Pitti for the benefit of de Brosse (who ignored them). But she also patronized French artists, notably Ambroise Dubois and Philippe de Champaigne and, through her Italian poet-protégé Giovanbattista Marino, Nicolas Poussin, then a young man with little to offer that anticipated the genius he was later to display.

Henry had attempted to involve his queen in the government of France in an apprentice role by inviting her to meetings of his council. Her lack of interest was such that he allowed her to retreat into the Italianate associations of her own household. In 1610, he tried again; haunted as he set off to make war in Germany by what might become of his nine-year-old heir Louis were he to be killed, he made Marie his regent. Next day the solitary assassin Ravaillac knifed him in his carriage.

Marie's thirst for authority, which had hitherto been the momentary response of pique, now became a steady preoccupation. As regent until 1614, with the forms but neither the glamour nor the permanence of power, she continued to rely on Concini, and to buy off the once mighty subjects who again sought to dominate the monarchy instead of trying to rally them behind the young Louis XIII. They became ever more truculent, and Henry's and Sully's careful savings dwindled. Her son himself dismissed her brusquely in 1617 to Blois after having Concini arrested and – though the arresting officer was possibly going beyond his orders – shot. Not long afterwards Leonora was executed after a trial that bore more witness to her unpopularity than to the strict processes of justice.

From that date, apart from brief reconciliations with her son, during the first of which, in 1622, she drew his attention to the abilities of her favourite, Richelieu, she remained a thorn in his side, plotting against him (and then against Richelieu) with members of his own court, sent packing, wearily being accepted again, dismissed at last in 1632 for good. She died in Cologne in 1642, unmourned.

17 Cosimo; relief by Verrocchio

18 Piero; bust by Mino da Fiesole

19 Lorenzo the Magnificent; death mask

20 Pan as the god of nature and as the god of music, painting by Luca Signorelli

21 Pietro as a young man; detail of fresco
by Ghirlandaio

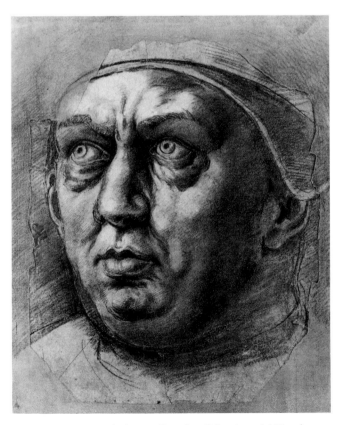

22 Pope Leo X; painting attributed to Sebastiano del Piombo

23 Giuliano, Duke of Nemours

24 Lorenzo, Duke of Urbino

25 Pope Clement VII;
painting by Sebastiano del Piombo

26 Ippolito; painting by Titian

27 Alessandro; painting by Vasari

28 Apotheosis of Cosimo I;
painting by Vasari

29　Francesco I; painting by Bronzino

30　Ferdinando I

31　Catherine, Queen of France

32   Cosimo II

33   Marie, Queen of France;
drawing by Rubens

34   Ferdinand II; painting by Justus Sustermans

35   Cosimo III   36   Gian Gastone

CHAPTER VI

The Decline of a Dynasty and the Growth of a Legend

Cosimo II, 1609–21 and Ferdinando II, 1621–70

The reign of Ferdinando I's son and successor does little more than indicate the downward slope between the end of a period of renewed initiative in internal and foreign affairs and the beginning of one in which Tuscany was to project an ever lower profile against the economic and political screen of Europe. Nineteen when he became Grand Duke, Cosimo II died in 1621 at the age of thirty from tuberculosis, and for much of the intervening time he was incapacitated by illness. The work of government was carried on by ministers trained by Ferdinando, and of diplomacy by men too experienced to be puzzled by a lack of instructions, and too much in sympathy with Ferdinando's desire to keep on good terms with both sides of the balance of power in central and western Europe to risk amending it. The chief obstacle to the efficient running of the state was not Cosimo's sickness or his lack of energy or intelligence, but the fretful intervention in governmental affairs of his mother Christine and the increasingly determined interference of his wife Maddelena. As his wife was the sister of an Austrian Emperor – Ferdinand II – and of the queens of Spain and Poland, while his mother was the descendant of kings of France, the young grand duke lived with the alarming spectacle of an allegory of Tuscan foreign policy being fought out within the Pitti itself. For the first time Medici rule was woman-ridden not by mistresses anxious to please, but by viragos determined to dominate. In this context – far beyond the control of Cosimo, whose time was much taken up with consulting witches or negotiating for relics to rub on his chest – the wife proved more powerful than the mother-in-law, not only routing Christine's influence in affairs of state but producing, in addition to an heir, a quadruple guarantee of the dynasty's continuance in the form of four more boys.

The regime became still more woman-ridden when Cosimo died in 1621. His puzzled inability to see past his own illness or beyond his immediate family circle was expressed in his will, under which Christine and Maddelena were made regents for the eleven-year-old

Ferdinando II. He had, indeed, left directions that they were to take no decisions without consulting the four councillors. Executive action was left to two tried secretaries of state, one for internal, the other for external affairs. The Senate and the Council of Two Hundred were still in existence, even if membership of either body was, without the challenge of collaborating with a respected leadership, little more than a social feather in the cap. But the double regency – especially as the two women fell into accord when neither had a husband living – harassed and confused a system perfectly capable of carrying on a routine, and was to emasculate Ferdinando's sense of independence well after he had reached eighteen, the age of legal maturity. His reign as an expression of his will and not as an echo of women's voices did not begin until Christine died in 1636.

Shortly after Ferdinando became titular ruler of Tuscany, his uncle, Cardinal Carlo, expressed his view of the chief aspects of grand-ducal history in its formative period by commissioning a fresco cycle for his house, the Casino Mediceo. Painted by a team that included Fabrizio Boschi, Michelangelo Cinganelli, Giovanni da S. Giovanni, Matteo Rosselli and Francesco Furini, the scheme allotted a room apiece to the celebration of Cosimo I, Francesco and Ferdinando I, and two to the recently dead Cosimo II. Cosimo I was remembered for the breaking of the exiles at Montemurlo, the acquisition of Siena and its territories, and his coronation by the pope as Grand Duke. Francesco is shown being entrusted with the regency and being crowned. After this stress on the legitimacy of his succession, he is portrayed in the regalia of a Knight of S. Stefano, and the Order's galleys are seen in action at the great victory over the Turks at Lepanto. Finally, he discusses Buontalenti's plan for the new city at Leghorn, and work is shown going forward on the courtyard of the Pitti Palace, headquarters of grand-ducal rule.

With Ferdinando I the emphasis of this pictorial history becomes more martial, as if to show that his search for peace was not the action of a coward. Several scenes show Tuscan galleys in action in the Mediterranean and Tuscan contingents fighting with the land forces of the Emperor Rudolf II and the Archduke Ferdinand on the Empire's Turkish land frontier. The allegorical figures which are part of the scheme stress the Imperial rather than the crusading aspect of this anti-Turkish activity: Neptune with the Medici arms, War holding the grand-ducal crown, Aeolus holding a sceptre and bit to symbolize Tuscan power by land and sea. The fortifications of Leghorn are shown being built around the new city. Significantly, however, there is no reference to the fortress of the Belvedere; Carlo chose instead to show Ferdinando's concern for the poor in distributing grain after the flood which devastated the city in 1589. Of the two rooms allotted to Cosimo II, one, again, was dedicated to naval operations against the Turks, the other to the Grand Duke as protector of science and the arts. Astronomy shows him the satellites of Jupiter discovered by Galileo's telescope; accompanied by Fame he wakens Painting from sleep. Finally, as a tribute to the family as a whole rather than to his own by no means impressive qualities, Justice, Plenty and Power pay him homage and the Virtues mourn at his tomb.

Within a generation, there was rich scope here for irony. Under Ferdinando II the Mediterranean became too full of interlopers, including English and Dutch, for his galleys to make a profit by raiding Turkish shipping, and he sold most of them. In an ever more priest-ridden atmosphere Galileo, whom his father had protected and encouraged, was allowed to be humiliated by the Inquisition even though Ferdinando himself was deeply interested in scientific pursuits. Above all, Power moved further away from the grand duke and Plenty positively turned her back.

From 1619–20 a long-term economic depression set in which affected most of western Europe but hit Tuscany particularly hard and, as it was to turn out, irreversibly. The demand for its chief industrial exports, processed silk and woollen cloth, fell drastically in the face of foreign competition based on lower wages and nimbler manufacturing and sales techniques than the clumsy Florentine guild structure could copy. Another wave of poor harvests – there was a real famine in 1621 – sent up the price of grain and pushed more and more families off the land and into a capital which had no work to offer them and decreasing public-ducal funds from which to feed them. Then in 1630 came plague, and when the last of its recurring bouts petered out in 1633 some ten per cent of the population had perished.

The economic effects of plague follow no rule. In theory, by striking at the dirtiest and most squalidly housed members of a society, it reduces the burden of paupers while only trimming the work force and leaving its directors, who have healthier bolt holes to retreat to, more or less intact. Information for Tuscany is unsatisfactory, but events do not appear to have followed this cruel logic. Florence in the late 1630s was still spending more than it earned.

Meanwhile, the two grand duchesses hampered the bureaucracy and discouraged Cioli, secretary for the interior, from suggesting any thoroughgoing reforms. Intensely pious, they took the side of the religious orders in the constant litigation involved in the purchase of land for new foundations. They arranged a marriage with Vittoria della Rovere, daughter of the Duke of Urbino, which made Ferdinando miserable and, above all, their presence, scolding and dominating, meant that he only once emerged from his natural inclination to live quietly and avoid troublesome confrontations with either individuals or ideas.

Marriage with the daughter of a mere Italian princeling was not the only humiliation which showed how closely allied power was to plenty. Lack of cash, as well as belief in his grandfather's policy of not taking sides, kept Tuscany from intervening to prevent the Spanish from sacking Mantua in 1630 and helping Naples to Piombino, the port coveted by the grand dukes since the days of Cosimo I. In 1631 Ferdinando watched helplessly while Pope Urban VIII annexed Urbino, to which his own claim by marriage was so strong. It was with this precedent in mind, when he was free from his pious grandmother and the pro-papal Cioli, that Ferdinando took the initiative for once with a grand militant gesture. In 1641 Urban annexed Castro, a territory on Tuscany's southern frontier which up to then had been governed unprovocatively by the Farnese. After waiting laboriously to make sure that the coast was clear of possible intervention from France or Spain, the grand duke led a large and motley army of mercenary troops and in 1643 swept Urban's forces out of Umbria. It was a famous victory, if only because it was the first time a Medicean army had operated in Italy since the war of Siena, ninety years before. But it did no more than restore the *status quo*, and it knocked the crutches from a crippled economy.

Since the early 1620s tax had been piled on tax, destroying the value of initiative and inflating the cost of living to a point which in more densely populated areas could have led to revolt. Industry was depressed and received no encouragement. The moneyed classes invested instead in land or state bonds and jockeyed for titles through the fitful good offices of the papacy or in the heraldic fleamarket that the kingdom of Naples had become under Spanish rule. Florence accelerated its metamorphosis from an emporium of wool and silk merchants into an art city full of low-budget barons and countesses. As unemployment grew, the urban poor became increasingly dependent on charity and government-sponsored work programmes. And as Tuscany was now fully fortified, and its marshlands reasonably well drained, it was difficult even to invent projects that might operate to the eventual benefit of the state. In the countryside, wages had begun to be paid in kind more regularly than in cash and a barter economy had reappeared in rural markets. Clearly the war could not be paid for with new taxes. Paying off the troops reduced public funds to a point at which bond-holders could not be paid the interest due to them. So the interest rate was dropped by three-quarters. This was a drastic and, since 1530, an unprecedented move. But its broader significance emerged only when it was found that few bondholders reacted by withdrawing their deposits: at so low an ebb was the Tuscan economy that there was nothing more attractive to reinvest in.

Against this background the Medici, as rulers with still large private fortunes or as elaborately beneficed princes of the Church, stood out in richer relief than ever; it was in the 1650s and 1660s that the family's cultural and social influence was at its most pervasive. Just as Cosimo I had been closely associated with the Florentine Academy of 1540 and the Academy of Design, his successors and their brothers kept in touch with the various academies and societies that followed it: the philo-logical della Crusca, the literary Alterati, the dramatic Immobili and Infocati, and the purely convivial and sporting Nobili. Both in country villas and in new palaces in Florence, such as the Casino Mediceo, the households of Cosimo II's brothers, Mattia and Cardinals Giovan Carlo and Leopoldo, amounted to satellite courts and extended the variety of intellectual aspirations that could identify with the ruling house, and the number of lightning rods that could render dissatisfaction with what it stood for harmless. It would be difficult to show that there was any deliberate policy involved, but it seems likely that the political tranquillity of the century did to some extent depend on this voluntary subjection of intellectual and social activity to the surveillance of the Medici.

In addition to scientific interests, which brought him the congratula-tions of the Royal Society of London, Leopoldo began the Medici collection of artists' self-portraits. Giovan Carlo, the least devout and most dissolute of all the family's 'political' cardinals, was an enthralled patron of music and drama. The less intellectual Florentines took their lead from Mattia, commander of the grand-ducal army and a passionate huntsman. Moreover Ferdinando, accustomed from his childhood to closet government, used his brothers as an informal family cabinet, deputing responsibility for financial affairs to Giovan Carlo, military matters to Mattia and leaning on Leopoldo's advice in diplomacy. There was no area of administration that did not involve consultation with some member of the family, hardly an aspect of leisure that did not find its apex in one of their homes, scarcely a topic, therefore, especially if it had political or moral implications, that could be speculated upon with real freedom.

It is doubtful whether anyone wished to raise the old topic of republicanism as arguably a preferable form of government. The price Cosimo I had decided to pay for Medicean influence in Rome rankled more deeply because it affected standards of living as well as ways of thought. His subjects had had to read the *Decameron* in a bowdlerized version which removed the gusto of its anticlericalism. Ferdinando I had had to watch the extension of the religious orders, especially the Jesuits, into Tuscany and the passing of more and more land out of his tax control and into the dead hand of the Church. By the 1660s there were getting on for 12,000 nuns in the old *dominio* alone, that is, Tuscany without the Sienese territories. The actual cost in diminished revenues to the state, the effect on the price of purchasable land, the cost to the individual in terms of contested wills and land titles: these calculations have still to be made and set against an undoubted religious fervour. The evidence of the courts suggests that the level of popular morality did not rise with the increasing number of clerics per square mile, and it was not a notable century in the annals of devotional literature or of the pulpit. Even an approximate balance has yet to be attempted. That it must take intellectual life into account is clear from the stifling of scientific inquiry at the University of Pisa and the handing over of the ageing Galileo to the Inquisition.

This episode is the sadder for being uncharacteristic. When Galileo discovered the satellites of Jupiter in 1610, he named them 'the Medicean stars' by way of compliment to his patrons. When the Accademia del Cimento, the first organized scientific society and predecessor of the English Royal Society, was established in 1657 by Ferdinando II and Leopoldo, one of its purposes was to provide experimental proof of some of Galileo's theorems. He had, for instance, suggested that a cannon ball fired horizontally from a tower would touch the ground simultaneously with one dropped vertically from it. This the *cimentisti* proceeded to demonstrate. Demonstration, mensuration, description: these were the aims of the society whose title means 'experiment' and whose motto was 'test and test again'. Among its members were two of Galileo's most productive and talented disciples,

Vincenzo Viviani and Evangelista Torricelli, but Ferdinando and Leopoldo themselves were not merely patrons. Both had laboratories and collections of scientific instruments of their own. Ferdinando's experiments included (prophetically) an attempt to isolate a poisonous substance in tobacco, and Leopoldo, with the aid of a skilled glass-blower, devised apparatus in connection with the Academy's work on the expansion of gases and liquids. Held back from making the links or conjectures that might challenge the official cosmology of the Church, scientific observation and experiment constituted the most original and least provincial aspect of the intellectual life of Ferdinando's time.

Under his and his brothers' care Tuscany followed its old administrative and diplomatic routines and, leaving the economy aside, came to no grave harm. Leghorn continued to be fostered. Cosimo II extended the harbour works and, under Ferdinando II, the port – its English consulate dates from 1634 – combined the cosmopolitanism of Venice with the ruffianly exoticism of Algiers; it was, indeed, the chief slave port of the northern Mediterranean. Though need as well as inclination kept Tuscany a backwater, its diplomatic history remained as complex and as full of nervous tension as ever and was even more widely extended, for so finely adjusted were the interests that made the difference between peace and war in Europe, and therefore the demands flung at the allies of the major powers, that Tuscany had now to take England and even Scandinavia into account. Like a small business fighting to retain its independence among the industrial giants of its day, Tuscany was forced to dodge and weave, here yield a little and there steal a minuscule advance, with an absorption as dedicated and time-consuming as that required of the chief competitors in the diplomatic market. The absence of major incident, which relegates Tuscany to a footnote in the history of international affairs, is a concealed tribute to assiduity rather than evidence of incompetence or indolence.

The war of Castro was Ferdinando's only adventure, but faced later in the 1640s by another Franco-Spanish confrontation on Italian soil, during which for a while there was French pressure against the flank of Tuscany through their occupation of Piombino, as well as Spanish pressure from the *presidii* in the south, he managed, without losing face, to stay neutral: he was even able to strengthen Tuscany's northern frontier by the purchase of Pontremoli from Spain. Though he was prepared to mobilize troops in order to give teeth to his diplomacy, it was always with the aim of obtaining a securer peace as quickly as possible. It was in those years that he commissioned Pietro da Cortona to decorate the Sala di Giove in the Pitti with its lunettes that portray Fury abandoning the earth, the Dioscuri leading their horses back into the Zodiac, Vulcan renouncing the forging of weapons and Mercury proclaiming an age of peace to all men.

Ferdinando, indeed, followed the Medici practice of commemorating themselves and their house in paint to delicious effect. Under the light brush-strokes of Giovanni da S. Giovanni, the doleful marriage with Vittoria became an ethereal celebration of a political union blessed by the goddesses of marriage and of love. He paid the family's final and most attractive homage to Lorenzo the Magnificent in the Pitti's Salone Terreno, where the same painter, together with Francesco Furini, showed how the Muses, scattered and desolate after the destruction of Parnassus, had been led back together into the political sanctuary of Laurentian Florence. And Ferdinando was not simply interested in the programmatic side of his commissions to painters; deciding to break with the weakly graceful style of the local Florentines, he brought in, with Pietro da Cortona, the bolder mode of baroque Rome.

As part of Vittoria's dowry, Ferdinando had received Titian's *Recumbent Venus* and Raphael's portrait of Pope Julius II. He added generously to the gallery of antique sculpture; among his acquisitions were the *Hermaphrodite* and the *Idolino*. And he swelled that vast collection-within-a-collection of little precious and ingenious objects, cabinets, clocks, mechanical toys and intricately carved fruit stones, which reflected the private lives of rulers who were often ill and who delighted in time-passers and talking points, who were fascinated by technology and the methods used in the luxury crafts of jewellery and stone-cutting.

Ferdinando cut a reasonably impressive figure among his fellow heads of state in his last years. Foreign ambassadors were unanimous in their praise of him as a man of culture and high intelligence. He had resisted the bullying of the most militant pope of the century, Urban VIII. Tuscan volunteer contingents earned golden opinions during their service with successive Emperors against the Turks. Ferdinando was one of the parties to the Treaty of the Pyrenees of 1659, the climax of so many attempts to bring a settled peace between France and Spain. Two years later his heir, Cosimo, able to look higher in the marriage market than had been possible for his father, was married to Marguerite d'Orléans, niece of Louis XIII, King of France. Buttressed by his private fortune and by the atmosphere of effortless splendour with which Pietro da Cortona irradiated the spacious new rooms of the Pitti, Ferdinando's reign closed in 1670 on a note of hazardous dignity. An English visitor who was in Florence during the last years of the reign declared the court 'clearly one of the best in Italy . . . The noble pallace, the prince, his title of Serenissimo, his train and retinue of noble officers and gentlemen, his store of pages, palfreniers, guards of Swissers with halberds, his troop of horse waiting upon him, make this court appear splendid.' The second Ferdinando had, like the first, done something to restore respect for the grand duchy after a reign that had been virtually an interregnum. What the situation now demanded was a new chapter of Medicean enterprise and energy. What it received was two rulers so dimly incompetent that the history of the last grand dukes can not unreasonably be seen as offering little more than the record of their personal eccentricities.

Cosimo III (1670–1723) and Gian Gastone (1723–37)

The grand dukes had no more use for the old family home in the via Larga once the Pitti had swollen to such a size that any visiting dignitaries could be accommodated there. Their brothers preferred to build town houses in the modern manner, airy and graceful. In 1659 Ferdinando II sold the empty Medici palace to the marchese Riccardi, who expressed his gratitude a generation later by commissioning Luca Giordano to paint what is at once the most winning and the most absurd of allusions to the greatness of the dynasty. The four figures who presided over its long-drawn-out conclusion ride the ceiling in jaunty apotheosis. Cosimo III feebly repeats the imperial gesture of Jupiter himself; on each hand his sons Ferdinando and Gian Gastone prance on their ponies; at his feet sprawls his brother, Cardinal Francesco Maria, as fatly dimpled as the clouds that support him.

Cosimo III ruled for fifty-three years, the longest of any Medici reign. It was also at once the least eventful and the most disastrous. Above all, it was a reign in which the Grand Duke's inattention to the worsening condition of his country means that the history of the Medici can, for the first time, be detached from the history of Florence and Tuscany without doing violence to the meaning of either. Were it not for this charge, it would be easier to sympathize with the disastrous run of bad luck he experienced in trying to ensure the dynasty's future, with the humiliation of his marriage to a high-spirited foreigner who hated him, and with the worried kindness at the core of his vanity and bigotry.

The bad luck that dogged him had commenced with his conception.

Had he not been the eldest surviving boy he would have become the family cardinal. Brought up, under his mother's influence, by priests, he would have made a far better churchman than his worldly younger brother. So timorous about physical contact with his wife that he was rumoured to be homosexual, he would have been happiest without any sexual challenge at all. As it was, he tried to inhibit it in others by legislation. He had Bandinelli's marble *Adam and Eve* removed from the cathedral, he issued an edict forbidding men to enter houses where there were unmarried girls, and tried, vainly, to revive the canon law prohibition of women actresses which had long been ignored even in Rome.

In the name of religion he became the first Medici to be a declared anti-Semite, forbidding Jews and Christians to live in the same households, let alone to marry; he forbade Christian wet-nurses to suckle Jewish children, and any prostitute entertaining a Jew was to be publicly flogged, stripped to the waist. In the same vein the University of Pisa was informed that 'His Highness will allow no professor . . . to read or teach in public or in private, by writing or by voice, the philosophy of Democritus, or of atoms, or any save that of Aristotle.' With this he coupled a law forbidding Tuscan residents to attend any other university.

Restlessly he moved about his dominions, but it was to touch relics, to promote the sale of indulgences, to give lustre to religious processions, not to inspect public works or hear complaints. On a visit to Rome, avid not only to see but to touch St Veronica's handkerchief with its mystic imprint of Christ's features, and informed that this was a privilege accorded only to the canons of St John Lateran, he persuaded the pope to make him a canon, displayed the relic in triumph to a crowd of pilgrims and had himself painted in ecclesiastical garb. In 1719, as though he were another Savonarola, he announced that God had revealed to him that henceforth his realm was to be dedicated to 'the governance and absolute dominion of the most glorious Saint Joseph'. His last senile years were spent trying to convert three obstreperous Cossack boys, sent to him as a present by the bishop of Cracow.

Cosimo went through the motions of continuing to play off France against Spain by an occasional loud *rapprochement* with Austria. But, as it was clear that he was determined to stay neutral at any cost, the prestige of Tuscany continued to wane. The military organization of the state had become as decrepit as some of its representatives: a muster of the Leghorn garrison in 1700 lists soldiers of seventy and eighty years of age; one 'has lost his sight', another 'requires a stick'. The navy amounted to three galleys and a few small craft with a total complement of 198. Cosimo, after frenetic negotiation, did extract from the Emperor the highest honour his family had ever obtained, the *trattamento reale* – licence, that is, to be referred to as His Royal Highness instead of His Highness, and to be addressed as Most Serene. But this was no more than an indulgent concession to powerlessness, and to Cosimo's grief neither France nor Spain took the slightest notice of his new dignity.

As for cultural propaganda, the grand duke left the marchese Riccardi to blow his trumpet for him. As a prince, his favourite painter had been Carlo Dolci, who had been patronized by his mother on religious rather than stylistic grounds. Thereafter, though he supported the studies of a number of young painters, and instructed his agents abroad to buy miniatures and medals as well as the items he marked in book catalogues, he took a consistent interest in only one artist, the ingenious waxwork-maker Gaetano Zumbo, whose plague victims and anatomical models were a source of fascination for Grand Tourists of both sexes in the eighteenth century. Physically tough, Cosimo nevertheless had waves of hypochondria, and it was in one of these moments, convinced that he would have to pass what time was left to him indoors, that he ordered the most famous of Medicean antiquities, the *Venus*, the *Arrotino* and the *Lottatori*, to be shipped from Rome to give more interest to his nervous perambulations through the galleries of the Uffizi. The marble encrustations of the new chapel inched upwards, but as Joseph Addison justly prophesied shortly after 1700, it 'will be perhaps the most costly piece of work on the face of the earth when completed, but it advances so very slow, that 'tis not impossible but the family of Medici may be extinct before their burial-place is finished.'

It was a possiblity of which Cosimo was not only aware but by which he was obsessed. For some forty years it absorbed much of the energy he had available for affairs of state. But in his search for a grandchild to carry on the family name, he was dealing with exceptionally recalcitrant genetic material, and by aiming for prestige rather than compatibility in his matchmaking he forced his children and his brother into marriages that were uniformly miserable as well as barren.

His first concern was naturally for Ferdinando. The character of the grand prince was a case history of the Eldest Son. Conscious of being cleverer than his father but denied any political role, he reacted by being disobedient, extravagant and self-consciously dissipated. From his affairs with women he contracted syphilis, from his ostentatious devotion to castrated opera singers he courted the reputation of being homosexual. With the wife Cosimo procured for him, Violante of Bavaria, he refused, or was unable, to beget an heir.

As a collector of paintings Ferdinando was the most perceptive and deliberate of the Medici and probably the only one who deserves fame as a connoisseur. In the hands of the ruling members of the family, painting had been used so consciously as propaganda support for their power that it is difficult to discern the quality of their personal involvement with painting simply as an art. Without power, Ferdinand patronized for pleasure, and his collections at Poggio a Caiano, Pratolino and in his apartments at the Pitti contained neither reference to the greatness of the dynasty nor allegories of Tuscany's grateful acceptance of its dominion. He was among the first collectors to revel in the quality of the paint as well as in the subject and style of a picture. He went back to styles which he found congenial in the past, purchasing Raphael's *Madonna del Baldacchino*, Andrea del Sarto's *Madonna delle Arpie* and, most imaginatively, the *Madonna del Collo Lungo* of Parmigianino. Increasingly he ignored the contemporary Florentines – though he bought Franceschini's most eccentric work, *La Burla del Pievano Arlotto* – in order to concentrate on the Venetians. When he did on one occasion use painting as propaganda it was simply to draw attention away from Florence to Venice, and from the academic formalism of most contemporary art to the lighter and more 'painterly' style the Venetians were introducing, as in the work of his favourites, Sebastiano and Marco Ricci. In 1706 he sponsored an exhibition of paintings. Held in the cloister of SS. Annunziata, it was to celebrate art, not a feast of the Church, and for the first time in Italy a printed catalogue was prepared. Ferdinando lent none of the Florentine works from his collection but concentrated on the Venetians. And apart from pioneering an approach to connoisseurship that was to spread throughout Europe later in the eighteenth century, Ferdinando was certainly the most musically sensitive of his family, being an accomplished executant and making Pratolino a Mecca for composers, Alessandro and Domenico Scarlatti among them.

Cosimo's daughter, Anna Maria Luisa, was long hawked about the princely marriage market in vain. She was turned down by France, Portugal, Savoy and Spain (twice) before being contracted to Johann

Wilhelm, the Elector Palatine. It was a union that brought her venereal disease and miscarriages, but no living child. Gian Gastone, Cosimo's younger son, was well aware of his responsibility. Ten generations of Medici looked from their tombs and portraits to this youngest descendant of Giovanni di Bicci for an heir. Nervous, an alcoholic and a homosexual, he might nevertheless have discharged this duty had it not been for the bride Cosimo eventually selected for him, Anna Maria Francesca, widow of the Duke of Saxe-Lauenburg. Stout, haughty, ignorant and a natural scold, she had little about her person to help him get over his physical dislike of women, and the revulsion was completed by her way of life. By nature an aesthete, he found himself bound to a wife who was happiest in the stables of her own estates at the dingy little town of Reichstadt, and who refused to leave them. Bored and disgusted, Gian Gastone began what was to be the pattern of his life, long debauched absences, usually in Prague, punctuated by miserable sojourns with Anna Maria when his father's letters of reproach and hortation had been backed up by the visit of a grand-ducal emissary to remind him of his duty.

By 1708, after eleven years of this match, it was clear to Cosimo that only a miracle could bring an heir to any of his children. He turned, then, to the family's one untried bachelor, the portly Cardinal Francesco Maria, who was nearing fifty. The protestations of this cheerfully raddled voluptuary, whose court at Lapeggi was a Bacchic inversion of the depressed religiosity of his brother's at the Pitti, were slowly overcome. He allowed himself to be dispensed from holy orders and married to Eleanora Gonzaga, daughter of the Duke of Guastalla. Aged twenty, guaranteed fruitful by her physician, who reported to Cosimo, she was so shaken by the sight of her bridegroom that she refused to sleep with him. Though finally forced to do so by the spiritual chiding of her confessor and the political pleading of the Grand Duke and her father, she found the incompatibility too great. The ex-cardinal's diseases further undermined his determination and he died, rejected and ridiculed, within two years, leaving Eleanora free, and childless.

The pathetic comic opera of Cosimo's efforts to prolong the Medici line took place against a sombre background. Cosimo I and Ferdinando I had both urged their heirs to avoid imposing fresh taxes were it possible to avoid doing so. Tuscany, like the other Italian states, needed both imagination and unremitting care to shore up an economy against which the balance of trade had tipped with some violence. Cosimo III's entourage included skilled and devoted diplomats and men whose wisdom troubled their courtiership: no reign that lasts more than fifty years can be painted entirely in shades of grey. The bureaucracy continued to function honestly and painstakingly. Justice was seen to be done to rich and poor alike, and the incidence of violent crime and brigandage was probably lower in Tuscany than elsewhere in the peninsula. Independence, the cause which had always been the most effective link between Medicean and republican days, was a practical, as well as historically a well-nigh sacred policy: Milan and Naples exemplified the economic hazards of satellitism.

But Cosimo, by neglecting internal strength – fortresses and the armed forces – and by adopting an obsequious posture towards powers that were not only political threats but possible sources of brides and grooms, was forced to pay for his neutrality. Subsidies to Austria alone came to be enormous. Partly because he was himself extravagant and partly for reasons of international prestige, the grand-ducal court was maintained with a quite unrealistic pomp. His gifts to religious foundations and his reluctance to fight any clerical claim to tax immunity was another issue his ministers found it vain to contest. For personal and dynastic reasons, therefore, Cosimo taxed the country until its resilience was broken. Certain families, indeed, continued to prosper. It was under Cosimo that the del Rosso brothers built up one of the finest collections of paintings in Florence apart from those of the Medici. It was late in the century when the Corsini built their enormous palace on the Lungarno. Taxes struck especially the multitude of smaller merchants, manufacturers and farmers on whom the country's prosperity depended. For reasons which demographers have not yet determined, the population declined. Agricultural land went back to waste, weeds broke through the flagstones of once thriving quarters of Pisa, Siena, even of Florence itself. 'As one goes over Tuscany', Gilbert Burnet, the historian, wrote from Florence in 1685, 'it appears so dispeopled that one cannot but wonder to find a country that hath been the scene of so much action, and so many wars, now so forsaken and poor.'

Though 'To let' signs were found posted mockingly in front of the Pitti after Francesco Maria's funeral, there was still Gian Gastone, who became grand duke on Cosimo's death in 1723, his brother Ferdinand having died ten years before. He was fifty-two, prematurely senile, often drunk in public, his wit and intelligence either soused in wine or muffled from contact with his officials by a crowd of hangers-on who kept him amused and catered (it was rumoured) for the most depraved of appetites. Increasingly he spent his time, months of it at a stretch, in bed. Yet the erratic sense of duty that had made him submit, from time to time, to the company of his coarse termagant of a wife, led to flashes of legislation that showed he understood the needs of Tuscany more clearly than his father had done: laws designed to halt Church inroads on the functions of the state, releasing the labouring or artisan poor from some of their tax burden, cancelling anti-Semitic edicts, restoring the privilege of free inquiry to the University of Pisa. With his death in 1737 the history of the Medici closed, if not particularly honourably, at least on a fitful note of common sense.

In his last years Cosimo III had considered solving the succession problem by bequeathing the grand-ducal sovereignty to the Florentines after the death of his children or, if they predeceased him, of himself, thus restoring the constitution to its republican form in the years before Alessandro became duke. Though this would have meant restoring Siena and its territories to the Empire, the idea was pushed energetically by his diplomats. Only the English and the Dutch listened with some initial sympathy, and Cosimo's own enthusiasm soon waned. Indeed, the extinction of the male line of any principate was conventionally looked on as an occasion for counter-claims and preparations for conquest on the part of others; land and titles were still attractive in themselves, quite apart from the profit to be derived from taxation, and that some profit could still be squeezed out of Tuscany appeared clear from the sums Gian Gastone was able to advance to the Imperial treasury and the contingents he could send to serve in the Emperor's ceaseless wars against the Turk. Realization that the grand duke would die without an heir coincided, moreover, with a new wave of Italian ambitions on the part of the European powers. In the economic doldrums as it was, Tuscany could not be expected to decide its own destiny.

Its fortunes were debated and settled far from the capital where Gian Gastone lay passively and at times disgustingly in bed. In 1731 England, Holland, Spain, Austria and Savoy decided among them in Vienna that Tuscany should fall to Don Carlos of Bourbon, duke of Parma, as soon as Gian Gastone died, a possibility which his own diplomats, as well as rumour, held to be imminent. Indeed, Don Carlos arrived in person to sit out the last throes, and brought with him 6,000 Spanish troops as if to show that everything the grand dukes had striven for since Cosimo I had persuaded Charles V to call off his garrisons was about to be reversed. But Gian Gastone lingered on and in 1733 the War of Polish Succession struck up the theme for another round of musical chairs. Don Carlos ended up in Naples as king of the Two Sicilies, and another decision was arrived at in Vienna. This time Tuscany was handed to Duke Francis Stephen, whose own duchy of Lorraine was transferred to the King of Poland. In 1736 Don Carlos's Spanish troops marched out, and in 1737 some 6,000 Austrian troops moved in to watch what was so slow in becoming an actual deathbed, and to support the substitution of Lorrainers for Florentines in the bureaucracy.

The grand duke could do nothing when he was told that it was forbidden to observe the holidays that symbolized Medici power: the birthday of Cosimo *pater patriae*, Giulio's election as Clement VII, the public acceptance of Cosimo I's rule. He could do nothing when the Lorraine garrison in the Fortezza da Basso turned the guns so that they were ready to fire into the city: the future of Florence was being decided, as in the days of Alessandro, by force. Francis Stephen was betrothed to Maria Teresa, heiress to all the Habsburg lands; this meant that one day he would be Emperor himself. What Gian Gastone did stir himself to do, and it was the most important single action of his career, was to extract the promise that Tuscany would never be considered part of the Imperial domains but would remain independent, though hereditary to a branch of the house of Lorraine. Shortly after extracting agreement to this compromise, he died at last in 1737. And though the decision was challenged, it held. By the Treaty of Aachen in 1748, Tuscan independence was guaranteed. In a sense, then, Cosimo I's ambition had been realized, though for the benefit of another, and an alien, dynasty.

Gian Gastone's death did not mean that the line of the Medici was quite extinct. His sister, Anna Maria, lived on in the Pitti until 1743, and only at her death was it known what was to become of the property, as opposed to the power, of her family. Her wish was the one Medicean decision that has never been criticized. She left the entire properties of her family, 'galleries, paintings, statues, libraries, jewels, and other precious things' to the new grand duke and his successors – under this condition, however: 'that these things being for the ornament of the state, for the benefit of the people and for an inducement to the curiosity of foreigners, nothing shall be alienated or taken away from the capital or from the territories of the grand duchy'.

The legendary afterlife of the Medici

It was, ironically enough, only in the generation that followed the family's extinction that 'the curiosity of foreigners' began to be strongly focused on the Medici themselves.

Previous to the middle of the eighteenth century, as far as Englishmen were concerned, little interest had been shown in the fifteenth-century members of the family, and references to the later Medici put them on the same footing as other petty princelings, singling them out as individuals merely in order to retail gossip of a dramatic or scandalous nature; more was known about Lorenzino, Cosimo I's alleged incest with his daughter Isabella, and Bianca Capello than about the nature of ducal and grand-ducal rule. Florence was little regarded by visitors; their attention was, for the most part, concentrated on Rome with its ancient ruins and its popes, on Venice, whose constitution was eagerly discussed as the supreme example of how a republic could hold its own in an age of monarchies, and on Naples, with its classical excursions and marvellous bay. Nor had Florence yet acquired its reputation as an art city; Florentine art was valued less than that of Venice, Rome and Bologna, so there was little temptation to consider the Medici in their role as patrons. It was upon the first Roman Medici, Leo X, that a nascent interest in the Renaissance rebirth of letters and arts was centred at first. Thus Alexander Pope could write in 1711:

> But see! each Muse in L E O's golden days,
> Starts from her trance and trims her wither'd bays,
> Rome's ancient Genius, o'er its ruins spread,
> Shakes off the dust and rears his rev'rend head.
> Then Sculpture and her sister arts revive;
> Stones leap'd to form, and rocks began to live.

From the middle of the century, however, the situation began to change. Pope's friend, John Boyle, Earl of Cork and Orrery, detained against his will for a year in Florence by gout, began to look about him, to read, and to listen to gossip. He expressed his conclusions in a letter of 1755. 'If you take a view of the princes of the Medici in a group', he wrote, 'you will feel reverence and respect at one part of the picture and be struck with amazement and horror at the remainder. To revere and know them you must consider their generosity, their benefactions, their policy, and their scientific institutions. To view them with horror and amazement, you need only to listen to the undoubted outrages of their private lives.'

Four years later, Horace Walpole, who heard much of Florence from his friend Horace Mann, England's diplomatic representative at the

Tuscan court, wrote of a subject 'which would make an agreeable work, both to the writer and to the reader, as any I could think of. It is the history of the House of Medici. There is an almost unknown republic, factions, banishments, murders, commerce, conquest, heroes, cardinals, all of a new stamp, and very different from what appears in any other country . . . What a morsel Leo the tenth! the revival of letters! that torrent of Greeks that imported them! Extend still farther, there are Catherine and Mary, Queens of France. In short, I know nothing one could wish in a subject that could not fall into this – and then it is a complete subject, the family is extinct.'

This project, too, came to nothing. But three years later no less a man than Edward Gibbon, casting round for a subject worthy of detailed and intensive study, hit upon two possibilities. One was *The history of the liberty of the Swiss*, the other *The history of the republic of Florence under the house of Medici*. The one would show a nation gallantly winning liberty for itself; the other would demonstrate the processes through which liberty, already possessed, could be lost. 'Both lessons', he observed in 1761, 'are, perhaps, equally instructive', and of the second he went on to say 'on this splendid subject I shall most probably fix, but *when*, or *where*, or *how*, will it be executed? I behold in a dark and doubtful perspective.'

Within a few years, then, the Medici were promoted from being excuses for scattered anecdote to being material for serious dynastic history. And for three main reasons: being dead, they offered a subject complete in itself; having become princes they offered scope for philosophical musing on the theme of political liberty; above all, they posed an alarming paradox, for while their attitude to power and their private morals had to be condemned, they were responsible for the fostering of a noble culture. Scarcely known about as individuals, the Medici were thus already on their way to becoming mythic figures, depraved, tyrannical – and yet enlightened. And though the depravity came to be played down when historians looked past gossip to the sources, the tyranny-culture paradox continued to exert a potent attraction.

With the publication in 1796 of the first full-scale scrutiny of a single member of the family, William Roscoe's *Life of Lorenzo de' Medici*, this attraction was increased by the addition of a further element; the combination of business acumen with discriminating patronage. Roscoe was himself a banker and an art collector; his enthusiasm for his subject was all the greater because he saw himself as a Medici in little. For him, Lorenzo was 'the most extraordinary man that any age or nation has produced'. Part of his book's phenomenal success was due to its catering to an interest in the fifteenth-century revival of art and letters in the city that was already being called 'the Athens of Italy'. But it also appealed to artists and writers; the patronage system was withering in England, and through Roscoe's pages they were invited to linger imaginatively in a society which had apparently been uniquely protective towards creative and scholarly talent. Finally, the self-made men of the Industrial Revolution were intrigued to learn that commerce and manufacture could be made respectable, even glamorous, in the eyes of posterity were they to include payments for paintings and manuscripts in their balance sheets.

The projects of Boyle, Walpole and Gibbon were actually put into effect in 1797, when Mark Noble produced his *Memoirs of the Illustrious House of Medici*, thus enabling the English-speaking world at last to see the family as a whole, but interest continued to be concentrated on Lorenzo and, to a lesser extent, Cosimo *pater patriae*. A sociology of art and literature being lacking, cultural changes were almost necessarily explained in terms of patronage. Cosimo and Lorenzo were seen as personally responsible for the rebirth of classical learning and for an approach to painting and sculpture which delivered the arts from their thraldom to stiff and unrealistic forms and made possible the achievements of a Raphael and a Michelangelo. 'When we speak of the house of Medici', wrote Robert Bromley towards the end of the eighteenth century, 'the name sounds sweetly to every ear; admiration, delight, and almost homage follow that love of letters and of the arts in that family, which gave so brilliant a resurrection to both, after a long extinction.' And this myth of personal responsibility grew still stronger as the nineteenth century wore on and men began actually to appreciate such artists as the Ghirlandaio, Donatello, the Lippi, Fra Angelico, Botticelli and Verrocchio rather than taking their excellence on trust from the opinions of Vasari. As late as 1901 a historian could say of Cosimo and Lorenzo that they were 'the agents selected to promote the development of the Italian Renaissance', and the stubborn attractiveness of the myth is shown by the comparatively recent destruction of the notion that Lorenzo had supported a form of art school where the taste of Michelangelo, among others, was formed.

This benign version of the Medici myth proved strong enough to ride out the storm of political opprobrium that broke over their heads. This had already been hinted at in Gibbon's project and was openly stated in the first large-scale history of Florence to be published in

England, volume 36 of the *Universal History*, which appeared while Gibbon was still imagining himself as the historian of the Medici. Written anonymously, the *Universal History* was England's answer to the point of view expressed in the contemporary French *Encyclopédie*. It, too, was a work of the Enlightenment, and the Medici were accordingly scourged as tyrants. Roscoe had tried to save the political reputation of his heroes by representing them as constitutional rulers of the stamp of George III, but the sympathy for small nations whose constitutions were perverted by Napoleon swept this cautious mood aside. In 1812, the year of Napoleon's attempt to clamp Russia to the continental blockade aimed to destroy Britain's trading economy, a writer in the *Quarterly Review*, seeking examples of resistance to tyranny, announced that 'in this view, the history of Florence presents more objects of importance than almost any other nation – we mean, not the history of Florence under the Medici, but during the ages of her *real greatness*.'

In 1818 it was the turn of the *Edinburgh Review* to remind its readers that Florence's constitution 'fell a sacrifice to the cunning arts of the Medici, whose patronage of letters and encouragement of the arts cannot redeem their name from the infamy of having subverted the most splendid republic that has existed since the days of Athens.' Fifty years later a history of Florence, that of Adolphus Trollope, could claim that on account of their political crimes the reputation of the Medici as patrons 'was but as the phosphorescent light that may be seen to float above the putrescent remains of organic matter in process of dissolution', and Mark Twain, reflecting, as many of his countrymen did, on the contrast between the splendour of the monuments of Florence – now firmly established as an art city to visit and even reside in permanently – and the poverty of its inhabitants, could crushingly refer to 'the dead and damned Medici who cruelly tyrannized over Florence and were her curse for over two hundred years.'

The 'white' myth: that the Medici bought the Renaissance of arts and letters into existence with money from their bank, is now exploded. The 'black' myth: that they inveigled liberty away from a democratic people, is at least seen in drastically less simple terms. The paradox: that an advancing culture, experimental in form and profound in content, can coexist with radically changing political institutions remains a challenge. Apart from the factual interest of their careers it is the controversial nature of their legendary afterlife that does much to explain the hold the dynasty has had, and will perhaps continue to have, over the imaginations of posterity.

Bibliography

The purpose of this selective bibliography is to indicate the chief areas of my indebtedness, and to enable the reader to follow up aspects of the subject I have only been able to deal with cursorily. It does not cover the history of art except for works directly concerned with the Medici, nor does it include histories of Florence or of Italy. Of these F.-T. Perrens, *Histoire de Florence depuis la domination des Médicis jusqu'à la chute de la république* (3 vols, Paris 1888–90), provides the fullest narrative up to 1531; vol. 3 of Romolo Caggese's *Firenze dalla decadenza di Roma al Risorgimento* (Florence 1912–13) the most useful narrative from 1531 to 1737; Nino Valeri, *L'Italia nell'età dei principati, 1343–1516* (Milan 1949), and Alessandro Visconti, *L'Italia nell'epoca della controriforma, 1510–1713* (Milan 1958), provide a clear general background.

For an extensive, though by no means exhaustive, bibliography of the Medici, there is Sergio Camerani, *Bibliografia Medicea* (Florence 1964). Of the fairly numerous general works dealing with the family as a whole, I will not pretend to find any satisfactory, but I have had constant recourse to Gaetano Pieraccini's encyclopedic *La Stirpe dei Medici di Cafaggiolo* (4 vols, 2nd ed., Florence 1947). Full genealogical tables, with valuable biographical entries, are in P. Litta, *Famiglie celebri italiane* (15 vols, Milan 1819–1902), 'Famiglia Medici di Firenze'.

Works used in more than one chapter are referred to by author and chapter number after the first entry.

CHAPTER I   *The First Steps to Power*

On Florence before 1434: Gene A. Brucker, *Renaissance Florence* (New York 1969); Lauro Martines, *The social world of the Florentine humanists* (Princeton 1968); Marvin B. Becker, 'The republican city state in Florence: an inquiry into its origin and survival', *Speculum* (1960) 39–50, and 'The Florentine territorial state and civic humanism in the early Renaissance', in *Florentine Studies*, ed. Nicolai Rubinstein (London 1968); Anthony Molho, 'The Florentine oligarchy and the *balìe* of the late *trecento*', *Speculum* (1968) 23–51; 'Politics and the ruling class in early Renaissance Florence', *Nuova Rivista Storica* (1968) 401–20, and *Florentine public finances in the early Renaissance, 1400–1433* (Oxford 1972); Dale Kent, 'The Florentine Reggimento in the fifteenth century', *Renaissance Quarterly* (1975) 575–638. Alberto Tenenti's brief *Firenze dal comune a Lorenzo il Magnifico* (Milan 1968) is fullest on the period before 1434, but serves as an alert guide to the social and economic background up to 1492. On the Medici before 1434: Gene A. Brucker, 'The Medici in the fourteenth century', *Speculum* (1957) 1–26, an article I have followed closely; B. Dami's thinnish *Giovanni Bicci de' Medici* (Florence 1899); Dale Vivienne Kent, *Political alignments on the eve of Cosimo de' Medici's rise to power, 1426–1434*, an unpublished University of London thesis which I have used for what I have said about the growth of a Medici 'party'. I am deeply grateful to Mrs Kent for her permission to read this important work. By the same author: 'I Medici in esilio . . .', *Archivio Storico Italiano* (1976) 3–63. For the early stages of the bank: Raymond de Roover's now classic *The rise and decline of the Medici Bank, 1397–1494* (Harvard 1963) and George Holmes, 'How the Medici became the popes' bankers' in *Florentine Studies,* cit. The best biography of Cosimo is Curt S. Gutkind, *Cosimo de' Medici, Pater Patriae, 1384–1464* (Oxford 1938). Fundamental to an understanding of his (and his successors' up to 1494) political role is a work I have relied on heavily, Nicolai Rubinstein, *The government of Florence under the Medici* (Oxford 1966), as I have on the same author's 'Florentine constitutionalism and Medici ascendancy in the fifteenth century', *Florentine Studies*, cit. Useful both for fact and insight is Lauro Martines, *Lawyers and statecraft in Renaissance Florence* (Princeton 1968). Some of the letters of Cosimo and his family are translated in Janet Ross, *Lives of the early Medici as told in their correspondence* (Boston 1911). Vespasiano da Bisticci's memoir of Cosimo is translated in *The Vespasiano memoirs* by William George and Emily Waters (New York 1926). And see B. L. Ullman and Philip A. Stadter, *The public library of Florence: Niccolò Niccoli, Cosimo de' Medici and the library of San Marco* (Padua 1972). On Cosimo as a patron of art, the best treatment is that of E. H. Gombrich: 'The Early Medici as Patrons of Art' in *Italian Renaissance Studies*, ed. E. F. Jacob (London 1960), supplemented by A. D. Fraser Jenkins, 'Cosimo de' Medici's patronage of architecture and the theory of magnificence', *Journal of the Warburg and Courtauld Institutes* (1970) 162–70. For the humanist atmosphere and the political assumptions which Cosimo inherited, see Hans Baron's celebrated work, *The crisis of the early Italian Renaissance* (Princeton 1966), and the significance of contemporary opinion is skilfully analyzed in Alison M. Brown's 'The Humanist portrait of Cosimo de' Medici, Pater Patriae' in *Journal of the Warburg and Courtauld Institutes* (1961) 186–221.

CHAPTER 2   *The Medicean Regime*

There is nothing of much biographical value on Piero, but see, for one important aspect, G. Pampaloni, 'Fermenti di riforme democratiche nella Firenze medicea del quattrocento', in *Archivio Storico Italiano* (1961) 11–61 and 241–81 (documents). More regrettable is the absence of a satisfactory biography of Lorenzo. Even the wisest of historians falter when they come to grips with the discrepancy between what ought to be knowable about so famous a figure and what is known. A political biography will have to wait for the publication of the fully annotated edition of Lorenzo's correspondence projected under the general editorship of Professor Rubinstein. Meanwhile, a sensible introduction is C. M. Ady, *Lorenzo dei Medici and Renaissance Italy* (London 1960), the pre-Pazzi Conspiracy years are covered as fully as possible by A. Rochon, *La jeunesse de Laurent de Médicis, 1449–1478* (Paris 1963), Lorenzo's 'succession' to Piero is discussed by G. Soranzo in 'Lorenzo il Magnifico alla morte del padre e il suo primo balzo verso la Signoria', in *Archivio Storico Italiano* (1953) 42–77, and there are domestic letters in Ross (1). For the constitution, Rubinstein (1) is indispensable. The treatment of foreign policy suffers most from the absence of the printed correspondence, as can be seen from N. Rubinstein and P. G. Ricci, eds, *Checklist of letters of Lorenzo de' Medici* (Florence 1964). However, there are E. Fiumi, *L'impresa di Lorenzo de' Medici contro Volterra* (Florence 1948), Caterina Bonello Uricchio, 'I rapporti tra Lorenzo il Magnifico e Galeazzo Maria Sforza negli anni 1471–1473', *Archivio Storico Lombardo* (1964–65) 33–49, Giovanni Cecchini, 'La guerra della congiura dei Pazzi e l'andata di Lorenzo de' Medici a Napoli', *Bolletino Senese di Storia Patria* (1965) 291–301, and R. Palmarocchi, *La politica italiana di Lorenzo de' Medici: Firenze nella guerra contro Innocenzo VIII* (Florence 1933). (Of the two books, Fiumi is too harsh, Palmarocchi perhaps too favourable to Lorenzo.) These works are best read in conjunction with G. Pampaloni, 'Gli organi della repubblica fiorentina per le relazioni con l'estero' in *Rivista di Studi Politici Internazionali* (1953) 261–91, and G. Pillinini, *Il sistema degli stati italiani, 1454–1494* (Venice 1970). For patronage of the arts, see Gombrich (1) and D. S. Chambers, *Patrons and artists in the Italian Renaissance* (London 1970). Richard A. Goldthwaite, 'The Florentine palace as domestic architecture', *American Historial Review* (1972) 977–1012, relates buildings to *mores* in a masterly way. A work less general than it might appear but important both for information and insight is André Chastel, *Art et humanisme à Florence au temps de Laurent le Magnifique* (Paris 1959); in most respects it has superseded the enthusiastic work by Enrico Barfucci, *Lorenzo de' Medici e la società artistica del suo tempo* (Florence 1965). In *Italian Renaissance Studies* (1) there are articles by C. M. Bowra and Cecil Grayson that discuss Lorenzo's songs and his attitude to the vernacular. Lorenzo's poems can be conveniently read in Lorenzo de' Medici, *Scritti scelti*, ed. E. Bigi (Turin 1955), and among a copious critical literature I would single out A. Momigliano, 'La poesia del Magnifico' in his *Ultimi Studi* (Florence 1954). On Lorenzo's one dramatic work: Sisto dalla Palma, *La sacra rappresentazione di Lorenzo il Magnifico* (Milan 1965). Among much that throws light on Florentine Neoplatonism, I would cite J. B. Wadsworth, 'Lorenzo de' Medici and Marsiglio Ficino: an experiment in Platonic friendship', *Romanic Review* (1955) 90–100, Edgar Wind, *Pagan mysteries in the Renaissance* (London 1958), and Erwin Panofsky, *Studies in iconology* (New York 1939). In *Italian Renaissance Studies* (1) there is an important article by L. F. Marks, 'The financial oligarchy in Florence under Lorenzo', and though it is not about the Medici, there is essential comparative material in Richard A. Goldthwaite, *Private Wealth in Renaissance Florence* (Princeton 1968). De Roover (1) remains the guide to the operations of the bank, and the wider economic scene is explored (and the gaps in it noted) by F. Melis, *Tracce di una storia economica di Firenze e della Toscana in generale dal 1252 al 1550* (Florence 1966).

CHAPTER 3   *Towards the Principate*

F. Catalano, 'La crisi italiana alla fine del secolo XV', *Belfagor* (1956) 393–414, 505–27, is stimulating for the Italian scene as a whole in the late fifteenth century. Rubinstein, *Government* (1), ends with a chapter on Piero. Invaluable, too, is his 'Politics and the constitution in Florence at the end of the fifteenth century' in *Italian Renaissance Studies* (1). Two useful articles on the republican 'interregnum' of 1494–1512 by Sergio Bertelli are 'Constitutional reforms in Renaissance Florence', *Journal of Medieval and Renaissance Studies* (1973) 139–64, and 'Pier Soderini "Vexilifer perpetuus reipublicae florentinae" 1502–1512' in *Renaissance: studies in honor of Hans Baron*, ed. Anthony Molho and John A. Tedeschi (Dekalb, Illinois, 1971). Three biographies help to provide narrative and political background: D. Weinstein, *Savonarola and Florence: prophecy and patriotism in the Renaissance* (Princeton 1970), J. R. Hale, *Machiavelli and Renaissance Italy* (revised ed., London 1972), and Rosemary Devonshire Jones, *Francesco Vettori, Florentine citizen and Medici servant* (London 1972). Basic to the chapter as a whole is R. von Albertini, *Das Florentinische Staatsbewusstsein im Übergang von der Republik zum Prinzipat* (Bern 1955, Italian tr. Turin 1970), which is especially useful for an analysis of the political thought of the period, though it is not as stimulating as the shorter *Machiavelli and Guicciardini: politics and history in sixteenth century Florence* (Princeton 1965) by Felix Gilbert. The best treatment of Leo X is still Ludwig Pastor, *The history of the popes* (vols 7 and 8, tr. R. F. Kerr, London 1908), supplemented by G. B. Picotti, *La giovinezza di Leone X, il papa del Rinascimento* (Milan 1927), and the brief but suggestive article by E. Dupré Theseider, 'I papi medicei e la loro politica domestica', in *Studi Fiorentini* (Libera cattedra di storia della civiltà fiorentina, Florence, n.d.). The cultural side of Leo's pontificate is covered well in E. Rodocanachi, *Le pontificat de Léon X, 1513–1521* (Paris

1931). On Lorenzo the Younger there is now Rosemary Devonshire Jones, 'Lorenzo de' Medici, Duca d'Urbino "Signore" of Florence?' in *Studies in Machiavelli*, ed. Myron P. Gilmore (Florence 1972).

CHAPTER 4 *The Principate Achieved*

The fullest account of Clement's pontificate is that given in Pastor (3), vols IX and X; there is a reasonably helpful survey in M. Monaco, 'Considerazioni sul pontificato di Clemente VII', *Archivio* (1960) 184–223, and for the general Roman background see P. Pecchiai, *Roma nel Cinquecento* (Bologna 1948). For Florence, Gilbert (3) and von Albertini (3) continue to be useful; the last supplemented with Felix Gilbert, 'Alcuni discorsi di uomini politici fiorentini e la politica di Clemente VII per la restaurazione medicea', in *Archivio Storico Italiano* (1935) 3–24. Cecil Roth, *The Last Florentine Republic* (London 1925), still unreplaced, covers the period 1527–30. Nor, for Alessandro, has more recent work replaced M. Rastrelli, *Storia d'Alessandro de' Medici primo duca di Firenze* (2 vols; Florence 1781), though A. del Vita presents a brief and moderate view in 'Alessandro de' Medici', *Il Vasari* (1942) 5–27, 55–9. There is also J. R. Hale, 'The end of Florentine liberty: the Fortezza da Basso', *Florentine Studies* (2). Another old but useful work is L. A. Ferrai, *Lorenzino de' Medici e la società cortigiana del cinquecento* (Milan 1891). Ippolito's career is reviewed in G. E. Moretti, 'Il cardinale Ippolito de' Medici dal trattato di Barcellona alla morte, 1529–1535', *Archivio Storico Italiano* (1940) 137–78. The first years of Cosimo's reign are admirably treated in Giorgio Spini, *Cosimo I de' Medici e l'independenza del principato medicea* (Florence 1945), and the linking comments make doubly useful the same author's *Cosimo I de' Medici: Lettere* (Florence 1940). In spite of the large scale of L. Carcereri's *Cosimo I granduca* (2 vols, Verona 1926) and its excellent treatment of foreign policy, an

older work still remains fundamental: R. Galluzzi, *Istoria del granducato di Toscana sotto il governo della casa Medici* (5 vols; Florence 1781; vols 1 and 2 for Cosimo), as it does for the reigns of his successors. Nor has recent work displaced A. Anzilotti, *La costituzione interna dello stato fiorentino sotto il duca Cosimo I de' Medici* (Florence 1910). Though the relationship between Florence and the rest of Tuscany is still unclear, there are Elena Fasano Guarini, *Lo stato mediceo di Cosimo I* (Florence 1973), Arnaldo D'Addario, 'Burocrazia, economia e finanze dello stato fiorentino alla metà del cinquecento', *Archivio Storico Italiano* (1963) 362–456, J. Ferretti, 'L'organizzazione militare toscana durante il governo di Alessandro e di Cosimo I', *Rivista Storica degli Archivi Toscani* (1929) 248–75, (1930), 58–80, 133–52, 211–19, and, wider in scope, the report on the work of a team of young researchers edited by Giorgio Spini, 'Architettura e politica nel principato mediceo del cinquecento', *Rivista Storica Italiana* (1971) 792–845, now published in full in *Architettura e politica da Cosimo I a Ferdinando I* (Florence 1976). The Siena campaign is described by Roberto Cantagalli, *La guerra di Siena* (Siena 1962). On the use of the arts for propaganda purposes, see A. Lensi, *Palazzo Vecchio* (Milan 1929); N. Rubinstein, 'Vasari's Painting of "The Foundation of Florence" in the Palazzo Vecchio', in *Essays in the History of Architecture Presented to Rudolf Wittkower*, ed. Douglas Fraser, H. Hibbard and M. J. Lewine (London 1967); Rudolf and Margot Wittkower, *The Divine Michelangelo: The Florentine academy's homage on his death in 1566* (London 1964); Michael Levey, *Painting at court* (London 1971); Kurt W. Forster, 'Metaphors of rule. Political ideology and history in the portraits of Cosimo I de' Medici', *Mitteilungen des Kunsthistorischen Instituts in Florenz* (1971) 65–104. On wedding festivals: Henry W. Kaufman, 'Art for the wedding of Cosimo de' Medici and Eleanora of Toledo', *Paragone* (1970) 52–67, Andrew C. Minor and B.

Mitchell, *A Renaissance entertainment* (U. of Missouri 1968) – also about the wedding to Eleanor, and Piero Ginori Conti, *L'apparato per le nozze di Francesco de' Medici e di Giovanna d'Austria* (Florence 1936). There is much interesting detail in R. W. Carden, *The Life of Giorgio Vasari* (London 1911), and a vivid picture of the conditions of patronage in Cosimo's Florence is given by Cellini's *Autobiography*. I mention Eric Cochrane, *Florence in the forgotten centuries, 1527–1800* (U. of Chicago 1973), last because though its chapter on Cosimo I is the alertest and best-based short treatment of his reign, the book reaches through to the end of Medici rule, not as a narrative history, but as a series of stepping stones from which individual Florentines, or temporary residents in Florence, look about them. Cosimo is the only Medici to be focused upon, but the work has been a most valuable stimulus to my chapters 5 and 6.

CHAPTER 5 *Grand-Ducal Tuscany*

Galluzzi (4) provides the main narrative. On Francesco there is Luciano Berti's excellent *Il principe dello studiolo: Francesco I dei Medici e la fine del Rinascimento fiorentino* (Florence 1967). A cluster of articles deal with the turn of the century: Samuel Berner, 'Florentine society in the late sixteenth and early seventeenth centuries', *Studies in the Renaissance* (1971) 203–46, and 'Florentine political thought in the late *cinquecento*', *Pensiero Politico* (1970) 177–99; Eric Cochrane, 'The end of the Renaissance in Florence' in a book edited by him, *The late Italian Renaissance, 1525–1630* (London 1970); and there is O. Silli, *Una corte alla fine del '500: artisti, letterati. scienziati nella reggia di Ferdinando I de' Medici* (Florence 1928). There is no adequate biography of Ferdinando I. R. Burr Litchfield, 'Office-holding in Florence after the republic', in *Renaissance: studies in honor of Hans Baron*, ed. Anthony Molho and John A. Tedeschi (Dekalb, Illinois, 1971) covers the period from Cosimo I to Gian Gastone. On economic affairs, see Goldthwaite (2), and Amintore Fanfani, 'Effimera la ripresa economica d Firenze sul finire del secolo XVI?' *Economia e Storia* (1965) 344–51; more recent (still inconclusive) research is summarized *passim* in Cochrane (4). On the economic importance of Leghorn there is the outstanding study by F. Braudel and R. Romano, *Navires et marchandises à l'entrée du port de Livourne, 1547–1611* (Paris 1951). On the anti-Turkish activities of the grand dukes, especially useful are G. Guarnieri, *I cavalieri di Santo Stefano nella storia della marina italiana (1562–1859)* (Pisa 1960), and chapter 4 of A. Tamborra, *Gli stati italiani, l'Europa e il problema turco dopo Lepanto* (Florence 1961). On fief-holders there is Giuseppe Pansini, 'Per una storia del feudalesimo nel granducato di Toscana', *Quaderni Storici* (1972) 131–86. A useful if not heartening survey of research into agrarian history in Tuscany is included in Aldo de Maddalena, 'Il mondo rurale italiano nel cinque e nel seicento', *Rivista Storica Italiana* (1964) 349–426. For the social significance of the Order of S. Stefano see Guarnieri's *L'ordine di S. Stefano nei suoi aspetti organizzativi interni sotto il gran magistero mediceo* (Pisa 1966). Religion is a neglected aspect of this period, but there is now Arnoldo D'Addario, *Aspetti della controriforma a Firenze* (Rome 1972), especially useful for its treatment of charitable organization. For pageantry and its propaganda value: Eve Borsook, 'Art and Politics at the Medici Court. 1: The funeral of Cosimo I de' Medici', in *Mitteilungen des Kunsthistorischen Instituts in Florenz* (1965) 31–54, which I have followed closely, G. Gaeta Bertelà and A. Petrioli Tofani, *Feste e apparati medicei da Cosimo I a Cosimo II* (Florence, exhibition catalogue, 1969), A. M. Nagler, *Theatre festivals of the Medici, 1539–1637* (New Haven 1964), and D. P. Walker, *Les fêtes du mariage de Ferdinand des Médicis et de Christine de Lorraine* (Paris 1963). See also Howard Meyer Brown, 'How opera began; an introduction to Jacopo Peri's *Euridice* (1600)', in Cochrane, *The late Italian Renaissance*, cit., and B. H. Wells, *The fountains of Florentine sculptors* (Cambridge, Mass. 1933). Remarkable for its steady intelligence among the lush literature of Medici private life is Mary G. Steegman, *Bianca Capello* (London 1913). There is a splendidly integrated portrait of European politics in J. H. Elliot, *Europe Divided, 1559-1598* (London 1968). Far and away the best single work dealing with any aspect of Catherine's rule is Lucien Romier, *Le royaume de Catherine de Médicis: la France à la veille des guerres de religion* (2 vols; Paris 1922). Among the latest of the several large-scale biographies of Catherine the most informative is Jean Héritier's *Catherine de' Medici*, tr. C. Haldane (London 1963), but none of them has replaced the earlier work by J.-H. Mariéjol, *Catherine des Médicis, 1519-1589* (Paris 1920). The best treatment of the St Bartholomew massacre is N. M. Sutherland, *The Massacre of St. Bartholomew and the European conflict 1559-1572* (London 1973). The same author's *The French Secretaries of State in the Age of Catherine de Medici* (London 1962) is indispensable for judging Catherine's competence as an administrator. The extent of Italian influence in France before and during her lifetime can be gauged from E. Picot, *Les italiens en France au XVIe siècle* (Bordeaux 1918), Franco Simone, *The French Renaissance: medieval tradition and Italian influence*, tr. H. Gaston Hall (London 1969), and Werner L. Gundersheimer (ed.), *French humanism 1470-1600* (London 1969), and Anthony Blunt, *Art and architecture in France, 1500-1700* (London 1953). In spite of its title, the best biography of Marie is Louis Batiffol, *La vie intime d'une reine de France au XVIIe siècle: Marie des Médicis* (2 vols; Paris 1931). For the political background, see Roland Mousnier, *L'assassinat d'Henri IV* (Paris 1964), and Victor L. Tapié, *La France de Louis XIII et de Richelieu* (Paris 1952). For Marie's Italian sympathies, see Marcella Paiter, 'Toscani alla corte di Maria de' Medici regina di Francia', *Archivio Storico Italiano* (1940) 83-108, and for her patronage of the arts, L. Bourgeois, 'Marie de Médicis et les arts', *Gazette des Beaux Arts* (1905) 441-52, (1906) 221-43. On the Concini, C. Giachetti, *La tragica avventura dei Concini: la fine del Maresciallo d'Ancre, 1600-1617* (Milan 1939).

CHAPTER 6 *The Decline of a Dynasty and the Growth of a Legend*

The absence of biographies – apart from Sir Harold Acton's delectable *The last Medici* (London 1932) which is somewhat too hospitable to contemporary gossip – makes Galluzzi (4) more useful than ever. For intellectual life, besides Cochrane (4) (especially for Galileo) and his *Tradition and enlightenment in the Tuscan academies, 1690-1800* (U. of Chicago 1961) there is W. E. Knowles Middleton, *The experimenters: a study of the Accademia del Cimento* (Baltimore 1972). The economic picture is still impressionistic in spite of R. Romano, 'À Florence au XVIIe siècle: industries, textiles et conjonctures', *Annales* (1952) 508-12, and José-Gentile da Silva, 'Au XVIIe siècle: la strategie du capital florentin', *Annales* (1964) 480-91; G. Guarnieri, *Il principato mediceo nella scienza del mare* (Pisa 1963), contains useful, if undigested, information about commercial ventures. The patronage of grand prince Ferdinando is admirably assessed in Francis Haskell, *Patrons and painters, a study in the relations between Italian art and society in the age of the Baroque* (London 1963), and there are articles by M. Campbell, 'Medici patronage and the Baroque: a reappraisal', *Art Bulletin* (1966) 133-46, and by Anna Rosa Masetti, 'Il Casino Mediceo e la pittura fiorentina del seicento', *Critica d'Arte* (1962) no. 40, 1-27 and nos 53-54, 77-109. On the reputation of the Medici: A. Chastel, 'Vasari et la légende Medicéenne', *Studi Vasariani* (Florence 1952), J. R. Hale, 'Cosimo and Lorenzo dei Medici: their reputation in England from the 16th to the 19th century', *English Miscellany* (1957) 179-94, and *England and the Italian Renaissance* (revised ed., London 1963).

List of Illustrations

Index

Numerals in italics refer to illustrations